SOCIOLOGY AND THE FUTURE OF WORK

For John Edward Ransome, 1927-1997
Although a very quiet man,
the silence he leaves behind is quite deafening

Sociology and the Future of Work

Contemporary discourses and debates

PAUL RANSOME
School of Social Sciences and International Development
University of Wales Swansea
UK

Ashgate

Aldershot • Brookfield USA • Singapore • Sydney

Published by
Ashgate Publishing Ltd
Gower House
Croft Road
Aldershot
Hants GU11 3HR
England

Ashgate Publishing Company
Old Post Road
Brookfield
Vermont 05036
USA

Ashgate website: http://www.ashgate.com

British Library Cataloguing in Publication Data
Ransome, Paul
    Sociology and the future of work : contemporary discourses
    and debates
    1. Industrial sociology 2. Industrial sociology - Philosophy
    3. Employment (Economic theory) - Social aspects
    I. Title
    306.3'6

Library of Congress Catalog Card Number: 99-73694

ISBN 0 7546 1159 0

Printed and bound by Athenaeum Press, Ltd.,
Gateshead, Tyne & Wear.

Contents

List of Figures

List of Tables

Preface

The world of work is not what it used to be. One doesn't have to be Brain of Britain to recognize that once familiar assumptions about having a job for life, of developing a life-long career structure, or that work is a predominantly masculine activity are largely things of the past. The typical picture today is of a much more fragmentary and insecure pattern of employment. The message from Government spokespeople, careers advisers and employers is to develop a portfolio of flexible skills which will, if we are lucky, allow us to find a series of niches of employment. It is up to us to meet the challenge of the new world of work, to redouble our efforts to find new opportunities for rewarding and creative employment. We no longer simply have to be prepared to work whilst at work, but to work at anticipating where the next job, the next contract, the next challenge will come from.

The aim of this book is to lay bare a number of the key dimensions of change which are taking place in the present, and to use this as a basis for analysing what the key features of work in the future are likely to be. In developing this analysis, the book is organized around a critical examination of some of the leading discourses which are currently being deployed in debates about the future of work. Although this book will describe a number of the most likely underlying features of the future of work, it is also, and perhaps primarily concerned, with understanding which are the most useful ways of approaching the study of the future of work. It is as much a book about how to study the future of work from a sociological point of view, as it is an account of what that future will be like.

Acknowledgements

Inevitably, any book builds upon the ideas and research of its predecessors, and I would therefore like to acknowledge the work of all those authors referred to in the text. I would also like to acknowledge the support of colleagues teaching sociology and social theory in the School of Social Sciences and International Development at the University of Wales Swansea. My debt to Nickie Charles and Chris Harris is already large and continues to grow. The errors and omissions in the following are of course entirely my own responsibility.

Introduction

A friend of mine commented that it should not take very long to write a book about the future of work. She wondered if perhaps it ought to be called '*is there* a future of work?' Despite the sarcasm of this comment there is a serious point here, since the answer depends a great deal on *whose* future of work one is talking about. As is often the case in looking at the social world we tend to assess things from our own vantage point. Thus, in asking questions about the future of work, our first response is likely to be framed in terms of our *personal* expectations of work. As sociologists however, we need to adopt a much more objective perspective, and to recognize that the future of work is actually made up of diversity of a views depending on which parts of the working population we are looking at.

Imagine for example, that we are standing in the High Street asking different kinds of people what they think the future of work will be. Our first respondents are an elderly retired couple. Ostensibly, our question might seem non-sensical to them as they themselves are no longer working. What they are concerned about is their pensions and the value of their savings. As long as the economic well-being of society remains constant, they can be reasonably confident about their future prospects. The prices they pay for basic utilities, food and clothing will not increase too rapidly, and the state will be able to continue to provide them with the medical and social services they need. Their perspective on the future of work is framed in terms of the overall economic position of the country. They are less concerned about precisely who is doing what kind of job, or with whether the practical content of this or that job has changed, than with a general hope that relative economic stability can be maintained.

The next person we speak to is a man in his mid forties. After spending much of his adult life working in a bank, he has recently lost his job as a consequence of restructuring. Where once he held a position of some responsibility, he now finds that the personal and organizational skills he had built up over the years are no longer needed by his employer. In looking around for another job, he finds that although valuable these qualifications and experience are no longer sufficient to guarantee him a job. He is a skilled professional man, but he is no longer employable on these grounds alone. His prospects of finding the kind of work he is used to doing are slim because restructuring has taken place across the whole of the industry in which he used to work. It is not that he himself has become a bad employee, but that the circumstances in which he is looking for work have changed. Besides, he knows that because he is by no means the only person in this position, he faces stiff competition from other former managers, and especially from those who are a few years younger than himself. For him, the future of work seems bleak. At a minimum he faces the prospect either of having to take a quite different kind of job, perhaps one which bears little relation to what he did before, or of having to spend some time outside employment while he tries to acquire new skills. In either case, he knows he will have to revise his expectations of what the future holds and to look again at the standard of living and lifestyle which he and his family can afford. He feels demoralised and disillusioned by the fact that the expectations he had of work, expectations which he used to take for granted, can no longer be met.

Next we meet a woman in her late thirties who has just taken her children to school. Ironically, she has just started working part-time in the bank where our previous respondent used to work. The job she does is not terribly exciting, but she was able to pick up the necessary word-processing skills quite easily, and enjoys the company of her colleagues. Although she does not receive a large wage, this is off-set by the fact that her hours of work are flexible and convenient - she can work while the children are at school - and because being at work provides her with a break from the sometimes lonely routine of household life. She is pleased to have this opportunity for returning to work after a period away from it, and is quite confident that there is a continuing and perhaps growing demand amongst employers for women like herself. She knows that her employability is largely based on her availability, and on the employer's perception of her as a reliable mature and responsible person. She does not feel that her future employment prospects are unduly threatened by younger people with more current qualifications. She also feels economically secure because her partner is working. If she should not be able to work for a while, they will still be able to pay the mortgage and household bills. They also have modest savings to tide them over in an emergency.

Also having just taken her children to school is a younger woman. She is in a hurry to get to work at the nearby fast-food restaurant because she has already been warned about being late. One of her children has been ill and her employer is less than sympathetic. She also works part-time, but resents the fact that because she is a single parent, and is heavily dependent on her earned income, she cannot be too choosy about the job she does. For her, opportunities for part-time working are more ambiguous, because she has to work despite the relatively poor conditions and low wages. She feels that her employer is taking advantage of her and the other young people she works with, since the firm can always find somebody else. This is partly because the work itself is tedious and very intensive so that some people can't stick it for very long, and partly because the relatively low levels of skill mean that the employer isn't investing much training in any particular employee. Staff turnover is not a problem. Although she knows that she could have found a better job if she had made more of an effort at school, and that she could go to the local college to gain some qualifications now, having to look after the children on her own makes this very difficult. Besides, most of her friends also left school as soon as they could, and either took unskilled jobs or expected to start a family. In her current circumstances she is more concerned about having some kind of income than she is about where exactly that income comes from. Her perception of the future of work is constructed almost entirely in terms of these immediate pragmatic necessities.

Two people who did decide to persevere with formal education are two young men in their early twenties. They are studying at university, and have a largely optimistic perspective on the future of work. Although neither of them has concrete plans about the kind of job they will find, they are confident that the general skills they are acquiring - working with computers, being responsible for organizing their work, being able to communicate effectively - will make them attractive to a prospective employer. They accept that they will have to be prepared to keep on top of new skills once at work, and that they are likely to move from one employer to another rather than staying with the same firm for the whole of their working lives. Whilst they are realistic about the fact that they may not be able to find continuous employment, they hope to be able to avoid serious financial problems by not taking on commitments which they cannot meet. Essentially they are flexible and positive in their attitude towards work and the kind of lifestyle they will be able to have once they leave university.

A quite different attitude is expressed by two other young men just crossing the road. They have gained some vocational qualifications at college, but have been unable to find work. To start with, they were not too concerned about this thinking that it was just a matter of time before a job came along. They hoped that the time they spent at college would pay them back, and that they would be able to avoid the long-term employment which both their fathers had experienced when the local engineering firm has closed down five years before. After two years on benefit though, they are becoming increasingly worried about their prospects. They feel that they are very much on the margins of employment. Either they have to take what ever kind of job they can, or have to take a chance on further training. The latter option has started to feel like a waste of time, since the qualifications they already have,

have not been very useful. They spoke about older friends who had spent several years passing from one training course to another only to find either that there just weren't any jobs, or that their skills always seem out of date. Like other members of their families, they are becoming quite fatalistic about the future of work. It sees that whatever they do, it is the general lack of semi-skilled jobs in the area which is the problem. Looking around, they know that with so many people chasing so few jobs, they actually have very little control over their future employment prospects.

Even from these few imagined examples, we can see that there is actually no single future of work, but a variety of different futures depending on who and how old you are, where you live, the kind of work you are looking for, and what your family obligations and circumstances are. Since we cannot specify what the future of work will be like for every single person, the most appropriate strategy to adopt is to identify and understand *the underlying patterns and trends* which are likely to be part of the structure and experience of work in the future. Sociologically, and without denying the individual and personal forms through which these features will be manifested, we are not so much interested in particular individuals as in the prevailing structures and patterns which will confront them as the future of work unfolds.

On the basis of what we already know about the nature and experience of work, we can anticipate the *key dimensions* along which these underlying patterns and trends will develop. In each case however, choices about *which* dimensions deserve our closest attention, and about *where* the balance of importance lies between one factor and another, are radically affected by the theoretical and discursive perspective, the particular kinds of argument and specific areas of debate with which the observer chooses to engage. In the same way that there is no single future of work, there is no single *analytical perspective* from which to develop an account of the future of work. Although some of these key dimensions will be common to a number of accounts - everyone would agree for example that in the advanced economies at least, fewer people will work in manufacturing, and that an increasing proportion of the workforce will be made up by women - the process of selecting those key dimensions, of deciding where to place the emphasis in the analysis, depends on the choices that various researchers have made between the different theoretical perspectives and their associated discourses which are available. In building up a comprehensive picture of the future of work, we need both to describe the leading trends and details, and to look critically at the different perspectives which are involved.

It will useful to begin by making a number of general observations about why different perspectives on work have been developed. As is the case in all

4

kinds of scientific investigation, knowledge is a process rather than a thing. What may seem to be 'received wisdom' at one point in time is likely to be regarded as 'old hat' at a later point in time; knowledge is thus provisional rather than absolute. Where we were once comfortable with, and indeed comforted by, a sense of surety in what we know about the nature and experience of work, important changes in the world of work are forcing us to reassess previous knowledge and to investigate new avenues of enquiry. As we shall see shortly, three of the clearest examples of this process of reassessment have emerged from feminist discourses on work, from those working within the tradition of cultural studies, and from those who are concerned with how work will be affected by the process of 'globalization'. As the former have pointed out, almost all accounts of the nature and experience of work carried out by industrial sociologists until the late 1970s, were done by male researchers about male employees. Given that women have always played an important part in both public and private economic life, we are bound to ask whether the knowledge developed in these earlier accounts is actually very 'knowledgeable' at all. Similar pressures for revision have come from cultural theorists, who propose that the practice and experience of work are deeply embedded in a much more complex and diverse range of cultural practices and experiences, many of which are to do with questions of identity. From a culturalist perspective, a lot more needs to be said about life outside the immediacies of work, and about the kinds of processes and connections which bind or splice working life into social and cultural life more generally.

This process of revision is given a further push in the back because of the particular characteristics of *social-scientific* knowledge and its subject matter. As Giddens has described it, our understanding of the social world in the late-modern period is 'reflexive' in the sense that we are constantly revising what we know (or more precisely what we think we know) in the light of new information about the social world. This knowledge doesn't stand outside its subject matter as something separate from it, but is more or less rapidly absorbed by social actors thus altering their future actions:

> Sociological knowledge spirals in and out of the universe of social life, reconstructing both itself and that universe as an integral part of that process.... Sociology (and the other social sciences which deal with extant human beings) does not develop cumulative knowledge in the same way as the natural sciences might be said to do. Per contra, the "feed-in" of sociological notions or knowledge claims into the social world is not a process that can be readily channelled, either by those who propose them or even by powerful groups or governmental agencies. Yet the practical impact of social science and sociological theories is enormous, and sociological concepts and findings

are constitutively involved in what modernity is. (Giddens 1990, pp.15-16, original emphasis)

Since the realm of work can be very responsive to the development of new ideas and perspectives, reflexively acquired and reflexively applied knowledge will almost inevitably result in the development of new discourses about work. Moreover, since the vast majority of the population are involved in work of one kind or another, these arguments and debates are not confined within the sometimes obscure world of the academy, but are very a much part of people's day-to-day lives. If for example, a company decides to introduce a different kind of management structure, or more dramatically, to re-locate its operations, these decisions and the knowledge on which they are based will have a very profound and immediate impact on the employees involved. New ideas about work and how it can be organized have practical rather than just academic consequences.

It is also important to consider why questions about the future of work have come to figure so prominently in the public imagination at the present time. A simple answer would be that people always have been concerned about the way they work and that the present concern is not new at all. A second answer might be that as we approach the beginning of a new century, people tend to become particularly conscious of the future and what it holds for them. The future of work is therefore simply part of our heightened future gaze. A more pragmatic answer however, is that people's present experiences of job insecurity and the more or less universal disappearance of the 'job for life', have seriously undermined our sense of economic well-being. If our only means of gaining the financial resources we need in order to live is through paid employment, then it is inevitable that instability within those means of livelihood will focus the mind quite sharply on what might happen next.

Although periods of instability, such as the great depression of the 1930s or the oil crises of the 1970s have happened before, these were largely followed by a resumption of work very much in the manner of what had gone before. What is different about the present crisis of employment, is that many of its key characteristics have changed radically and rapidly and at the same time. The widespread restructuring and reorganization of industry, the development of powerful new technologies, the displacement of established patterns of work by new occupations and new ways of working, important changes in the composition and distribution of the workforce, and new pressures from the increasingly global character of economic planning and practice, are generating a fundamental transformation of work. Important aspects of the future of work will be quite unlike the past of work.

In addition to these practical changes in the nature and organization of work, we are also concerned with changes in people's *perceptions* of what work will be like in the future. The future of work may involve significant changes in people's ideas about what work is, and how it fits into their lives as a whole. How for example, will these likely changes hinder or help the eradication of gender and other forms of segregation and discrimination? What impact will they have upon social, personal and familial relationships outside the immediate work environment? How readily will we accept that the earlier perception of work as a predominantly male, skilled and full-time activity has being displaced by a gender-neutral conception which acknowledges the growing dominance of part-time service occupations? If leisure and consumption are displacing work as the primary basis of self- and social identity, does this mean that the future or work will be one where work itself is of diminishing importance?

In recognizing the importance of work and the employment structure in the character and development of modern industrial societies, the question of the future of work occupies a prominent position in academic and theoretical debates. Whilst earlier debates over the nature of the capitalist labour process have been revived, these have been supplemented by new, and in some cases more complex theoretical perspectives, which seek to plot the likely future trajectory of recent changes.

From a Marxist perspective, important questions arise as to whether these changes signify the 'final' crisis of capitalism as the dominant system of economic production and exchange, or whether they are simply the latest stage in its historical development. If capitalism is moving from a Fordist to a post-Fordist phase, then it is necessary to understand the characteristics of this transition in order to make an informed appraisal of how further inequality and exploitation can be challenged and reversed.

From a liberal-pluralist perspective, it is largely accepted that capitalism is here to stay, and that recent changes can be accommodated within the present system as long as a number of the challenges they present are met in the correct way. The rightist conservative view holds that further relaxation of restraints on market forces is the best way forward, whilst the leftist social-democratic view argues that a new balance needs to be struck between the free market and the supportive structures of the welfare and social systems. From a economistic-managerial perspective, the primary concern remains one of how best to use the new methods of work organization in maintaining and increasing profits. If economic efficiency demands greater flexibility, then the further segmentation of the workforce between a specialized 'core' and a number of less specialized 'peripheries' is simply part-and-parcel of the development of more fluid patterns of employment and 'employability'.

From a broader social-theoretical perspective, the future of work debate cuts across a number of currents in theories of modernity. In tracing the underlying dynamics of 'late' or 'high' modernity for example, Giddens (1990) has stressed the importance of the twin processes of *capitalism* defined as 'a system of commodity production, centred upon the relation between private ownership of capital and propertyless wage labour', and *industrialism* defined as 'the use of inanimate sources of material power in the production of goods, coupled to the central role of machinery in the production process' (Giddens 1990, pp.55-6). To the extent that late-modernity is characterized by a particularly energetic combination of these institutional structures and practices, transition in the economic structure inevitably has an important bearing on the direction of modernity itself. In addition, the somewhat disruptive way in which current changes in the world of work are unfolding and the sense of uncertainty and fragmentation which this generates, are very much part of what modernity is. Giddens conjures up the image of a juggernaut to capture these feelings of opportunity and uncertainty:

> The juggernaut crushes those who resist it, and while it sometimes seems to have a steady path, there are times when it veers away erratically in directions we cannot foresee. The ride is by no means wholly unpleasant or unrewarding; it can often be exhilarating and charged with hopeful anticipation. But, so long as the institutions of modernity endure, we shall never be able to control completely either the path or the pace of the journey. In turn, we shall never be able to feel entirely secure, because the terrain across which it runs is fraught with risks of high consequence. Feelings of ontological security and existential anxiety will coexist in ambivalence. (Giddens 1990, p.139)

Experiences of loss of direction and control, a sense of being carried along by events in a discontinuous rather than evolutionary way, and the feeling of having to cope with unfamiliar pressures, are affecting all aspects of our lives. Against such a background it would certainly be surprising if we were *not* concerned about the future of work.

In developing our account of the future of work we need to keep a firm grip on reality. It is all too tempting to drift into a romanticized preview of the more glamorous and eye-catching features of the high-tech future of work. In such an account we would find a simple description of the kinds of work and employment which are typically available in the 1990s. We would read about the fact that many more people now find employment in service-type work, that brain has largely superseded brawn in the balance of activities at work. Within the diminishing realm of employment in manufacturing, we would read about how sophisticated automated and computer-controlled machines have displaced the need for manual labour. The grime and noise associated with heavy industry and manufacturing have been replaced by a much more convivial working environment closely regulated by the technology's need for cleanliness.

Amongst white-collar employees, we would read about office workers 'interacting' within a world saturated by data. Information technology in the form of telephones, fax machines, and computer modems provide the means of living within this information-intensive environment. In terms of the organization of work, we would read about how hierarchical vertical systems have been replaced by democratic horizontal systems where people are networked into groups. Team-working, target-setting and opportunity maximization are the new canons of the culture of the enterprise. Employees are no longer represented as functionaries and operatives, but as dynamic human resources who must be nurtured and stimulated.

This kind of account might provide the background for a speculative description of the more exotic possibilities for work in the future. In what we can call the *Star Trek* scenario, the tedium and stress of work are overshadowed by fantastical images of virtual reality, the internet, working from home, the electronic cottage, automated factories populated by intelligent machines working night and day. At last we will have achieved the kind of Utopia described by H.G.Wells at the end of the nineteenth century:

> But now that the new conditions physical science is bringing about, not only dispense with man as a source of energy but supply the hope that all routine work may be made automatic, it is becoming conceivable that presently there may be no need for any one to toil habitually at all; that a labouring class - that is to say, a class of workers without personal initiative - will become unnecessary to the world of men.... [Were] our political and social and moral devices only as well contrived to their ends as a linotype machine, an antiseptic operating plant, or an electric tramcar, there need now at the present moment be no appreciable toil in the world, and only the smallest fraction of the pain, the fear, and the anxiety that now makes human life so doubtful in its value. There is more than enough for every one alive. (H.G. Wells, *A Modern Utopia*, 1905, p.56)

Despite the attractiveness of these images, we have to accept that they are still just fragments of a much more complex and less glamorous whole which will continue to include very many low-tech mundane activities which our grandparents, let alone our parents, would find familiar. Whilst it is certainly true that many features of work are changing, that microelectronic technologies are by their nature extremely flexible and adaptable, and that whatever else it is, modernity is profoundly dynamic and full of momentum for change, it is also true that many aspects of people's working lives and expectations of work are likely to remain constant. Most importantly, we have to accept that people *need* work, are *motivated* to work, and have *basic expectations* of work, which are unlikely to be discarded simply because of the introduction of e-mail or a more sophisticated photo-copying machine.

Although new technologies can change many aspects of work, they don't have the magical capacity to change everything. In a hospital or school for example, many working activities are by their nature physical and manual and are likely to remain so. Whilst looking for evidence of change therefore, and whilst trying to predict what these changes tell us about the future, we also need to discuss those features which are changing much less quickly.

Understanding the future of work therefore requires an assessment of where the balance lies between the established and the new, between high-tech and low-tech, between the familiar and the unfamiliar. It means accepting that the future of work is as much about *continuity* as it is about *change*.

The Scope of the Analysis

Turning to a number of the terms used in the following account, the first thing which needs clarifying is the word 'work'. Although it can be argued that our definition of work can include a very wide range of activities, and that the future of work debate is itself partly about redefining the category of activities which we include under this heading (see Ransome 1996), we are primarily concerned here with activities for which people receive direct financial remuneration in the context of a discernible and legally sanctioned employment structure. For present purposes then, work is defined as formal paid employment.

Secondly, what do we mean when we talk about the *future* of work? The future stretches from the immediate present to infinity. In terms of this analysis however, we are talking about a more limited period of time associated with the unfolding of recent developments in the nature and organization of work. Although the conclusions reached will certainly have an important bearing on the longer term future, perhaps stretching up to the middle of the next century and beyond, our immediate focus is on developments which are likely to take place during the next twenty to thirty years. A period which could be seen as equivalent to the most active working years of a twenty-five year old person entering the workforce during the late-1990s.

Although this might seem to be a relatively short period of time, it is well to remember that in many crucial respects, the dramatic pace and scope of recent changes in the world of work are such that a great deal can change even within a period of two or three years. Indeed one of the features of the changes which are taking place, is precisely that new orthodoxies and practices are following one upon the other much more rapidly than in any previous period of industrial development.

Thirdly, *whose* future of work are we talking about? Again the potential scope could be very large indeed if it sought to include all the peoples of the world, and the diverse ways in which they organize their economic life. Enforcing our definition of work as formal paid employment, and concentrating on transformative trends many of which are driven by technological advance, we are primarily concerned with the nature and organization of work in societies which already have an advanced industrial infrastructure. Whilst accepting that a number of societies, particularly the Southeast Asian economies of the Pacific Rim, are developing these facilities at an accelerated rate, and bearing in mind the increasingly global dimensions of the' division of labour, our main evidence will be based on the situation in Europe and the USA.

Plan of Chapters

Having set a number of preliminary limits to the analysis, the next task is to consider which dimensions of change deserve our closest attention. As already noted, getting a proper grip on the subject means more than simply describing current changes and projecting them into the future. In terms of general approach, and as already discussed above, two broad themes will be present throughout the analysis. The first, is that the future of work involves a combination of continuity and change. There is no point in developing a glitzy sci-fi image of the future of work only to find that the privileged few who are working from home in their electronic cottages, are vastly outnumbered by the millions whose experience of work is still closely circumscribed by the routines and pressures of conventional forms of working. For every graphic designer working with advanced computer-aided-design or virtual-reality software, there are literally thousands of people serving in shops, packing things into boxes in warehouses, driving things from one place to another, or tending to the young, the old and the sick.

The second, is that work involves a combination of ideas and practicalities, of conception and execution. If for example, we observe a technician in a factory or a labourer on a building site, we can produce a

11

detailed exterior account of *what* they are doing. We can describe their actions and the skills they use, how their work fits in with that of their colleagues and so on. Less easy to describe is their *experience* of work, their *ideas* about what they are doing, and their *expectations* of work. To unlock these interior consequences of work we need theories and methods which are suited to this particular kind of analysis.

The book is structured around a chapter-by-chapter analysis of the leading perspectives and associated discourses and debates which are currently being used in looking at the future of work. As already noted, there is more than one way of looking at the future of work, and thus more than one future of work that can be described. To get the ball rolling we can make a broad distinction between narrative perspectives which tend to adopt a story-telling approach encompassing a number of themes at the same time, and issue-specific perspectives which tend to concentrate on one issue or closely related set of issues. In highlighting the narrative aspects of some perspectives it should be emphasized that we are not only interested in them because of the detailed descriptions they provide, but also because they offer interesting theoretical insights and useful analytical tools which we might want to use in our own analysis of the future of work. From a sociological point of view, the question is as much about *how* and *why* things change as it is about *what* has changed; we need to understand the nature of the underlying processes involved as well as the details. This brings us into the realm of theoretical frameworks and suppositions, and towards a deeper consideration of the methods used and the type of evidence deployed. Since we cannot be certain about what will happen until it actually is happening (and even then opinions will differ), it is quite legitimate to develop theoretical means of predicting what is most likely to happen. An important part of our investigation then, is to look again at what previous theorists have had to say, and to see whether their theoretical propositions continue to apply.

We can identify three main narratives on work which will be discussed in the first two chapters. The first, which we can call the narrative of industrialism, was a response to the emergence of industrialism during the latter years of the nineteenth and early years of the twentieth centuries. The key contributors here are Karl Marx, Max Weber and Emile Durkheim. The second was a response to the possible transcendence of industrialism by post-industrialism during the 1960s and 1970s. Contemporary debates over technological change, post-Fordism and the so-called flexible future constitute the third narrative which we will be looking at. As we shall see, it is by no means coincidental that these three narratives emerged at precisely the time when the repercussions of the first phase of industrialism (the industrial revolution), the second phase centred around Fordist-style mass production and automation, and the third phase centred around the development of microelectronic technologies had really taken hold throughout the labour process. The authors of these narratives didn't seek explanations of what was going on just for the sake of it, but because they recognized the significance of the widespread changes which were taking place around them. The same can be said for the author of this book and most likely for all those who are currently concerned about what the repercussions of present changes will be.

Turning to what we are going to call issue-specific perspectives and accepting that these are by no means free of narrative content, we will look in turn at the following. Firstly, and deliberately picking up on issues of a practical nature, chapter three looks at arguments and debates which are based around the idea of the emergence of a new 'technological paradigm'. Whilst these obviously start out from a concern with technological change, they also embrace its impact on issues of skill and quality of working life, on management practices, and on organization and control.

Chapter four looks at the future of work from a feminist perspective. The importance of this perspective is that it has made the most forthright attempt to understand both the increasing role of women in formal paid employment - what some have called the 'feminization' of work - and to consider whether this development has actually been very successful from the point of view of women themselves. Serious concerns are being expressed for example, about an evident concentration of women in particular occupations, many of which are poorly paid and insecure, and about how the labour market operates with various levels of discriminatory segregation. Writers in this field have also made a very significant contribution in bringing into the open important questions about how ideologies of work are gendered, about the role of the household in social reproduction, and of how 'work' should be defined under circumstances where much of the 'work' that women do within the household is effectively done 'for free'.

In chapters five and six we turn our attention towards two of the most important perspectives which have emerged in recent years. We can group the first under the heading of culturalist and identity perspectives which place a firm emphasis on the role of work in providing people with an extensive range of outcomes which have typically been left out of account by traditional labour-process approaches. Here, the main concern is not so much with the practical and material outcomes of work as with the personal, experiential and thus less visible outcomes. These approaches also attempt to reassess the role and meaning of work both in terms of its impact on people's sense of identity, and in terms of where the balance lies between people's activities as workers

13

and their activities as consumers. If we are drifting towards a more consumption-oriented outlook on life, then important questions arise as to whether the whole experience of work become less important to us.

Chapter six looks at how processes of economic globalization are affecting our perceptions of what the future of work will be like. Whilst it is certainly true that international capitalism has always and necessarily operated between and across nation-states, recent developments have made the global dimension much more explicit. As part-and-parcel of the process of modernity itself, and greatly facilitated by information and other technologies of communication, economic processes and relationships are increasingly being affected by pressures which operate at a global level. Whilst these developments are being interpreted by some as signifying a radical shift in the nature of global economic activity, others have argued that the case for an all-encompassing and convergent notion of economic globalization has been grossly overstated.

In the final chapter a number of conclusions will be drawn about the problematical nature of making clear predictions about the future of work. It will be argued that the various perspectives tend to offer competing views of what the future will be thus underlining the fact that the future of work is a plural rather than singular thing. We will also reconsider briefly the continuing usefulness of the various narrative approaches to the future of work we looked at in the opening chapters, and emphasize that a tension will continue to exist between changes in the structural aspects of work - the practicalities of work and how it is organized, and changes in its ideational aspects - what we think about work and how we would like it to change. It will be argued that ideational flexibility is one of the most important features of the future of work.

1 The Narrative of Industrialism

A Typical Narrative of Work

The first three perspectives we shall be looking at involve a largely *narrative account* of the future of work. Typically within this type of account the future is framed or constructed out of an understanding of what has happened in the past. Notwithstanding the problematical nature of 'knowledge' just discussed, this kind of approach is attractive because we all like a good story. It is also comforting because it reassures us that despite our present difficulties we are all going to live 'happily ever after'. This optimism amounts to a continual refurbishment of the idea of progress. Not only are things going to turn out right in the end, they are going to be bigger and better than they were before. The idea of progress has occupied an important position within both the popular imagination and sociological theory ever since its inception during the nineteenth century. Picking up on one of the leading ideas of the European Enlightenment (see for example Hampson 1990, ch.2, Swingewood 1984, chs. 1 and 2 and Morrison 1995, ch.1), humankind reinvented its own image of itself as 'master' of its own destiny.

Our capacity for creative action motivates us to improve ourselves as time goes by, an improvement which is not random, is not an unfolding of blind chance or fate, but is deliberate and directed towards fairly definite goals which we have set for ourselves. Instead of being fixed in the present, or obsessed with the past, human endeavour became focused on the future. Although the final outcome cannot be known, this merely adds to the excitement of finding out what *can be* achieved. Since society is essentially a product of human effort, human progress means social development. If social scientists could discover the underlying processes of social development, this opened the possibility of using this knowledge to intervene in the next stage of progress. Social-scientific knowledge itself becomes a key ingredient of social development. As Francis puts it:

> At the heart of sociology lies the idea that human behaviour is conditioned by social environment.... Armed with [a scientific understanding of man and history] mankind would no longer be at the mercy of blind historical processes. It would be possible to control the course of history by reconstructing society in accordance with the laws of human behaviour. By

15

perfecting man's social environment one could perfect man himself. (Francis 1987, p.3)

In one of the earliest attempts to define the 'positive' potential of the new science of sociology, Auguste Comte is quite explicit that knowledge of the past has an important bearing on understanding what lessons the past holds for the future:

> The aim of every science is forethought. For the laws established by observation of phenomena are generally employed to foresee their succession. All men, however little advanced, make true predictions, which are always based on the same principle, the knowledge of the future from the past.... Manifestly, then, it is quite in accordance with the nature of the human mind that observation of the past should unveil the future in politics, as it does in astronomy, physics, chemistry, and physiology. The determination of the future must even be regarded as the direct aim of political science, as in the case of the other positive sciences. Indeed, it is clear that knowledge of what social system the elite of mankind is called to by the progress of civilization - knowledge forming the true practical object of positive science - involves a general determination of the next social future as it results from the past. (Comte 1822, 'Plan for scientific work necessary for reorganising society', quoted in Kumar 1983, pp.23-4)

In addition to all of this, the arrival of the idea that human society develops through time, provided a conceptual framework for understanding the past. Previous periods in history, previous manifestations of society, could be understood as the earlier stages, the stepping stones, of social *evolution*. Having taken humankind out of history, having separated humankind from nature and fate, it could now be put back into history, and the social and the biological aspects of development could be reconciled. Kumar goes so far as to suggest that the idea of *biological* evolution actually developed out of the idea of *social* evolution:

> Indeed it isn't far-fetched to suppose that the attention to change brought by the idea of progress stimulated inquiries in an evolutionary direction in the natural sciences. At any rate, to complement the theory of social evolution ... there was now a highly satisfactory theory of natural - geological and biological - evolution. The natural and social world could now be seen as continuous; human social evolution was a special case of biological evolution in general; the principles of order and change in the one applied equally to the other. (Kumar 1983, pp.18-19)[1]

One justification for Kumar's suggestion, is that Darwin's theory of 'natural selection' was published *after* the social theorist and 'gentleman scholar'

16

Herbert Spencer had popularised his idea that the principal mechanism of biological and social development was through 'the survival of the fittest' (described in *Social Statics*, 1851).

In brief, Spencer identifies three types or levels of evolution and the categories of scientific knowledge and modes of investigation which go with them: the natural sciences (geology, physics and astronomy) are concerned with identifying the mechanisms of evolution of inorganic matter; the biological sciences are concerned with organic matter, and sociology is concerned with the mechanism of evolution of society itself. Sociology then, is the study of the 'super-organic' - a level of knowledge which seeks to unite theories of inorganic and organic evolution into one complete system of knowledge. As Spencer puts it:

> The study of Sociology [is] the study of Evolution in its most complex form.... Throughout [the work of sociologists] there runs the assumption that the facts, simultaneous and successive, which societies present, have a genesis no less natural than the genesis of other classes [of phenomena].... Using the analogy supplied by human life, we saw that just as bodily development and structure and function, furnish subject matter for biological science... so social growth and the rise of structures and functions accompanying it, furnish matter for a Science of Society... we saw, on comparing rudimentary societies with one another and with societies in different stages of progress, that they do present certain common traits of structure and of function, as well as certain common traits of development. (Spencer in Thompson and Tunstall (1971), pp.33-43)

Although Spencer's highly naturalistic view of social evolution has been largely rejected by contemporary theorists (Goldthorpe in Raison (ed.) (1979), it is difficult to cast off completely the idea that we and the society in which we live are evolving towards some 'higher' state.

Applied to the world of work a typical narrative might run something like this. Humankind emerged from a primitive state of hunting and gathering during the early stone age (from around 600,000 to 100,000 years BC) into a more settled state of agrarian communities during the middle and late stone age (up to around 10,000 BC). These communities began to coalesce into larger rural and semi-urban settlements during the bronze (3,500-800 BC) and iron ages (from 800 BC), characterized by a more elaborate division and specialization of tasks. Metalworking and thus tool making enabled significant increases in production to take place, which in turn led to the beginnings of non-local trade. The emergence of new hierarchies and distinctions in economic life (for example between slaves, labourers, craftsmen, proprietors and lords), together with the need for governmental structures and administrative systems, was accompanied by the emergence

17

and consolidation of social and cultural hierarchies. Despite the rather faltering rate of 'technological' progress during the medieval period (typically from the end of the Roman Empire in 476 to the Ottoman conquest of Constantinople in 1453) these relationships reached a level of maturity based on the authority of private ownership of land.

The period from the Renaissance in Europe around 1450, up to the emergence of the first industrial revolution in Northern Europe around 1750 was a period of transition, in which many of the constraints of feudal society were gradually displaced and subsequently replaced by industrial society. As far as economic life was concerned, and apart from continuing innovations in agriculture, the most important developments were a considerable expansion of entrepreneurial activity both within Europe and between Europe and the recently discovered 'new worlds', and the expansion of non-agricultural industries in, amongst other things, the mining of coal and other necessary minerals and ores, and in the manufacturing of other desirables such as glass, paper and gunpowder. The earth-bound nature of many of these new activities meant regional concentration of industry. In the same way that it is not practicable to graze sheep in places where there is no grass, it is not possible to mine coal where there is none.

Between 1750 and 1900 industrial society really shifted into top gear. Beginning in the textile industries, the application of new technologies and ways of organizing industrial work in factories massively increased the economic output of the key European players.[2] By 1781 Arkwright's Cromford factory employed nearly 1,000 workers, while by the turn of the century there were in excess of 150 water-powered factories in northern England and the midlands. By the nineteenth century, the size of the workforce in the average mill was around 500, and steam-power had almost completely replaced water-power. As a measure of production in cotton textiles, imports of raw cotton increased from around 2 million lbs in the 1730s to over 33 million lbs in the 1790s.

Similar dramatic developments took place in iron and steel production (which in England increased from 68 thousand tons in 1788 to 6.5 *million* tons in 1873 and upwards of 9 million tons in 1914), and in coal production which rose from 8 to 50 millions tons between 1750 and 1850 to over 130 million tons by 1875.[3] The massive canal- and road-building projects of the 1790s, together with the development of the steam railway (by 1860 over 12,000 miles of track had been laid in Britain) represented both the symbolic and the practical completion of the transition to a fully industrialized economic infrastructure.

With the coming of industrial society the land-based authority of the old feudal aristocracy was more or less completely displaced by the capital-based authority of the industrial entrepreneur. Increasing output in manufactured goods generated large amounts of capital which was eagerly re-invested in new ventures. At the lower end of the social hierarchy, the mass of the working population was settling down to an urban rather than a rural way of life. The natural rhythm of the seasons and cycles of cultivation were almost entirely replaced by clock-based time (Thompson, E.P., 1967). Working had become a distinct realm of activity, a calibrated portion of the day spent at the place of work.

This transition was accompanied by a qualitative change in the nature and experience of work, because now that the worker was paid in relation to the time spent at work, rather than in terms of the product itself, the relationship between the doing of the work and the work done was much more abstract. The most extreme case was in the highly mechanized factory, where mass production was, by definition, concerned with producing large numbers of identical components or products. It therefore mattered very little which individual had produced which particular item. The division of labour in industry therefore required workers who were prepared to forfeit any real or direct conception of how their effort and skill manifested itself in the final product.

This shift into mechanized and factory-based working also brought about an explicit separation of the place of work from the home of the worker. Work had become a public rather than private activity. The new pattern of work also involved a change in the division of labour between men and women as the earlier self-sufficiency of the household based on a sharing of activities between men, women and children, was replaced by a dependent household characterized by a much more explicit division of work between family members (Thompson, E.P., 1963, Anderson 1974, Pahl 1984).

At the turn of the twentieth century, the pattern of development which had begun in Britain replicated itself across Northern Europe and the United States. The industrial revolution had established an economic system based on the production and sale of manufactured goods. The merging of the large industrial firms into a small number of joint stock companies, corporations and industrial conglomerates, together with the development of ever more sophisticated and reliable international networks of transportation and communication, meant that industrialism had become a truly 'global' affair. A rise in standards of living, first amongst the expanding middle classes, and later amongst the working classes, provided an essential market for the increasing variety of manufactured goods.

The spiral of supply and demand of manufactured goods for domestic consumption meant that industrial society was also 'consumer society'. This was a new kind of commercial ethos in which passive response to traditional tastes was superseded by actively developing new products and stimulating new consumer demands. The division of labour was extended to include a new range of functions performed by a new strata of non-manual employees as firms now had to devote an increasing proportion of their resources to planning, advertising and sales. As both the quantity and quality of information about the firm and its various interlocking functions increased, managers required more and more support from white-collar clerical staff. The intellectual information-handling paper-based occupations of the office, had become at least as important as the manual materials-handling machine-based occupations of the workshop and factory floor.

Outside private industry, demand for people to work in the public sector also increased as the state became the major provider of education and other forms of health and social welfare thus establishing career structures in government and public administration, education and health, and later in social and welfare services. With good career prospects, relatively high levels of pay, and rising social status, these new 'service sector' occupations, consolidated the shift away from heavy manual industrial occupations.

Technological advance in sources of power, communications, and in new manufacturing processes and products continued to stimulate economic development. Within industry, and following the lead taken in motor manufacture and chemicals, automated production lines and continuous processing techniques became the new model. Within the manufacturing sector, and to an increasing extent outside it, the demarcations between blue and white-collar occupations which had begun to emerge a few decades earlier, become firmly established, with a growing proportion of the workforce engaged in technical, design, managerial, administrative and clerical tasks. Outside manufacturing, the service sector continued to grow in importance, both in response to industry's need for business and other financial services, and in response to the new demands of the welfare state in Europe and the United States.

With near full employment during the 1950s and 1960s came rising prosperity, prosperity meant affluence, and affluence meant even more consumption. Whereas work had once been seen as an unremitting struggle for survival, people now came to expect that there would be sufficient income left over to achieve the better things in life. With the help of the mass media, the horizon of pleasure and images of the good life moved onwards and upwards. Even if work did involved some sacrifice of personal autonomy, this was the necessary price one had to pay for membership of consumer society.

While the 1960s and early 1970s represented the high point of industrialism in the established economies of the West, the 1980s and 1990s have been characterized by a considerable levelling-off and subsequent decline in their economic fortunes. Internally, the dominant theme is one of industrial and economic transition, characterized by a widespread feeling of uncertainty and perplexity. The very considerable, and in some cases total contraction of traditional heavy industries (mining, steel manufacture, ship building), combined with the widespread automation and restructuring of manufacturing enterprises (car manufacture, engineering, assembly and production firms) has resulted in severe shortages of employment and mis-matches between 'old' skills and 'new' jobs. The hoped-for increase in service-type occupations has proved to be only temporary as this sector has itself completed a period of restructuring with the associated shedding of jobs and reorientation of skills.

Externally, the balance of economic power in the global economy has shifted away from the regions which became dominant during the first wave (industrial revolution) and second wave (Fordism) of industrial innovation, towards regions whose industrialization coincided with the third wave of innovations based on microelectronic technologies. These technologies (including information technologies), and the new methods of working they require, have been adopted much more quickly by the economies of the Pacific Rim, and particularly in Japan, than they have been in the mature industrial economies, which have been reluctant to modify the techniques and working practices which underlay their own success earlier in the century. Rather than simply providing convenient markets for western goods, the rising economies have become major exporters in their own right. Western dominance over the world market, and the sense of security and confidence which this allowed, have had their day.

How does this kind of narrative account help us in approaching our study of the future of work? The first point to make is that it shows us that work is *always* undergoing a process of refinement and development. During periods when the rate of change is particularly slow, it may *appear* that work is constant and unchanging, but this apparent constancy is simply relative compared to times when change is more rapid. We should not be surprised therefore to discover that our working futures will also be characterized by change.

It also alerts us to the fact that since such developments are characterized by a constant shifting between old and new occupations, between established and innovative patterns of work, there will always be winners and losers. We

21

may be fixated with the idea that changes in work will always be positive, that transition represents an upwards leap from a lower to a higher level, but history contains at least as many examples of great civilizations and economies which have collapsed and been replaced by far less sophisticated ones.

Secondly, perceptions of change are governed by the span of time covered by the narrative. If instead of describing the whole history of work we had concentrated only on events during the medieval period, we would have got much more excited about the introduction of the iron plough sheer, the use of fertilisers, and the introduction of the three-field system of crop rotation. These particulars would have become much more important and might even be described as 'revolutionary'. In our more condensed account however these innovations don't even get a mention.

In describing change then, we need to keep our eye on the ball and not overestimate the *relative importance* of one development compared with another. It may sometimes be that gradual changes, those which are barely noticed at the time, have a more significant impact than those which hit the headlines. One current example of this is the hype which surrounds the genetic 'engineering' of animals for the production of food. Although scientifically important, they are unlikely to have much of an impact on working practices or the experience of work.

Thirdly, and related to the above, narrative accounts are very good at identifying what we can call 'periods of transition'. By deliberately taking the longer view they help us to understand not only what these transitions are made of, but how their ramifications work themselves through into the periods which follow. This approach is not however without its dangers since the desire on the part of the author to keep the story going may lead him or her into giving the impression that a particular event 'altered the direction' of work, how this or that period was one of 'dramatic change'. For example, the transcendence of feudalism by industrialism, which actually took a couple of centuries to complete, becomes 'a watershed', 'a great leap forward' in human economic affairs. Stripped of the surrounding detail, it appears to be a sudden event, a before and an after.

Perhaps the clearest example of such a dispute surrounds accounts of the timing of the 'industrial revolution' itself. Lane explains that scholars are divided over whether the term 'revolutionary' is actually very appropriate on the grounds that industrialism followed a much longer and more gradual path. He quotes two leading authorities on the period to illustrate this apparently contradictory reading of events:

When, on looking back we find that the revolution has been going on for two centuries, and had been in preparation for two centuries before that... we may begin to doubt whether the term... has not by this time served its turn. (George Unwin quoted in Lane 1978, p.3)

The word "revolution" implies a suddenness of change that is not, in fact, characteristic of economic processes. The system of human relationships that is sometimes called capitalism had its origins long before 1760, and attained its full development long after 1830; there is a danger of overlooking the essential fact of continuity. But the phrase 'Industrial Revolution' has been used by a long line of historians and has become so firmly embedded in common speech that it would be pedantic to offer a substitute. (T.S.Ashton *The Industrial Revolution 1760-1830*, quoted in Lane 1978, p.3)[4]

A major consideration in identifying these great transitions is the *content and scope* of the events themselves. Essentially what we are looking for is a *combination* of changes or developments whose effects move beyond the particular to the general. In this sense, the period from 1760 to 1830 counts as a 'great transformation' because the ingredients of industrialism came together in such a way as to *irreversibly alter* the patterns, structures and experiences of working life. On its own the steam engine or the industrial entrepreneur or the factory system could not have done this. In combination they undoubtedly did.

The term *industrial* revolution gives the game away about the kinds of factors which are regarded as the most important in developing narratives about the future of work. What we have to be interested in are those factors which directly affect and characterize working life. Amongst the most important are technological innovation, the day-to-day organization of work, economic relationships both national and global, and between different groups within society, and attitudes towards, and expectations of work. When we come across such a combination, then, on the basis of our knowledge of similar events in the past, we are justified in labelling such a period as 'transitional' or 'revolutionary'.

For economic historians of the future, it is extremely likely that the 1990s will be described as just such a period of transition. Already we can imagine how an historian writing in 2050 will record these events. This was a period in which the paradigm of microelectronics became fully integrated into the organization of work. It was a period of transition similar in scale and scope to that which developed in the nineteenth century with the development of steam power, and earlier in the twentieth century with the introduction of Fordist methods of mechanization and automation. The shift away from

23

manufacturing towards services reached full maturity. With increasing efficiency of production, combined with a shifting of labour-intensive employment away from the relatively expensive developed regions in the North and West towards the emerging regions in Southeast Asia and Eastern Europe, enterprises concentrated on meeting the growing demand for ever more varied commercial and personal services to relieve the tensions created by intensified globalized economic activity.

These services came to play a leading role in the ability to compete. One of the most vigorous areas of development was at the level of organization. Constraints on productive capacity shifted up from the practical challenges of making machines do various tasks, to the challenge of deciding how best to organize the overall business of the enterprise. As the life-expectancy of process and product innovations continued to shorten in anticipation of the next set of developments and changes in consumer demand, the main challenge was to remain competitive in the context of fluid and organic approaches to management.

The 1980s and 1990s was a period in which the rapid growth in state-funded employment during the 1960s and 1970s was checked and reversed. Whilst state spending on national defence continued to fall, increasing domestic tensions between the wealthy minority and the less prosperous majority resulted in a shift of resources towards internal security. This was also the period in which the stereotype of work as a predominantly male-dominated full-time and life-long activity which dominated economic life during the nineteenth and early twentieth centuries, was gradually displaced by a much more gender-neutral stereotype of work as time-flexible, contract-based and periodic. It is amusing to think that people were once reluctant to accept this more open and reflexive orientation to work.

The main protagonists of the first narrative account we shall be looking at are Karl Marx, Max Weber and Emile Durkheim. Although for convenience we are grouping their contributions together under the single heading 'narrative of industrialism' it is important to note at the outset that the focus of interest does vary from one to the other. The main difference is that whereas Marx and Weber place particular emphasis on *the relationship between* industrialism and capitalism, Durkheim is interested in the development of industrialism defined more neutrally as a particular *set of techniques* of production and economic organization. In some accounts, the former are therefore described as 'theorists of capitalism', and the latter as a 'theorist of industrialism'.

These differences in both *their own* substantive analyses, and in *the later interpretation* of their work derive in part from the intellectual ancestry of the concepts they use. Building respectively on concepts developed within Hegelian Idealism, British Political Economy, and French Socialism, and on philosophical and methodological debates discussed by the neo-Kantians Wilhelm Windelband and Heinrich Rickert, and the more 'cultural' issues raised by Werner Sombart and Georg Simmel, Marx and Weber are explicitly concerned with the wider social and historical implications not only of industrial development itself, but of how these developments are implicated in the development of capitalism as a *specific historical type* of social formation.

In contrast, Durkheim's principal intellectual ancestors, Henri Saint-Simon and Augusts Comte, led him towards as less politicized and more sociologically neutral concern with how modern societies develop out of pre-modern societies.[5] What each of these accounts does have in common however, is that their different interpretations express a shared concern with the ways in which the productive process plays a pivotal role in economic and social development.

In the context of our present discussion of the future of work, it will be useful to focus on the advantages of each approach in understanding four types of issues: (i) the role of the economic structure within society; (ii) the technical and organizational dimensions of work; (iii) the nature of working relationships, and (iv) the qualitative and experiential aspects of work within the industrial division of labour.

Karl Marx

For Marx, material production lies at the very heart of social life: 'As individuals express their life, so they are. What they are, therefore, coincides with their production, both with *what* they produce and with *how* they produce. The nature of individuals thus depends on the material conditions determining their production' (Marx and Engels 1970, p.42). If we want to understand social development first we have to understand the development of the labour process.

Although as we shall see later in this chapter, more recent approaches have tended to down grade the importance of this relationship, it is quite unrealistic to suppose that the labour process of the future will have anything other than a very considerable impact on social development. If this were not the case, if changes in the world of work were merely incidental to social development, then people might not be very interested in the future of work at all.

Taking this as his starting point, Marx goes on to observe that economic and thus social development is not random, is not something which just happens as if by accident, but is instigated and regulated by the dynamic of what he calls 'the productive forces' of society:

> No social order ever perishes before all the productive forces for which there is room in it have developed; and new, higher relations of production never appear before the material conditions of their existence have matured in the womb of the old society itself. Therefore mankind always sets itself only such tasks as it can solve; since, looking at the matter more closely, it will always be found that the task itself arises only when the material conditions for its solution already exist or are at least in the process of formation. (Marx, Preface to *A Critique of Political Economy,* in McLellan 1977, p.390)

There are two important messages for us here. The first is that in our search for clues about what will happen in the labour process of future we have to begin by looking at the labour process of the present. The second is that *the pressure for change* is itself generated by *the limitations* of present practices.

At first glance this seems rather obvious because if there was nothing wrong with current working practices, then why should we want to change them? The much more subtle and important point that Marx is making however, is that there are *concrete reasons* why this should be the case, reasons which have a definite historical pattern to them. Although Marx bases his analysis on one particular episode of technical development - the transcendence of small-scale handicraft-based manufacturing by what he calls Modern Industry in the first decades of the eighteenth century - the basic principles of what he has to say can be applied just as effectively *to any* historical period including the present one.

The Productive Forces

In his analysis of the capitalist labour process of the mid-nineteenth century, Marx identifies two aspects of the productive forces which are reaching their limits; the practical organization of work, and the economic relationships which constitute the labour process. With regard to technical and organizational change, he explains that each new development contains remnants of previous developments. Initially things progress quite nicely as an accommodation can be reached between the old and the new. After a while however, problems emerge as attempts to make further improvements in the advanced parts of the process are more and more constrained by the inherent limitations of the more rudimentary processes onto which they were grafted.

He illustrates this with a detailed account of how Modern Industry first built upon, and then superseded the craft-based system of small-scale manufacturing which had prevailed in the earlier part of the eighteenth century. For Marx, Modern Industry, which is variously defined as 'the collective machine', 'a huge automaton', 'an automatic system of machinery'; 'attains its most highly developed form in the organised system of machinery in a factory' (Marx 1954, *Capital I*, p.372). He continues:

> Here, then, we see in Manufacture the immediate technical foundation of Modern Industry. Modern Industry produced the machinery, by means of which Modern Industry abolished the handicraft and manufacturing systems in those spheres of production that it first seized upon. The factory system was therefore raised, in the natural course of things, on an inadequate foundation. When the system attained to a certain degree of development, it had to root up this ready-made foundation, which in the meantime had been elaborated on the old lines, and to build up for itself a basis that should correspond to its methods of production.... Modern Industry became technologically incompatible with the basis furnished for it by handicraft and Manufacture. (Marx 1954, *Capital I*, pp.361-2)

Having described the stages through which each new level of technical innovation must pass, Marx then explains where the desire for improvement comes from. The simple answer is that it is in our nature always to be looking for new ways of doing things. This stems partly from our creative consciousness (of which more below) and partly from our near obsession with the idea of progress referred to earlier in this chapter.

More precisely however, Marx suggests that the desire for change increases as a direct result of increases in the potential of the technology to make new things possible. The greater the possibilities offered by the technology, the more forceful is the desire to realize those possibilities. When we catch glimpses of what might be possible, the main question in our minds is not so much why, as why *not*? As far as Marx is concerned, it is precisely because the techniques of Modern Industry are so full of potential for change, that they represent such an important step forward in human history - they are in fact 'revolutionary':

> Modern Industry never looks upon and treats the existing form of a process as final. The technical basis of that industry is therefore revolutionary, while earlier modes of production were essentially conservative. By means of machinery, chemical processes and other methods, it is continually causing changes not only in the technical basis of production, but also in the functions of the labourer, and in the social combinations of the labour-process. At the

same time, it thereby also revolutionises the division of labour within the society, and thereby also launches masses of capital and of workpeople from one branch of production to another. (Marx 1954, *Capital I*, p.457)

The emergence of the factory system of Modern Industry with its mechanization of production and ever more sophisticated division of labour necessarily has powerful implications for the second set of limitations discussed by Marx, namely those associated with 'traditional' patterns of working and working relationships. Accepting that the relations of production, characterized by the division of labour, are part of the 'productive forces' of industrial society,[6] they are necessarily heavily involved in the implementation of technical change in the labour process. The application of new techniques cannot be achieved without also changing the way that work is organized. In the same way that Modern Industry has to overcome the limitations of early manufacturing, it also has to overcome the limitations of earlier manifestations of the division of labour. It is not just the spinning wheel or loom which have to be mechanized, the worker too has to be automated:

> Modern Industry... sweeps away by technical means the manufacturing division of labour, under which each man is bound hand and foot for life to a single detail-operation. At the same time, the capitalistic form of that industry reproduces this same division of labour in a still more monstrous shape; in the factory proper, by converting the workman into a living appendage of the machine. (Marx 1954, *Capital I*, p.455)

Under circumstances where relatively minor changes are involved this may not pose much of a problem. Asking a clerical worker to use a word processor rather than a typewriter, or an assembly worker to use a digital rather than a mechanical tool hardly constitutes a revolution in the forces of production. However, the introduction of major changes is likely to be much more problematic as, quite naturally, people are suspicious of changes which may undermine the familiarities of the work they do and the established ways in which they interact with other people. This resistance to change constitutes a considerable problem for enterprises which are trying to upgrade from an older system to a newer one (Burns and Stalker 1961, Silverman 1970, Salaman 1981, Donaldson 1985, Thompson and McHugh 1990).

It is at this point that Marx's specific analysis of the industrial labour process coincides with his wider critique of capitalism as a particular type of social formation. Without attempting a complete review of what he has to say about these complex issues, the important point to grasp is that in order to understand the process by which change takes place within the labour process, in order to identify the kinds of limitations which may hinder its future progress, we have to be aware of the wider social relationships which exist between employers and employees.

At one level we can study industrialism simply as a set of ways of organizing work in the most efficient way possible. Adopting this detached view, we can develop reasonably accurate theories about how the labour process will develop in the future. What Marx shows in his analysis of Modern Industry however, is that some of the limitations to technical progress are a direct result of the fact that the industrial labour process is also a *capitalist* labour process. In brief, Marx argues that within a capitalist system, the key to the productive relationship is whether an individual does or does not own the means of production, meaning the skills, tools, premises and other resources necessary for earning a living. The concentration of ownership of the means of production into the hands of the capitalist class means that the majority are forced to work in particular ways because they have no choice. The vast majority cannot make a living without exchanging their time, effort and skills for wages.

This compulsion is compounded by the fact that the wages received do not adequately reflect the true value of the workers' contribution to the final value of the product. The surplus value or profit taken by the factory owner or employer is not therefore simply a function of the difference between what the product costs to produce and its sale value, but is in part made up of wages which have in effect not been paid to the workforce (see Meek 1973). The need for surplus value is justified on the grounds that it is constantly necessary to reinvest in new machinery, plant, premises and so on, so that the cycle of production can continue. Without profit the incentive to invest in industry would be lost, and, in the long run, the workforce will be unable to find work.

Within the Marxist scheme of things, the inherently exploitative and conflictual nature of the capitalist division of labour will reach a final crisis when the proletariat becomes fully conscious of its key role in the labour process, and overturns the capitalist system in favour of a socialist or communistic system, where ownership of the means of production is in the hands of the majority. Industrialism as a method will continue, but this time in the context of equal and non-exploitative economic and social relationships. Although this might sound like a rather old fashioned way of looking at things, it remains the case that many of the problems we are facing at the end of the twentieth century about how new ways of working can be introduced without causing major economic and social instability, are still to do with the limitations of the capitalist system.

Quality and Experience

Turning to the qualitative and experiential aspects of work, Marx's account is also useful in that it provides important reference points against which we can understand both the motivation to work, and the degree of satisfaction which derives from working. Marx begins by suggesting that human activity is of a higher order than that of other animals, since humans not only act reflexively in response to physiological need but also in accordance with their own *conscious preconceptions*:

> We pre-suppose labour in a form that stamps it as exclusively human. A spider conducts operations that resemble those of a weaver, and a bee puts to shame many an architect in the construction of her cells. But what distinguishes the worst of architects from the best of bees is this, that the architect raises his structures in imagination before he erects it in reality. At the end of every labour-process we get a result that already existed in the imagination of the labourer at its commencement. He not only effects a change of form in the material on which he works, but he also realises a purpose of his own that gives the law to his modus operandi, and to which he must subordinate his will. (Marx 1954, *Capital I*, p.174)

Through exercising this unique ability to preconceive in consciousness and to realize these preconceptions through co-operative actions with others, individuals are able to give form to their overwhelming desire *to act*. Since work is evidently a form of action, we can gain useful insights into the underlying motivations of work by looking at the kinds of motivations, purposes and intentions which underlie action in general.

This characterization of work also provides what we can call a framework of *motivational priority*, in the sense that some consequences or outcomes of work are more urgent or more 'needed' than others. The question of 'needs' is extremely complex since the range of desired outcomes, and thus the range of actions is potentially very large indeed. In discussing material needs for example, Durkheim suggests that the human predisposition for new appetites makes the notion of need almost limitless:

> But how determine the quantity of well-being, comfort or luxury legitimately to be craved by a human being? Nothing appears in man's organic nor in his psychological constitution which sets a limit to such tendencies. The functioning of individual life does not require them to cease at one point rather than at another; the proof being that they have constantly increased since the beginning of history, receiving more and more complete satisfaction, yet with no weakening of average health. (Durkheim 1952, p.247)

Distinctions have been drawn between 'vital' or 'basic' needs and 'existential', 'psychic' or 'acquired' needs (Marcuse 1964, Fromm 1955, Seve 1978, Godelier 1980, Gorz 1989), needs have been arranged into different 'hierarchies' (Maslow 1970, Herzberg 1968, Vroom 1964) and have been used as ammunition in various policy-related debates (Plant *et al*. 1980, Soper 1981, Doyal and Gough 1984 and 1991, Lodziak 1995, Jordan 1996, and Pierson 1996). As we shall see in chapters four and five, work also satisfies needs for relative social status and for our sense of identity.

The main contribution of Marx's analysis is that it suggests that however extensive the range of needs is, and however elaborately we are able to describe them, it is still possible to prioritize between different outcomes since it is undeniably the case that we must be alive in order to act at all:

> An animal only produces what it needs immediately for itself or its offspring; it produces one-sidedly whereas man produces universally; it produces only under the pressure of immediate physical need, whereas man produces free from physical need and only truly produces when he is free thus from. (Marx 1963, *Early Writings*, p.128)

'True' human production then, only develops in the context of *freedom from immediate physical need*. The satisfaction of this basic vital physiological need is the *prerequisite* for all other higher forms of activity, since without it people would not exist at all:

> The first premise of all human existence, and therefore of all history [is] that men must be in a position to live in order to be able to "make history". But life involves before everything else eating, drinking, a habitation, clothing and many other things. The first historical act is thus the production of the means to satisfy these needs, the production of material life itself. (Marx and Engels 1970, p.48)

This might seem like an incredibly obvious point to make especially in a context where, in the 'first world' at least, the vast majority have come to take their physical survival more or less for granted. It cannot be emphasized too strongly however, that however much we might want to highlight the consequences of employment for our consumer lifestyles or for our sense of identity, there are a great many people who simply don't have the luxury of being able to foreground these aspects of working. The satisfaction of basic survival needs will remain as much a feature of the future of work as it always has been in the past; one cannot have 'a sense of self' unless one has a 'self' to have a sense of. We will return to this point in chapter five.

Taking Marx's analysis a stage further, it follows that the level of satisfaction people get from work (both intrinsically and extrinsically) is closely related to whether work does or does not provide them with adequate opportunities to meet the expectations they have of it; expectations which are ordered in terms of what they consider to be their most pressing needs. The central explanatory device here is the concept of alienation. This refers to a situation where the act of producing does not allow the individual sufficient scope for creativity and autonomy, and where the products of work no longer relate to the needs and purposes of the person carrying them out:

> The worker feels himself only when he is not working; when he is working he does not feel himself. He is at home when he is not working, and not at home when he is working. His labour is therefore not voluntary but forced, it is *forced labour*. It is therefore not the satisfaction of a need but a mere *means* to satisfy needs outside itself. Its alien character is clearly demonstrated by the fact that as soon as no physical or other compulsion exists it is shunned like the plague. External labour, labour in which man alienates himself, is a labour of self-sacrifice, of mortification. (Marx 1975, *Early Writings* p.326. Original emphasis).

If work does provide opportunities for individual creativity, social development, a sense of achievement in the work done and so on, it can be regarded as 'valuable' and 'useful' to the person doing it. If it does not provide these outcomes, then it will be experienced as dissatisfying or alienating work characterized by feelings of frustration, resentment and loss of purpose.

More concretely, and following the largely unambiguous findings of empirical research into these matters carried out during the 1970s and 1980s, we can state that the most important expectations which people bring with them into the workplace are for: material and ontological security (principally income and continuity of employment); opportunities for creativity (i.e. having interesting and challenging work), and for social contact (i.e. people like being at work because it is socially stimulating).[7]

A final point to raise here, is that since people evidently do have a range of intrinsic and extrinsic reasons for working, it is remarkable that 'work' is almost always defined in terms of the single criterion of whether one gets paid for doing a particular thing. Being paid is the lowest common denominator for categorizing an activity as 'work'. Under circumstances where work of this kind is easy to come by, we may as well leave it at that. However if, as has already happened for a significant minority of people living within the once dominant economies of the West, opportunities for income through formal paid employment continue to diminish, alternative means will have to be found of providing people with the financial means of ensuring their survival.

A number of contemporary critics (Jordan 1992 and 1996, Gorz 1989 and 1992, Van Parijs (ed.) 1992) argue for example, that one of the main limitations of capitalism is its tendency to assess the worth and value of all activity according to the criteria applied to working activities. This tends to foreclose the possibility of investigating how people might be able to satisfy their daily needs through a combination of paid and non-paid activities rather than through 'formal paid employment' alone. Although there is a distinct lack of imaginative discussion about the means-ends relations of work within present discussions about work, this remains an extremely important avenue of enquiry which we shall return to in due course.

Max Weber

In common with Marx, Weber doesn't think that capitalism simply fell out of the sky at some magic moment during the eighteenth century, but was the result of a highly significant coming together of historical circumstances. He also recognizes that developments in the industrial labour process play a leading role in, and are a defining characteristic of, modern social formations. Where they differ in their explanations is that while Marx places great emphasis on the *practical and material* aspects of the labour process, Weber focuses on the *conceptual and ideational* aspects of the labour process.

In this sense, and although Weber does give us his own narrative *description* of the concrete form of industrial capitalism, he is not really a labour-process theorist, but a theorist of the intellectual/cultural *origins* of capitalism. For Weber, it is not so much the invention of the steam engine or the factory which accounts for the emergence of modern industrial capitalism, but the development and spread of a new commercial and spiritual orientation towards life which originated in Northern Europe during the sixteenth and seventeenth centuries.

Rationality and the Development of Capitalism

One of the most important and recurrent themes which forms the basis of Weber's analysis of the origins of modern capitalism, is his argument that it developed where and when it did because of the emergence of a peculiarly 'rational' approach to life. For Weber, it is entirely false to suggest that capitalism is unique to the modern world. Much of his historical analysis is concerned with showing that different forms of capitalistic behaviour have persisted throughout history (see for example Weber 1976 and 1978). This is why he rejects the Marxian idea that modern industrial capitalism is simply the latest, and inevitable, stage in a long process of historical development. A development which will continue into a socialist and subsequently communist stage.

Whilst Weber agrees that modern industry and all that goes with it (the factory system, technological advance and the division of labour) is certainly a defining characteristic of modern capitalism, he suggests that there is nothing inevitable about its development. Modern industrial capitalism in other words, is just one type, one variety, of the different kinds of capitalism which, under different historical circumstances, *could have* developed. Modern industrial capitalism is thus contingent upon a range of environmental, intellectual, legal, political and religious factors, and not simply upon developments within the economic sphere. The economic sphere certainly played a leading role, but not an exclusive one as Marx and his followers suggested.

Whilst not wishing as he puts it, to substitute 'a one-sided spiritualistic causal interpretation of culture and of history' for 'a one-sided materialistic interpretation' (Weber 1992, p.183), he does want to emphasize that developments in the labour process come about as a result of a *combination* of intellectual and material factors, rather than as a result of material factors alone.

In trying to understand the origins of modern capitalism then, it is also necessary to look at developments in the other spheres of social activity (specifically the political, legal and religious spheres), and at the sometimes corresponding and sometimes conflicting beliefs, motivations and interests which are expressed through them. Despite the somewhat perplexing range of material and intellectual phenomena being suggested as worthy of analysis by Weber, the theme of rationality pervades all of them. If we were looking for a single hook on which to hang Weber's analysis of both the nature and the origins of modern capitalism, it would be 'rationality'. In Lowith's words:

> Weber conceived of this rationality as an original totality - as the totality of an "attitude to life" and "way of life" - which is subject to a variety of causal conditions but is nevertheless unique: as the occidental "ethos". This determinant ethos manifests itself in the "spirit" of (bourgeois) capitalism as well as in that of (bourgeois) Protestantism. Both religion and the economy are formed in their living religious and economic reality within the current of this determinant reality, and they, in turn, concretise this totality by leaving their imprint upon it. The form taken by the economy is not a direct consequence of a particular faith, nor is this faith an "emanatistic" consequence of a "substantive" economy. Rather, both are shaped "rationally" on the basis of a

34

general rationality in the conduct of life. In its primary economic significance, capitalism *per se* cannot be regarded as the independent origin of rationality. Rather, a rational way of life - originally motivated by religion - let capitalism in the economic sense grow into a dominant force of life. (Lowith 1982, p.42)

Unfortunately, Weber is by no means consistent in his use of the term 'rationality'.[8] Brubaker suggests that 'no fewer than sixteen apparent meanings of 'rational' can be culled from [a summary] of Weber's characterization of modern capitalism and ascetic Protestantism: 'deliberate, systematic, calculable, impersonal, instrumental, exact, quantitative, rule-governed, predictable, methodical, purposeful, sober, scrupulous, efficacious, intelligible and consistent' (Brubaker 1984, p.2).

Before looking at the specific features which allowed Weber to distinguish between modern 'rational' capitalism and earlier varieties of 'non-rational' capitalism - a distinction which led him both to *define* modern capitalism, and to *account* for its development, it will be useful to consider briefly Weber's general use of the terms 'rationality' and 'rationalization', and the distinction he draws between 'formal' and 'substantive' rationality.

Rationality and Rationalization

The basic difference between the first of these terms, is that *rationality* describes a collection or constellation of tendencies of thought and organization which are applied across all spheres of society - the economy, politics, legal and religious life - whilst *rationalization* describes *the consequences* of this application. The rationalization of the economy for example, is a consequence of the application of particular rational techniques to the organization of production. Similarly, the rationalization of the political and legal institutions of society is a consequence of the practical application of rational principles of organization and decision making. These result in the emergence of bureaucracy, which is thus a defining characteristic of modern society.

Weber felt that the overriding tendency of the modern period was the desire to rationalize everything and he thus uses the term rationalization to capture the overall effects of rational activity in the different spheres of social action. The rational approach imposes a particular framework for understanding the world, a framework based on making rational judgements about things. Following Morrison, we can summarise the basic characteristics of the rational approach as follows:

(i) the principle of development inherent in the process of civilization and Western society; (ii) the stress on the rational containment of everyday life; (iii) the widespread use of calculation as a strategy of social action; (iv) the freeing of social action from all magical thought: (v) the emphasis on a practical orientation to empirical reality; and (vi) the widespread use of technical and procedural reasoning as a way of controlling practical outcomes and mastering everyday life. (Morrison 1995, p.218)

Up to a point, Weber is suggesting that the driving force of human historical development, is precisely the tendency towards rationality and rationalization. Whilst property relations, class conflict and developments in the means of production clearly play an important part in driving history forward, each of these is, according to Weber, a kind of vehicle for, and a manifestation of, the underlying urge to become increasingly 'rational'.

There is a tendency to assume that in describing the key characteristics of modern rational capitalism, Weber somehow approves of these developments and their consequences. Quite unlike Marx, he does not supplement his *narrative* about the origins and nature of capitalism with a *critique* of capitalism. Nor does he wish to offer any suggestions about how things could be organised differently. What he does do however, is to make an important distinction between the 'internal' or 'formal' rationality or rational logic of a particular activity, and the validity or 'substantive' rationality of claims about whether it is desirable to apply them. For example, it is clear that in many respects the industrial division of labour is more efficient than feudal agriculture. It is a more rational organization of work. What is less clear however, is whether the decision to apply this type of organization is actually an entirely rational one. In this sense, the industrial division of labour is simply *a* division of labour rather than *the* division of labour understood in a more universal sense.

Brubaker usefully identifies two important points about rationality: 'First, rationality does not inhere in things, but is ascribed to them. Secondly, rationality is a relational concept: a thing can be rational (or irrational) only from a particular point of view' (Brubaker 1984, p.35). What this means is that making decisions about what is the most rational way of achieving a particular end depends upon whether or not one feels that those ends are actually desirable. Running a business in a calculating instrumental way to accumulate profit is rational (both in terms of the decision about what to do and in terms of how to carry it out) so long as one feels that profits are worth making. If one does not, then arguably the decision and the actions which flow from it are *irrational*. Crucially, there is no binding logical basis upon which to make final decisions about which ends are worth pursuing and which are not. It is a matter of *judgement*. Again quoting Brubaker:

> Formal rationality is a matter of fact, substantive rationality is a matter of value. Formal rationality refers primarily to the *calculability of means and procedures*, substantive rationality primarily to the *value* (from some explicitly defined standpoint) of ends or results.... The formal rationality of the modern social order is a matter of fact; whether or not this social order is substantively rational, in contrast, depends on one's point to view - i.e. on the ends, values or beliefs one takes as a standard of rationality. (Brubaker 1984, pp.36-7)

The significance of all of this for Weber's analysis of capitalism, is that the tendency towards rationality has, since its detachment from the religious ethic of Protestant asceticism, become a highly complex set of means to no particular end. In the absence of any agreement about the substantive end to which it is a means, it has become an end in itself. Paradoxically then, the end to which the rationalization of the social world is a means, is the further rationalization of the social world itself: 'It is this substantive neutrality, this indifference to all substantive ends and values, that makes the rationality of the modern Western social order "specific and peculiar"' (Brubaker 1984, p.38).

Whereas Marx accounts for tension and conflict within the capitalist labour process in terms of the struggle over access to the means of survival, Weber accounts for it in terms of this 'substantive indifference'. It was the apparently indissoluble nature of these tensions between the formal and substantive rationality of modern society, and between the rationalities of the different spheres of social action, which caused Weber to be extremely pessimistic about what the future might hold. Increasing the efficiency of economic production meant increasing the alienation of the working class; increasing the efficiency of social institutions through bureaucratization meant increasing people's sense of anonymity, and increasing the efficiency of the governmental and legislative spheres meant increasing people's sense of loss of liberty and freedom.

The Rationality of Modern Capitalism

Turning from general issues to the specifics of the 'rational' industrial labour process, the following quotation more or less summarises Weber's analysis of what is peculiar about modern capitalism. 'In the last analysis' he says:

> The factor which produces capitalism is the rational permanent enterprise with its rational accounting rational technology and rational law, [complemented

by] the rational spirit, the rationalisation of the conduct of life in general and a rationalistic economic ethic. (Weber 1983, p.128)

In contrast to earlier forms of profit making, the modern 'rational' form tries to reduce risks to a minimum, behaves in a highly calculative way when making business and investment decisions, and perhaps most essentially, it continues to make profit even when the individual has already done enough work to satisfy her or his immediate and particular needs. In this sense, profit making within modern rational capitalism becomes an end in itself rather than a means to an end. (In Marx's terms, we can equate this shift with the shift from the production of use-values to the production of exchange-values, from concrete production of actually needed commodities, to the more abstract production of commodities almost irrespective of whether they express or satisfy a need).

We can list a number of the basic features of this rationality as it is directly applied to the labour process. First is the use of rational calculation as the basis of action. This is a means-ends relation, meaning that decisions about what to do are based on a concrete and usually mathematical calculation of costs and benefits. It is an instrumental orientation. Second, the medium for achieving this level of economic instrumentalism and regulation is money:

From a purely technical point of view, money is the most 'perfect' means of economic calculation. That is, it is formally the most rational means of orienting economic activity. Calculation in terms of money is thus the specific means of rational economic provision. (Weber, *Economy and Society* 1978, p.86: quoted in Brubaker 1984, p.11)

Third, in order to be able to calculate accurately, the capitalist also needs ownership, or at least complete control over the business, and access to reliable technical and scientific knowledge: 'its rationality is to-day essentially dependent on the calculability of the most important technical factors... it is dependent on the peculiarities of modern science, especially the natural sciences based on mathematics and exact and rational experiment' (Weber 1992, p.24).[9]

The fourth basic feature described by Weber addresses the issue of working relationships. Although he is more interested in the relationships between one capitalist and another than in the division of labour as such, he is quite explicit that in order to be able to complete the rationalization of the labour process, the capitalist must also have access to a source of 'free labour' which he or she can force to work:

People must be available who are not only legally in a position to do so but are also economically compelled to sell their labour on the market without restrictions. Only where in consequence of the existence of workers who in the formal sense voluntarily, but actually under the compulsion of hunger, offer themselves to work for a wage, can the costs of production be unambiguously determined in advance. (Weber 1983, p.110) [10]

Furthermore, the capitalist must impose a strict discipline over the workforce. Brubaker quotes Weber's approval of the techniques of Taylor's 'scientific management' (the essence of 'Fordism') to ensure a sufficiently high level of calculability:

Discipline in the factory has a completely rational basis. With the help of suitable methods of measurement, the optimum profitability of the individual worker is calculated like that of any material means of production. On this basis, the American system of 'scientific management' triumphantly proceeds with its rational conditioning and training of work performances, thus drawing the ultimate conclusions from the mechanization and discipline of the plant. The psycho-physical apparatus of man is completely adjusted to the demands of the outer world, the tools, the machines - in short, it is functionalised, and the individual is shorn of his natural rhythm as determined by his organism; in line with the demands of work procedure, he is attuned to a new rhythm through the functional specialization of muscles and through the creation of an optimal economy of physical effort. (Weber, *Economy and Society* 1978, p.1156: quoted in Brubaker 1984, pp.14-15)

We can note that Weber's description of the situation of the worker in the capitalist labour process as living 'under the compulsion of hunger', and having their 'psycho-physical apparatus completely adjusted to the demands of machines' is very similar to Marx's description. Weber also reiterates another point raised earlier about how established or 'traditional' patterns within the division of labour can inhibit or limit the development of new patterns:

A man does not "by nature" wish to earn more and more money, but simply to live as he is accustomed to live and to earn as much as is necessary for that purpose. Wherever modern capitalism has begun its work of increasing its intensity, it has encountered the immensely stubborn resistance of this leading trait of pre-capitalist labour. And to-day it encounters it the more, the more backward (from a capitalistic point of view) the labouring forces are with which it has to deal. (Weber 1992, p.60)

Finally, and looking at developments which had taken place after the time that Marx was writing, Weber describes how the desire to rationalize the organizational features of modern institutions was resulting in a massive expansion of bureaucracy. In the same way that the division of labour emerges as the most efficient means of production, bureaucracy emerges as the most efficient means of organising the enterprise as a whole. Since the main purposes of bureaucracy is to manage information, and since the amount of information to be managed was increasing very rapidly during the first decades of the twentieth century (a tendency which has of course continued), there is bound to be an increasing need for bureaucracy and for bureaucrats.

In strictly practical terms there is nothing unexpected about this, since its application was both formally rational (i.e. it was the best way to do something) and substantively rational (i.e. it fitted in with the kind of rationality which is to do with deciding the general objectives and meanings of action). Culturally and politically however, Weber was very concerned that bureaucracy was 'irrational' in the sense that it had a tendency to override individual freedom and integrity. He feared that the bureaucracies and the bureaucrats who ran them, would envelop or smother personal freedoms amounting to what he famously called the emergence of a 'new iron cage of serfdom'. As Lowith puts it:

> That which was originally a mere means (to an otherwise valuable end) becomes itself an end or an end in itself. In this way, means as ends make themselves independent and thus lose their original "meaning" or purpose, that is, they loose their original purposive rationality oriented to man and his needs. This reversal marks the whole of modern civilisation, whose arrangements, institutions and activities are so "rationalised" that whereas humanity once established itself within them, now it is they which enclose and determine humanity like an "iron cage". Human conduct, from which these institutions originally arose, must now in turn adapt to its own creation which has escaped the control of its creator. (Lowith 1982, pp.47-8)

Bureaucracy thus becomes a system of domination and control rather than simply a means of rational organization and management.

In addition then, to the exclusion or 'expropriation' of the majority of the workforce from direct access to the means of production identified by Marx, Weber adds that it is also, and perhaps more seriously, 'expropriated' from the decision-making and administrative dimensions of the organization as well. Alienation, discontent, a feeling of being trapped in the iron cage is not simply caused by the fact that the proletariat (or indeed any other section of the population) are expropriated or divested of their direct access to the means of production, but that they are expropriated from *all forms* of control over society; bureaucratic specialization is exclusionary at the level of administration and authority:

40

In the modern state, 'expert officialdom, based on the division of labour' is wholly expropriated from the possession of its means of administration. 'In the contemporary "state" - and this is essential for the concept of state - the "separation" of the administrative staff, of the administrative officials, and of the workers from the material means of administrative organisation is completed'. (Giddens 1972, p.35, quoting Weber 1968, p.82)

Although Weber says very little about the day-to-day experiences of working within the capitalist labour process - whether people enjoy it, how satisfying it is, what kinds of conflicts are likely to arise - he does have a number of interesting things to say about the underlying motivations of action.

Whereas Marx largely accounts for this motivation in terms of the desire to satisfy various categories of need, Weber is much more interested in the kinds of values and beliefs which people feel they are expressing through their actions. In order to understand why people behave in the way that they do - both at and outside work - it is not enough simply to describe their actions; we have to pay at least as much attention to *interpreting* their subjective and value-laden reasons for doing them.

In brief, Weber's analysis of action draws on his comments about the spread of rationality. Given the rationalization of the world associated with modernity, there is a clear implication that 'traditional' and 'affectual' forms of action (determined respectively by habit and emotion) are being displaced by 'rational' action. He distinguishes between two forms of rational action; *wertrational* or 'value-rational' action which is regarded by the actor as valuable or desirable in itself (means-as-ends), and *zweckrational* or 'purpose-rational' action which is intended to achieve a desired result (means-to-an-end):

> *Wertrational* action is oriented to an act's intrinsic properties, *zweckrational* action to its anticipated and intended consequences. *Wertrational* action presupposes a conscious belief about the intrinsic value or inherent rightness of a certain way of acting, *zweckrational* action conscious reasoning in terms of means and ends. (Brubaker 1984, p.51)

Picking up on our earlier discussion of rationality, we can see that increases in the techniques of formal rationality in the labour process (new techniques, the division of labour, rational accounting procedures, a formalised legal system, bureaucratic organization and so on), increase the scope for purpose-rational action. We can more easily achieve particular desired ends because modern industry and science are full of useful and formally rational techniques for doing so. Our prospects of acting in a rationally means-to-an-end kind of way are increased because real and practical changes make this kind of action available to us.

In this sense, a general shift towards purpose-rational action is a *structurally determined feature* of economic and social development - a feature which was not available in previous periods of history. (This does not mean of course, that previous ways of acting were irrational, but that pre-modern rationality was a *different kind* of rationality). Again we are reminded of Marx's observations about how Modern Industry offers great potential for future development because of its scientific/technical prowess.

Whilst we can make empirical observations of, and objective assessments about, this or that action in terms of whether it is the best way of achieving a particular end - is this division of labour more effective than the previous one, is the word processor more efficient than the typewriter - we can only make very approximate exterior assessments of the experiential and value-laden aspects of activity because they are inherently *subjective* phenomena.

For example, a concert pianist presumably *enjoys* playing the piano as well as *needing* to play the piano in order to make a living. Whilst we can describe the act of playing and count the fee, only the player can assess whether the act of playing is rational in terms of satisfying all the other value-laden reasons she or he has for playing:

> Whether or not an action is objectively rational depends on the judgement of a scientific observer - i.e. one who is able to ascertain empirically the appropriateness of the actor's conduct as a means to some end. This end may be the one intended by the actor, or it may be one of which the actor is unaware but toward which his conduct in fact tends.... Whether or not an action is subjectively rational [in contrast] depends on the actor's self-understanding.... It is the *perceived* appropriateness of the means, not their *actual* appropriateness, that makes action subjectively rational.... (Brubaker 1984, pp.54-5)

The application of these ideas to economic action allows Weber to make his case for the role of ideas, values and beliefs in economic development. Modern capitalism developed where and when it did not only because of the availability of new techniques but also because of the ideational orientation of the emerging entrepreneurial bourgeoisie. What was this ideational orientation? Ascetic Protestantism. For Weber, the motivation of this group derives from their wholehearted belief that they were fulfilling a religious purpose. Their 'calling' was to prove their spiritual salvation by glorifying God through productive earthly toil. The more diligently they pursued their economic ends, the more certain they were of their spiritual salvation. They regarded what they were doing as both formally rational in the sense that their business methods were efficient and productive, and substantively rational in the sense that they were fulfilling their religious duty:

> The valuation of the fulfilment of duty in worldly affairs as the highest form which the moral activity of the individual could assume... The only way of living acceptably to God was through the fulfilment of the obligations imposed upon the individual by his position in the world. That was his calling. (Weber 1976, p.80)

Since enjoyment of wealth was also considered sinful, the only legitimate use for excess revenue was as a reinvestment to perpetuate the cycle of worldly success and thus heavenly salvation. For Weber, it is this coincidence within the Protestant Ethic between frenetic working activity and an ascetic attitude towards the wealth it generates, which lies at the heart of the 'elective affinity' between Protestantism and capitalism:

> When the limitation of consumption is combined with the release of acquisitive activity, the inevitable practical result is obvious: accumulation of capital through ascetic compulsion to save. The restraints imposed upon the consumption of wealth naturally served to increase it by making possible the productive investment of capital. (Weber 1976, p.172)

Whilst this particular system of beliefs has had its day,[11] the important message from our present point of view, is that in trying to understand what the future of work will be like, we have to take a wide spectrum of subjective and ideational features fully into account. As we shall see in chapter five, one of the most important current developments in debates about the future of work has been a more forthright recognition of the fact that people's expectations of work are heavily influenced by a range of value-laden experiences centred around issues of consumption, lifestyle and identity. In this respect, those who adopt an orthodox labour-process perspective have been accused of overlooking experiences and expectations which are crucial to understanding the role of work in people's lives.

Emile Durkheim

The issue of how the labour process is implicated in the 'moral' aspects of modern life also plays an important part in Durkheim's analysis. Where he differs from Weber however, is that whereas Weber sees the moral/spiritual motivations of work as spreading outwards from the individual towards society, Durkheim sees these values as being generated by 'society' itself.

For Durkheim, society has a reality and a moral integrity of its own which exist over and above the individuals who occupy it. This is obviously a contentious point, since it is difficult to understand how this morality could be expressed if it were not for the presence of real acting individuals. What Durkheim is getting at here, is the idea that although individuals may feel that they are acting autonomously, their actions are always governed by the social context in which they find themselves, a context which exists before they themselves enter the world at all. Moreover, unless one does understand the social dimensions - both enabling and constraining - which surround social action, then one cannot actually reach a full understanding of what it means to be an individual.

The logical extension of this argument is that the very notion of 'the individual' is something which follows on from, or emerges out of, 'society'; 'the individual' and 'society' should not be regarded as distinct and separate entities which can be analysed independently of each other, but as two parts of a larger organic whole. Understanding what this organic whole is, is the task of the sociologist. In *The Rules of Sociological Method* (1895) he claims to have uncovered 'a category of '"social" facts' consisting of 'ways of acting, thinking, and feeling, external to the individual, and endowed with a power of coercion, by reason of which they control him' the source of which 'can be no other than society' (Durkheim 1964, pp.3-4):

> A social fact is every way of acting, fixed or not, capable of exercising on the individual an external constraint; or again, every way of acting which is general throughout a given society, while at the same time existing in its own right independent of its individual manifestations. (Durkheim 1964, p.13, emphasis removed)

He gives a number of examples of the kinds of social phenomena which we freely use but which are external to us:

> When I fulfil my obligations as brother, husband, or citizen, when I execute my contracts, I perform duties which are defined, externally to myself and my acts, in law and in custom.... The system of signs I use to express my thought, the system of currency I employ to pay my debts, the instruments of credit I utilize in my commercial relations, the practices followed in my profession etc., function independently of my own use of them. And these statements can be repeated for each member of society. Here, then, are ways of acting, thinking, and feeling that present the noteworthy property of existing outside the individual consciousness. These types of conduct or thought are not only external to the individual but are, moreover, endowed with coercive power, by virtue of which they impose themselves upon him, independent of his individual will. (Durkheim 1964, pp.1-2)

For these reasons, Durkheim severely criticised the whole thrust of 'individualistic' social theory, and particularly of 'utilitarian individualism' of the kind put forward by Jeremy Bentham and John Stuart Mill, on the grounds that it was quite inadequate to presume that the only motivation for human action was the selfish desire for personal gain. Whilst it is certainly the case that individuals do pursue material gains, often at the expense of other people, these are not the only aims which guide and govern their actions. Following Saint-Simon and Comte, Durkheim sees these other motivations very much in terms of our 'moral' sense of what is right or wrong. We don't simply do things on the basis of a dispassionate calculation of costs and benefits, but because they 'feel' right.

Durkheim's analysis of the labour process in *The Division of Labour in Society* (1893) is framed almost entirely in terms of his attempt to understand how the 'integrity' of society can be maintained under circumstances where individuals seem, at one and the same time, to become more autonomous and yet more dependent on society:

> This work had its origins in the question of the relations of the individual to social solidarity. Why does the individual, while becoming more autonomous, depend more upon society? How can he be at once more individual and more solidary? Certainly, these two movements, contradictory as they appear, develop in parallel fashion. This is the problem we are raising. It appeared to us that what resolves this apparent antimony is a transformation of social solidarity due to the steadily growing development of the division of labour. That is how we have been led to make this the object of our study. (Durkheim 1933, p.38)

He argues that this development is possible because of a corresponding change in the kind of *social solidarity* which binds individuals and society together. The core of his argument is quite simple. The transition from pre-modern to modern societies is accompanied by a corresponding transition from one kind of social solidarity to another, from 'mechanical solidarity' to 'organic solidarity'.

In pre-modern societies, mechanical solidarity is established through the presence of a *conscience collective* or shared consciousness, which binds individuals together 'automatically' as a consequence of the intimate, simple and relatively unchanging social reality in which they live. In modern societies, organic solidarity is primarily brought about by the social division of labour, which, although more anonymous, complex and dynamic, establishes a realisation of interdependence with, and reliance upon, others.[12]

The increasing individuation or separating out of social relationships is accompanied in the moral sphere by an increased acceptance of individual freedoms and appetites - forms of expression and motivation which were largely inhibited within mechanical solidarity. In terms of the role of the economic structure and the organization of work, the significance of the division of labour is that it both stimulates *a need for* new forms of social solidarity - a need to fill the vacuum left by the decay of mechanical solidarity - and provides *the basis of* that new form of solidarity.

On this understanding, developments which originate in the labour process and subsequently become generalized across all social functions and institutions, are absolutely fundamental to social transition. They are not simply one change amongst many others, but are singularly significant. Furthermore, the nature of these changes, in particular the increasing individuation of functions and the growth of a sense of individuality and individual rights and responsibilities, stamp themselves on the whole of society. Modern societies are not simply pre-modern societies made over but are fundamentally different:

> Nothing seems easier to determine, at first glance, than the role of the division of labour. Are not its effects universally recognized? Since it combines both the productive power and the ability of the workman, it is the necessary condition of development in societies, both intellectual and material development. It is the source of civilisation... the most remarkable effect of the division of labour is not that it increases the output of functions divided, but that it renders them solidary. Its role in all these cases is not simply to embellish or ameliorate existing societies, but to render societies possible which, without it, would not exist. (Durkheim 1933, p.50/61)

In common with Marx and Weber however, Durkheim was less than optimistic about just how positive a contribution the division of labour was making to the moral integrity and social solidarity of industrial society. He attributes this failure to the fact that organic solidarity based on the division of labour remained incomplete, and was thus dysfunctional or 'pathological' rather than functional and 'normal'.

These deficiencies resulted in 'anomie', a state of moral limbo and uncertainty caused by the transition from one form of social solidarity to another. Firstly, he suggests that given the importance of our (socially bequeathed) sense of individuality, it is essential that we feel that we ourselves occupy a place within the social division of labour which suits our own needs and predispositions. It is not enough simply to offer people a choice about their occupational and other social roles at the intellectual or ideological level, these choices have to be *real* choices at the material level. If we are not able to make these choices for ourselves, then in effect we are being 'forced' to do something against our will. If we are forced to occupy an economic or social role which we would prefer not to occupy, then we are inclined to regard the choices available to us as 'false', and to regard the system which gives rise to these 'choices' as illegitimate. In order to be legitimate, and *to be seen to be legitimate*, the social division of labour has to offer genuine choices which people can actually make.

This lack of choice may, under some circumstances, give rise to the kind of social conflict described by Marx. In the world of work for example, people may join trade unions and take industrial action in order to restore their right to make choices about the kind of work they do and how they do it. Beyond the economic sphere, lack of real choice may give rise to strong claims for 'equality' such as those pursued successfully by the women's movement during this century. Durkheim felt that the impending social conflicts of industrial society were a result of the fact that the corrective balance between a strong and progressive state and the occupational associations (or corporations) of civil society, had not yet matured.

Up to a point then, the anomic tendencies of the experience of industrial work is a feature of the developmental process itself, rather than an ultimate consequence of it. With increasing maturity comes greater intervention by employers' and employees' organizations, and thus a levelling out of economic and other social differences. In the present context, one is bound to make the observation that many of these conflicts have not been resolved in the hundred years since Durkheim's analysis first appeared. This strongly suggests that the underlying inequalities and inconsistencies of industrialism are extremely resilient, and that new approaches will have to be found if they are to be resolved at all.

Secondly, he thought that individuals may loose a sense of their actual relationship or connectedness to society precisely because the division of labour has become so advanced. We loose a sense of how our individual and individualized actions actually fit in either with our own sense of what we are trying to achieve, or with the actions of other people. At this level, the idea of anomie is very close to Marx's notion of alienation. Where Marx constructs his critique around the idea that modern industry deprives people of their sense of purpose by dislocating or removing the necessary connection between conception and execution (thought and action), leaving them frustrated and perhaps vengeful, Durkheim argues that the division of labour (both within and outside the economic sphere), deprives people of their sense of moral purpose and moral unity with other people.[13]

Durkheim's critique of the excesses of the division of labour also reminds us of Weber's critique of the tendency of bureaucracy to become an end in itself. It can be seen as a particular example of the general kind of social disharmony which Durkheim observes is a major problem for all forms of complex social organization based on the division of labour. These shared concerns give rise to similar recommendations at the political level, i.e. what practical steps can society take to solve these problems. For Weber, it is the State which needs to intervene in order to overcome the tendency for bureaucracy to stifle democracy. For Durkheim, the State has an important role in increasing the moral regulation of the relationships between for example, employers and employees within the economy, or between the economy and the polity in general.

Thirdly, and as a result of the above deficiencies, Durkheim is concerned that the urge towards individualism, the almost obsessive sanctioning of individuality over sociability, may lead to a situation where people no longer understand the importance of the idea of society. In pursuing their desire for autonomy and freedom, individuals actually begin to undermine the very source of their individuality, namely society itself.

Industrialism and the Future of Work

Until quite recently, it has been very unfashionable to look at the work of Marx, Weber and Durkheim in the search for clues about how to understand what the future of work might be like. One of the reasons for this has been a rejection of the Enlightenment/modernist idea that society is somehow bound to progress and that the trajectory of this progression or evolution can be determined in advance.

It has been suggested instead that what characterizes post- or late-modernity is a sense of fragmentation and uncertainty within which a much more diverse range of futures might be possible. We may not, as Marx and Durkheim, and to a lesser extent Weber implied, be moving inexorably onwards and upwards in our economic and social development. However, although as Giddens has pointed out 'history does not have the "totalised" form attributed to it by evolutionary conceptions [and] cannot be seen as a unity, or as reflecting certain unifying principles or organization and transformation', this does not mean that we should get carried away with the idea that the future can take on any form that we choose to give it; 'There are definite episodes of historical transition... whose character can be identified and about which generalisations can be made' (Giddens 1990, pp.5-6).

What this means for us in studying the future of work, is that we can learn a great deal from the theorists discussed in this chapter precisely because the 'generalisations' they made in studying the transformation of work during the nineteenth and early-twentieth centuries, can also be applied to the 'historical transition' which is taking place today. Without denying the limitations of their analyses, and whilst accepting as we shall see in subsequent chapters, that new and important analytical perspectives have been incorporated into current debates, it remains the case that very many of the insights developed by them still apply. The following points are not simply historical suppositions and theoretical speculations, they are *facts*. Any study of the future of work worth its salt *must* take them into account.

(i) The Role of the Economic Structure within Society

- Changes in the industrial labour process *always* have a very profound impact on the nature of society. It is quite inadequate to suppose that the world of work is somehow 'separate from' or 'independent of' the wider society.
- The mutuality of this relationship means that new ideas and intellectual orientations (including spiritual or religious ones) move from the economic realm to the social and political realms and vice versa. One of the most important of these in modern societies is the desire to find ever more 'rational' ways of doing things: rationalization is as much a social and intellectual orientation as it is a scientific or economic one.
- The division of labour in industrial societies is one of the key mechanisms for maintaining social stability, coherence and 'solidarity'. The autonomy of each individual is based simultaneously on a recognition of other people's individuality and on the sense we have of being mutually interdependent. The individual is a social actor.

(ii) The Technical and Organizational Dimensions of Work

- A recurrent pattern within the process of development is that innovation always has to overcome the limitations (both technical and relational) of the practices and kinds of organization which preceded it. In trying to understand what will follow, we must understand how things have developed so far. The *outcomes* might be different, but the *process of development* will be very similar.
- A defining characteristic of industrial (as opposed to pre-industrial) technologies and their applications, is that they are inherently dynamic. Unless we choose not to use them at all (which is highly unlikely) their capacity for perpetual development means that we will always be looking

for new ways to realize their potential. There is no end point to technological innovation, and thus no *technical* limit to how they might affect the longer-term future of work.

(iii) The Nature of Working Relationships

- Working relationships are just that: *relationships*. Whilst it is interesting to describe the actions and circumstances of a particular worker, the division of labour is a collective social undertaking.
- All economic relationships are circumscribed by the wider social, political and cultural context within which they take place. In order to understand properly the nature of economic relationships it is also necessary to understand the complex ways in which these various contexts interact with one another.
- A dominant characteristic of economic relationships within *capitalist* social formations is the conflict of interests between those who control access to the means of making a living and those that do not. Access to employment, autonomy over how one works, and receipt of the proceeds of working *are not equally distributed*.

(iv) The Qualitative and Experiential Aspects of Work

- Although particular identifiable criteria are applied to that category of activities we label 'work', these activities are still part of, and should be seen in similar terms as, activity in general. In common with all activities, and however minimally, work is value-laden.
- People work in order to meet a complex variety of expectations derived from a range of intrinsic and extrinsic needs. Some of these needs may be a practical expression of spiritual or religious beliefs and values.
- People order or prioritize these expectations in accordance with their perceptions of what they most need. The main expectations of work stem from the need for material and ontological security, for creativity and for social contact.
- Judgements about the quality of working experiences are made on the basis of whether work does or does not meet these expectations. The degree of satisfaction is conditional upon the extent to which a particular expectation is prioritized by the individual. For example, if a worker is mainly interested in earning a high wage, he or she may have reduced expectations for creativity and self expression.

50

- A lack of satisfaction results in alienation or anomie characterized by a profound sense of frustration, loss of purpose, futility and ontological insecurity.
- People generally express 'formal rationality' in their orientation to work in the sense that they see it as the most effective means to a desired end. This kind of action can be observed empirically and assessed objectively. Whether people are 'substantively rational' in their orientation to work is a much more open question since this is very much a personal matter which lies beyond the reach of empirical observation. There is no absolute way of resolving disputes between different claims to substantive rationality.

2 The Narrative of Post-Industrialism, Post-Fordism and Flexibility

Post-Industrial Society

In the same way that the narrative of industrialism was an attempt to uncover the origins of industrial capitalism, and to describe its effects on the labour processes of the late-eighteenth, nineteenth, and early-twentieth centuries, the narrative of post-industrialism/post-Fordism emerged during the and 1970s and 1980s when astute observers noticed that the labour process had entered yet another period of transition.

In recounting the story of post-industrialism/post-Fordism we need to clarify one or two initial points. The narrative of post-industrialism/post-Fordism is not so much a distinct narrative with historically bounded conclusions and diagnoses all its own, as an attempt to identify and account for what its authors see as a general shift in the direction of industrialism proper. The basic subject-matter (what does industrialism entail in practice, how is work organized, how does it affect the experience of work) and underlying concerns (does industrialism help or hinder the development of a more productive and equitable society) are the same in both types of account.

Secondly, and although casually they can all be regarded as part of the discourse of 'post-industrialism', it is important not to confuse 'first-phase' theories of post-industrialism which emerged during the 1960s and 1970s, and 'second-phase' theories of post-Fordism/flexibility which first emerged during the 1980s. Unlike the discourse of industrialism which can be attributed to a small number of key thinkers, both phases of post-industrialism are made up of a bundle or collection of narratives which have quite divergent origins and intentions.

This is particularly the case in the first phase where we find conservative and liberal American writers such as Daniel Bell (1974, 1976) and J.K.Galbraith (1969, 1972, 1994) who viewed the changes of the post-second-world-war period in an optimistically neutral light, rubbing shoulders with writers such as Schumacher (1974), Illich (1971, 1973, 1975), Bahro (1984,

1985), Toffler (1970, 1980) and Gorz (1976, 1982, 1985) whose humanist-socialist perspective led them towards being much more critical of these developments. Somewhere between these positions, we come across the accounts of Marxist academics such as Alain Touraine (1974) and Serge Mallet (1975) who thought they had identified the emergence of 'post-industrial' class formations, the government-funded 'futurologists' who confidently tried to make long-range forecasts about where society was actually going, and the 'Atari Democrats' which Frankel (1987) uses as a label 'applied to those politicians and theorists who combine technocratic solutions with the rhetoric of small-is-beautiful'.

Trying to capture exactly what 'post-industrialism' is, is a bit like being a photographer watching an impressive array of talent attending a film premier. Although brilliant in their own right, you suspect that the only thing they really have in common is the revolving door through which they come and go. This sense of synthetic togetherness is reinforced by the adoption of the term 'post-industrialism' itself. Unlike 'industrialism' which usefully and literally describes a real thing - an historically distinct combination of technology and divisions of labour used in the mechanized production of goods - the term 'post-industrialism' is dangerously misleading since clearly it is not the case that advanced economies suddenly became 'un-industrial' or 'non-industrial' at some dramatic moment during the 1970s.

This lack of clarity over terminology became almost endemic as a range of quite absurd alternatives such as 'post-capitalist', 'post-maturity', post-economic', 'post-collective', 'information society', and 'technetronic society' also came and went.[1] As we shall see shortly, the term 'post-Fordism' is not without its critics either. The issue of the extent to which post-Fordism constitutes an entirely separate phase of development following a novel logic or trajectory of its own devising is very much part of the current debate. Clearly our glitterati were not all reading from the same script. In order to capture the fact that the labour process of the 1980s and 1990s is located within a different historical period but is still characteristically 'industrial' the term 'late-industrialism' seems much more sensible. We can also note in passing that *even if* a cogent argument could be made to say that post- or late-industrialism is a different kind of animal altogether, it would still be necessary to explain the linkages between industrialism and *capitalism*. One of the most worrying aspects of some uses of the term post-industrialism is the implication that capitalism died quietly in its sleep while we were busily getting on with our post-something lives.

Bearing these difficulties in mind, and without attempting to provide a comprehensive summary of all the positions of first-phase post-industrialism in the manner of Kumar (1978) and Frankel (1987), it will be useful to identify a number of specific themes which link the narratives of industrialism and post-Fordism. Since these are most evident in the work of Daniel Bell who first popularized the term 'post-industrial society', and of J.K.Galbraith, we will begin by taking a brief look at what they have to say about shifts in the concentration of economic activity and employment towards the service sector, the role of scientific/technical knowledge, and increases in the organizational complexity of large-scale institutions. These contributions can be regarded as providing an epilogue to the kinds of issues raised in the previous chapter, and a prologue to the more rigorous debates around post-Fordism and flexibility which will occupy us for the remainder of this chapter.

Post-Industrialism and the Service Sector

Bell's narrative is firmly situated within the story-of-work tradition, and true to form he immediately notes that changes in the labour process have had a profound impact upon the kind of society in which people live. Along with the emergence of 'new relations between theory and empiricism, particularly science and technology', he is clear that: 'the concept of the post-industrial society deals primarily with changes in the social structure, the way in which the economy is being transformed and the occupational system reworked' (Bell 1974, p.13). No surprises there. He goes on to list five components of post-industrialism - all of which are features of the labour process - that make it different from earlier manifestations of industrialism: 'the change from a goods-producing to a service economy... the pre-eminence of the professional and technical class... the centrality of theoretical knowledge as the source of innovation and of policy formulation... the control of technology and technological assessment... the creation of a new "intellectual technology"' (Bell 1974, p.14).

Taken together, these developments allow Bell to explain that whereas 'the design' of pre-industrial societies took the form of 'a game against nature', and industrial societies of 'a game against fabricated nature', the *modus vivendi* of post-industrial societies is 'a game between people', in which 'an "intellectual technology", based on information rises alongside of machine technology' (Bell 1974, p.116). Although Bell doesn't actually use the word 'evolution' there is a clear implication here that these 'games' are stages which must necessarily follow one after the other (a game against fabricated nature cannot take place until something has been fabricated), and that each stage is somehow 'better than' or more progressive then the one that preceded it.

54

As to what causes this transition, Bell suggests that the change from a 'goods-producing' to a 'service economy', and of the growing importance of the 'professional and technical class' which necessarily accompanies it, is a result of the fact that the expanding sectors are more productive and profitable than those which they displace. In addition to transportation and distribution services which developed during its earlier stages, post-industrial economies are characterized by a massive expansion in demand for personal services, business services (particularly 'banking and finance, real estate, insurance'), 'transportation, communication and utilities', and 'health, education, research and government' (Bell 1974, p.15).

In terms of the occupational profile of the population then, Bell's account seems clear enough. Post-industrial societies are ones in which an increasing proportion of the population is employed in services. In the same way that the industrial sector replaced the agricultural sector during the nineteenth century, the service sector replaced the industrial sector during the twentieth century as it was here that the largest profits could be made.

On closer inspection however, there are a number of points which need further clarification. Firstly, and perhaps in order to enhance the drama of his narrative by representing these developments as an 'epoch-making transition', Bell tends to exaggerate the extent to which they represent some kind of radical departure from the typical developmental path of industrialism. Kumar argues for example, that viewed from within a larger historical perspective, the transition from office to factory employment is far less decisive than 'the mass movement from farm employment to service employment; a difference compounded by the fact that this has equally been a movement from the countryside to the city' (Kumar 1978, p.203).

Although Kumar is correct to caution us against seeing the rise of the service sector during the post-war period as being in the same league as the coming of industrialism itself, and that we should remember that 'there is a constancy and continuity in the history of industrial work experience of the industrial societies' (ibid), we cannot ignore the fact that employment in services has increased both in absolute numbers and as a proportion of the workforce, and that as a generator of income within the economy, the service sector continues to grow in importance. In the UK for example, and expressed as a percentage of those in employment, the proportion employed in manufacturing fell from 36.4 per cent in 1971 to 20 per cent in 1994, while the proportion employed in services rose from 52.5 per cent to 74 per cent (a movement of some 4 million jobs from one sector to the other) (see *Social Trends* no.21, 1991, table 4.11; and *Annual Abstract of Statistics*, no.127,

1991; and no.131, 1996, table 6.1. For international comparisons see Castells 1996, tables 4.1 to 4.21).

We should however agree with Kumar that Bell certainly goes too far when he implies that these developments give rise to an entirely new experience of work, and that economies with a vigorous service sector have been wrenched clear of their industrial moorings and started to follow an entirely new course of their own. The emergence of a more service-oriented labour process is a twist in the story of industrial development not a new story altogether.

This tendency towards exaggeration on Bell's part raises a second point about the extent to which employment in services is more rewarding and satisfying than employment in industry. It clearly suites Bell's conservative stance to suggest that if more people are employed in services, and if this kind of work is more satisfying, then the shift towards post-industrialism is also a shift towards a better quality of working life. Unfortunately, Bell's notion of 'services' is far too blunt an instrument to justify these kinds of claims: he fails to distinguish between *different types* of service-sector employment, and then implies that the more attractive and glamorous attributes of the professional and scientific elite are generalized amongst service workers as a whole.

On the first point, Gershuny and Miles (1983) have usefully distinguished between service *industries* and service *occupations*. Service-industry employment refers to those individuals who are 'grouped according to the particular *industrial branch* that employs them... from an "industrial" point of view, any worker in a service industry is a service worker irrespective of the actual work undertaken'. So, for example, all employees of the Education Service are classified as 'service' workers irrespective of whether their activities are manual or non-manual or of whether they produce tangible commodities. In referring to service *occupations* however:

> We often have in mind, not only the nature of the final product of their industrial branch, but something much more immediate: the nature of the particular job they engage in. A service worker in this second sense is anyone who engages in work whose immediate output is typically either non-material or ephemeral. Thus white-collar workers, sales workers, catering, cleaning, security, even transport workers, could all be considered to be in service employment. (Gershuny and Miles 1983, pp.47-8) [2]

In looking at 'services' then, we have to be clear whether we are talking about non-manual typically white-collar clerical occupations both within and outside manufacturing industries, or whether we are talking about manual and non-manual jobs, clerical or otherwise, in industries which make up the 'service sector' of the economy. Given the importance of 'services' in his characterization of post-industrialism, it is surprising that Bell rather recklessly lumps all of these types of work together under a single heading.

This unclarity cannot help but undermine his suggestion that 'services' typically require higher levels of education and intellectual skill and thus offer higher levels of satisfaction. Whilst it is certainly the case that white-collar work has a different ambience than manual work, and often does require higher levels of educational, organizational, and decision-making skills, a large body of empirical research has shown that this is by no means always the case (e.g. Thompson 1983, Wood (ed.) 1982, Crompton and Jones 1984).

Despite the fact then, that late-industrialism is certainly characterized by a significant increase in the number of people holding white-collar jobs in the service sector, the majority of these jobs largely involve routine clerical and latterly data-entry tasks requiring little in the way of advanced skills and offering only marginal improvements in satisfaction and creativity. Under circumstances where the experience of service-type tasks has turned out to be 'remote indeed from the humanized, personalized, and self-fulfilling pattern envisaged in the post-industrial scenario' it would be very foolhardy to accept Bell's suggestion that post-industrialism inevitably constitutes 'a reversal of the trends towards alienation and depersonalization in the large corporations of the industrial society' (Kumar 1978, p.205/209).

Post-Industrialism and Scientific/Technical Knowledge

Although Bell's general claims about the epoch-making potential of the shift towards services and increases in the quality of working life are unsatisfactory, his observations about *one particular category* of 'services' have turned out to be much more promising, namely service occupations in 'education, research and government'. For Bell 'it is the growth of [this] category', 'the pre-eminence of the professional and technical class which is decisive for post-industrial society. And this is the category that represents the expansion of a new intelligentsia - in the universities, research organizations, professions, and government' (Bell 1974, p.15). What is outstanding about this sub-sector, or as Kumar numbers it 'quarternary sector' of services,[3] is 'the centrality of theoretical knowledge as the source of innovation and of policy formulation... the control of technology and technological assessment... the creation of a new "intellectual technology"' (Bell 1974, p.14).

What Bell is getting at here, is that these service-professions are important not just because of their facility for handling day-to-day information, but because the knowledge they use increasingly takes the form of *theoretical knowledge*:

> What has now become decisive for society is the new centrality of *theoretical* knowledge, the primacy of theory over empiricism and the codification of knowledge into abstract systems of symbols that can be translated into many different and varied circumstances. Every society now lives by innovation and growth, and it is theoretical knowledge that has become the matrix of innovation.... If the dominant figures of the past hundred years have been the entrepreneur, the businessman, and the industrial executive, the "new men" are the scientists, the mathematicians, the economists, and the engineers of the new intellectual technology. (Bell 1974, pp.343-4)

Although theoretical knowledge is most evident in science-based industrial research, it has also become a *generic* type of knowledge which is being applied in *all* types of problem-solving both within and outside the labour process. This new kind of knowledge is as much to do with understanding *the relationships* between phenomena as it is to do with understanding phenomena in isolation.

Picking up on the theme of rationality described in relation to Weber's analysis in the previous chapter, 'theoretical knowledge' can be seen as providing both a new and improved conception of what 'rational' knowledge is, and a new set of tools for exercising scientific/technical rationality in complex situations. By developing 'intellectual technology', modern institutions try 'to define rational action and to identify the means of achieving it':

> All action takes place under conditions of certainty, risk, or uncertainty.... In all these situations, the desirable action is a strategy that leads to the optimal or "best" solution; i.e. one which either maximizes the outcome, or depending upon the assessment of the risks and uncertainties, tries to minimize the losses. Rationality can be defined as judging, between two alternatives, which one is capable of yielding that preferred outcome. (Bell 1974, pp.30-1)

Given that organizational complexity and the volume of information which feeds into the decision-making processes of the labour process have increased very dramatically, it follows that those groups and institutions who hold theoretical knowledge and are able to control and implement it, are likely to play a leading and dominant role in economic development:

> In effect, theoretical knowledge increasingly becomes the strategic resource, the axial principle, of a society. And the university, research organisations, and intellectual institutions, where theoretical knowledge is codified and

enriched, become the axial structures of the emergent society. (Bell 1974, p.26)

There is a clear continuity here with the more recent contributions of Giddens and Beck. The former suggests for example, that 'expert systems' - 'systems of technical accomplishment or professional expertise that organize large areas of the material and social environments in which we live today' - are one of the most important 'disembedding mechanisms' of modernity, mechanisms which involve 'the "lifting out" of social relations from local contexts of interaction and their restructuring across indefinite spans of time-space' (Giddens 1990, pp.21/27):

> Expert systems are disembedding mechanisms because... they remove social relations from the immediacies of context.... An expert system disembeds... by providing "guarantees" of expectations across distanciated time-space. This "stretching" of the social system is achieved via the impersonal nature of tests applied to evaluate technical knowledge and by public critique (upon which the production of technical knowledge is based), used to control its form. (Giddens 1990, p.28)

Further still, our willingness to participate in social and economic relations governed or bounded by the disembedding mechanism of expert systems requires us to exhibit 'faith' and 'trust' in those systems and the knowledge claims they make. In this sense, 'trust may be defined as confidence in the reliability of a person or system, regarding a given set of outcomes or events, where that confidence expresses a faith in... the correctness of abstract principles (technical knowledge)' (Giddens 1990, p.34).

Whilst at least up until the 1980s, technical knowledge and expert systems were generally viewed positively both within enterprises and amongst the general public, this cosy situation has now changed.[4] As Giddens and Beck have pointed out, public perceptions of the trustworthiness and reliability of such knowledge is now much more sceptical and critical. For Beck, this pessimism and distrust arises out of a growing disjuncture between knowledge based on 'scientific rationality' and knowledge based on 'social rationality'. As people have become more aware of the 'hazardous potential of civilization' - meaning in particular the ecological dangers arising from industrialism - the knowledge claims of the scientific and technical elite are no longer accepted as beyond question: 'the two sides talk past each other. Social movements raise questions that are not answered by the risk technicians at all, and the technicians answer questions which miss the point of what was really asked and what feeds public anxiety' (Beck 1992, p.30).

In a similar vein, Giddens emphasizes that although knowledge in both the natural and social sciences has increased very dramatically in the period of late modernity/late-industrialism, this knowledge is not concrete and unidimensional but is essentially 'reflexive knowledge' which is constantly being revised and altered:

> The reflexivity of modern social life consists in the fact that social practices are constantly examined and reformed in the light of incoming information about those very practices, thus constitutively altering their character.... Modernity is constituted in and through reflexively applied knowledge, but the equation of knowledge with certitude has turned out to be misconceived. We are abroad in a world which is thoroughly constituted through reflexively applied knowledge, but where at the same time we can never be sure that any given element of that knowledge will not be revised. (Giddens 1990, pp.38-9)

The accumulation of knowledge then, is not as Bell and others have suggested a benign and uncontested feature of late-industrialism, but is a much more complex phenomenon which by no means guarantees that we can exercise greater control over the natural and synthetic environments. Essentially we live in a world of well-informed confusion and doubt rather than of increasing 'absolute' knowledge.

The tension which Beck identifies between 'scientific' and 'social' rationality is again highly reminiscent of Weber's distinction between 'formal' and 'substantive' rationality. Whereas it is possible to make objective assessments about which is the best way of doing a particular thing (scientific rationality), it is much more difficult to settle disputes over whether the thing is worth doing in the first place (social rationality):

> Even such simple questions as the extent to which an end should sanction unavoidable means, or the extent to which undesired repercussions should be taken into consideration... are entirely matters of choice and compromise. There is no (rational or empirical) scientific procedure of any kind whatsoever which can provide us with a decision here. (Weber, *The Methodology of the Social Sciences*, quoted in Brubaker 1984, p.59)

Beck's thesis on the problems facing 'risk society' is grounded precisely in this kind of dilemma; whereas the goals of economic growth and prosperity, of technological advance and progress, were once almost universally accepted as being 'a good thing', now, and having had time to reflect more fully on some of the negative and unintended consequences of industrialism, a rival discourse claiming to be even more 'rational' has touched the public conscience.

The same concerns are clearly expressed by Bell and Galbraith. The former for example, recognizes that the 'economizing mode' of industrialism has a number of crucial defects since unintended social costs of production such as pollution and urban congestion highlight the potential conflict between 'public goods' for social consumption and 'private goods' for consumption by individuals:

> Thus, if one is trying to assess welfare (or the quality of life) in some optimal fashion, the problem is not only the simple commitment to economic growth, but the nature of accounting and costing system of the economizing mode which has served to mask many of its deficiencies. Our fascination with Gross National Product is a good illustration. (Bell 1974, p.280)

Similarly, Galbraith develops the idea of 'social balance' to distinguish between 'the supply of privately produced goods and services and those of the state' (Galbraith 1969, p.225):

> By failing to exploit the opportunity to expand public production, we are missing opportunities for enjoyment which otherwise we might have had. Presumably a community can be as well rewarded by buying better schools or better parks as by buying bigger automobiles.... It is scarcely sensible that we should satisfy our wants in private goods with reckless abundance, while in the case of public goods, on the evidence of the eye, we practice extreme self-denial. (Galbraith 1969, p.229)

Although Bell still hopes to conclude his story with a happy ending, and so suggests that the economizing mode is being displaced in post-industrial society by a new 'sociologizing mode' in which a more direct effort is made to 'judge society's needs in more conscious fashion' (Bell 1974, p.283), he seems less than optimistic about how effective such an effort can be:

> A post-industrial society cannot provide a transcendent ethic - except for the few who devote themselves to the temple of science. And the antinomian attitude plunges one into a radical autism which, in the end, dirempts the cords of community and the sharing with others. The lack of a rooted moral belief system is the cultural contradiction of the society, the deepest challenge to its survival. (Bell 1974, p.480)

To the echoes of Weber we can now add the echoes of Durkheim. Bell's comments on the 'cultural contradictions' of capitalism in a subsequent volume, could just as easily have been written by his erstwhile predecessor:

> Every society seeks to establish a set of meanings through which people can relate themselves to the world.... The loss of meanings... creates a set of incomprehensions which people cannot stand and which prompt, urgently,

their search for new meanings, lest all that remain be a sense of nihilism or the void. (Bell 1976, p.146)

Post-Industrialism and Organizational Complexity

A third important theme associated with both Bell's and Galbraith's accounts of late-industrialism, is the organizational form through or within which the scientific/theoretical knowledge characteristic of 'expert systems' is expressed. According to Galbraith the power and influence of the scientific/technical elite within business organizations had given rise to what he calls a new industrial 'technostructure':

> This is the association of men of diverse technical knowledge, experience or other talent which modern industrial technology and planning require. It extends from the leadership of the modern industrial enterprise down to just short of the labor force and embraces a large number of people and a large variety of talent. It is on the effectiveness of this organization... that the success of the modern business enterprise now depends. (Galbraith 1972, p.58)

Most importantly, the technostructure emerged as a direct and (formally) rational response to the increasingly complex technological and organizational demands of the contemporary labour process, particularly the need for organizations to be able to co-ordinate their decision-making functions:

> The need to draw on, and appraise, the information of numerous individuals in modern industrial decision-making has three principal points of origin. It derives, first, from the technological requirements of modern industry.... The second factor requiring the combination of specialized talent derives from advanced technology, the associated use of capital and the resulting need for planning with its accompanying control of environment.... Finally, following from the need for this variety of specialized talent, is the need for its coordination. Talent must be brought to bear on the common purpose. (Galbraith 1972, pp.60-2)

The internal functioning of the modern technostructure also gives rise to new ways of working as individual decision-making is increasingly replaced by group and team working. As part of his narrative, Galbraith regards this change of approach as signifying the decline of the 'entrepreneurial' corporation (early-twentieth century) where decisions were made by charismatic individuals and the emergence of the 'modern' corporation (mid- to late-twentieth century) where the decision-making function is absorbed by the team-working technostructure:

In the industrial enterprise, power rests with those who make decisions. In the mature enterprise, this power has passed, inevitably and irrevocably, from the individual to the group. That is because only the group has the information that decision requires. Though the constitution of the corporation places power in the hands of owners, the imperatives of technology and planning remove it to the technostructure. (Galbraith 1972, p.98)

Whilst it is certainly the case that many more people work outside rather than within the giant corporations described by Galbraith, and that since he made these observations during the 1960s and 1970s the rigidly hierarchical organization of work has been displaced by a more open horizontal structure, it is also true that many of the structural and organizational problems he identifies continue to preoccupy managers of the 1990s. As we shall see in the following chapter, complex decision-making procedures are an inherent feature of the late-industrial labour process.

It should be clear from this account that the 'grand narrative' of first-phase post-industrialism leaves a lot to be desired. Of the two authors Galbraith certainly has more to offer, not least because he seems less willing to overlook the evident shortcomings of the labour process of the 1970s in the hope of providing us with a happy ending. Bell's account suffers because his notions of a service-oriented and service-dominated labour process are insufficiently strong to bear the weight of economic and social transition which he attributes to them.

Amongst the debris though, we can salvage important prototypes of the debates which followed. Firstly, it is certainly true that industrial societies are less 'industrial' in the sense that many more people are employed in non-manual occupations than was the case during the 1960s and 1970s. The *range* of service-type occupations has also increased in response to increases in the organizational and administrative demands of industry, to the growing demand for 'social' services, and the commercialization of 'personal' services (i.e. the kinds of services which are now organized on a commercial footing rather than being provided 'free of charge' to ourselves or by others).

Secondly, the structure and internal organization of business enterprises has continued to change partly in response to the increasingly close association between scientific research and development and technological innovation in industry, and to the increasingly dynamic nature of competition in the market place.

Thirdly, the kind of knowledge upon which decisions are made has tended to become embedded within expert systems of one kind or another. Because this knowledge is not available to most people, we are more or less obliged to have 'faith' or 'trust' in these systems both as workers and as consumers.

Finally, and as an opening shot in the debates we will be looking at in the remainder of this chapter, we can note the remarkable correspondence between the concerns of theorists writing about the industrial labour process during the first decades of this century (Weber and Durkheim), those writing during the 1970s (Bell and Galbraith), and the 1990s (Giddens and Beck). The historical contexts surrounding what they have to say may be different, but the substance of those concerns has barely altered at all. This adds a good deal of weight to the view that despite the important changes which have taken place in the labour process during the past hundred years or so, the basic defining characteristics of industrialism have remained very much the same. Post- or late-industrialism *is* different from early- or 'high'-industrialism, but not *that* different.

Post-Fordism and Flexibility

Despite the failure of first-phase accounts of post-industrialism to provide a fully convincing account of how and why the industrial labour process was changing, it was quite evident that there was still an important story which needed to be told. Nobody even vaguely considered appending the words 'The End'. The main problem with the earlier narrative was that key parts of its plot - shifts from manufacturing to service industries and occupations, a revised form of scientific/technical rationality, and changes in organizational form - were not strong enough to support the idea that a fully-developed post-industrial society had emerged. Although thoughtfully described, these features seemed to be *consequences* of something else, something more fundamental and dynamic. *Why was it* that employment had shifted into the service sector? *What was* the origin of the new rationality? *Why were* organizations having to change?

The answer, which seems embarrassingly obvious today, was technological innovation. Debates about work always have given an important role to technology of course, but the capacity of the wave of microelectronic-technologies which became continuously available from the mid-1970s onwards to literally transform the labour process ensured that it would now take on a starring role. The second-phase narratives of post-industrialism/post-Fordism which emerged during the 1980s and 1990s have been almost entirely dominated by the theme of the effects of technological innovation in general and of one of its main characteristics 'flexibility'. New theories (or at least revised versions of established theories) have been put forward which not only seek to *describe* the changes which are taking place,

64

and to *explain* the underlying reasons for them. Surrounded by the very large quantity of empirical material now available, the task of making reliable predictions about what the final impact of flexibility on the labour process will be is even more dependent on how one chooses to interpret this evidence than was the case a few years ago.

Given that a number of comprehensive accounts of the detailed picture are now available (Wood (ed.) 1989; Gilbert *et al.* (eds.) 1992; Amin (ed.) 1994; Amin and Thrift (eds.) 1994; Kumar 1995, and Storey (ed.) 1994), the following account will consider the merits of the arguments which have been put forward in terms of the cogency of the underlying theoretical perspectives which support them. In doing this, it will also be possible to emphasize areas of similarity between the various perspectives rather than being drawn into a somewhat unrewarding and unnecessary exaggeration of their differences.

The Terms of the Debate

In expressing solidarity with their immediate predecessors, contemporary debates in labour process theory and the sociology of work, have centred around the question of whether the late-industrial labour process has passed from a phase of 'Fordist' production based around the earlier paradigm of mechanized and semi-automated mass production, to an entirely new or perhaps higher stage of 'post-Fordist' production based on the paradigm of flexible production (the notion of a 'technological paradigm' is discussed in more detail in the following chapter). As Jessop puts it:

> A minimum condition for referring to post-Fordism is to establish the nature of the continuity in discontinuity which justifies the claim that it is not just a variant form of Fordism but does actually succeed Fordism. Without significant discontinuity, it would not be *post*-Fordism; without significant continuity, it would not be post-*Fordism*. (Jessop 1994, p.257)

As we shall see, and quite irrespective of whether any final agreement can be reached about the delimiting characteristics of these two stages, there is no disagreement over the fact that the late-industrial labour process has entered an important period of transition, or that the momentum for change and the consequences of it are here to stay; the narrative of post-Fordism/flexibility is not offering us a choice about what we would *like* to happen, as much as it is about telling us what *is* happening. It will be useful to begin by looking briefly at what the notion of 'flexibility' entails, and at some of the critiques which suggest that although there is evidence of change, a widespread and clearly focused transition towards 'flexibility' is more questionable.

Following Gilbert *et al.* (eds.) (1992), the flexibility debate can be seen as involving three distinct but closely related strands. Firstly, and operating at a general and more overtly theoretical level, a number of authors working within what has been labelled 'the regulation school' have proposed that a transition is taking place away from the established patterns of economic organization labelled 'Fordism', toward a new pattern labelled 'post-Fordism'. Secondly, Piore and Sabel (1984) have put forward the idea that at the level of the productive process itself, manufacturing industry is moving away from large-scale mass production of standardized products, towards smaller-scale production of specialized products. Thirdly, and at the level of managerial strategy, it has been argued that employers are deliberately introducing policies aimed at securing a highly skilled 'core' for performing essential tasks, while less skilled tasks are given over to a more casually employed and largely unskilled pool of 'peripheral' employees.[5] We will look at each of these strands in turn.

Fordism and Post-Fordism

The regulationist perspective on the transition form Fordism towards post-Fordism (or perhaps more accurately, from Fordist to post-Fordist capitalism: Aglietta 1979; Lipietz 1985 and 1987; and Jessop 1992(a), 1992(b)), takes as its point of departure the fact that the capitalist mode of production has historically been able to maintain an increasing level of economic growth and relative prosperity despite the fact that it is also subject to periods of crisis. They have developed the concepts of a 'regime of accumulation' and 'mode of regulation' to describe the way in which an economic system embraces not only the practicalities of the labour process in pursuit of profit, but also the economic, social and political institutions which are developed in support of it. Esser and Hirsch explain that 'each capitalist development of society is characterized by a specific *mode of accumulation* (accumulation regime) and a *method of regulation* associated with it':

> By "[regime] of accumulation", we mean a form of surplus value production and realization, supported by particular types of production and management technology.... This includes investment and capital devaluation strategies, branch structure (in particular the ratio between the producer goods sector and consumer goods sector), wage condition, consumer models and class structures, the relations between the capitalist and non-capitalist sectors of work in society and the mode of integration into the international market.

[Mode of] regulation describes the way in which the elements of this complex relationship between production and reproduction are related to each other socially, i.e. based on the behaviour of the social participants.... It includes a multifaceted configuration of economic and sociopolitical institutions and norms, which gives a certain equilibrium and stability to the reproduction of the system as a whole.... (Esser and Hirsch 1994, pp.73-4)

Regulationists argue that the economic crises of the 1970s signified that the relatively settled methods of production and structural organization of the economy which had allowed for reliable accumulation of capital during the 1950s and 1960s had come to an end. Since capital accumulation is the driving force of the capitalist enterprise (a point which Bell had made earlier about the expansion of the service sector), the avoidance of a more or less fatal decline in economic growth and prosperity required a thoroughgoing restructuring not only of the methods of production, but also of the regulatory socio-political institutions and mechanisms which were conducive to these changes:

Regulation theory characterises the postwar boom in terms of a Fordist regime of accumulation based upon techniques of mass production buttressed by a mode of regulation consisting of mass consumption and the Keynesian welfare state. The theory suggests that in recent years the process of restructuring we have been witnessing is a symptom of the "crisis of Fordism" and the emergence of post-Fordism. (Gilbert et al. (eds.) 1992, p.3)

Post-Fordism then, is seen as the most recent attempt by the owners of the means of production and their agents, to accommodate practical and organizational changes in those means, whilst at the same time manipulating the socio-political framework in such a way as to renew the process of capital accumulation. If successful, it was to be expected that a new period of growth and stability would emerge. Focusing on changes in the means of production, the re-establishment of stability is tied to the transcendence of Fordism, with its reliance upon 'mass production and mass consumption and mass public provision', by post-Fordism which is characterized by:

Homology between "flexible" production techniques, differentiated and segmented consumption patterns, a restructured welfare state and postmodernist cultural forms. The breakdown of Fordism and the emergence of post-Fordism is conceptualised primarily in terms of a search for greater levels of economic flexibility. (Gilbert et al. (eds.) 1992, p.3)

In political terms, and in sharp contrast to the Keynesian mode of the Fordist period, where government and state actively intervened in economic management, post-Fordist regulation is characterized by attempts by

67

government to 'deregulate' legal and other constraints on business practices, contracts of employment and working conditions, by attempts to undermine the strength of trade unions, and arguably by increasing (or at least failing to reduce) the pool of employees who can be hired and fired at short notice (the maintenance of a reserve army) thus shifting the balance of power from employee to employer.

In social and cultural terms, and again in contrast to the mass consumption and universalized domesticity of Fordism, post-Fordism is characterized by the notion of the sovereign consumer, the emergence of personalized life-styles and the withdrawal of individuals into their private worlds, what could be called the 'privatisation of personal space'.[6] Although the regulationists tend to concentrate on the structural aspects of the socio-political and socio-cultural dimensions of the mode of regulation, we should note that these dimensions also play an important part in maintaining what we can call the *perceived legitimacy* of the labour process (regime of accumulation). People's willingness to participate in the mechanisms of employment, to have a sense of trust in their ability to meet their expectations of work, is just as crucial. We will look at the consensual aspects of this participation by introducing the idea of the *work paradigm* towards the end of this chapter.

Flexible Specialization

Although the regulationist approach is as much concerned with the broader historical and political dynamics of the regeneration of capitalism as it is with the more immediate practicalities of the labour process, it assumes nonetheless, that significant changes have taken place in the practical organization of work. What after all, is post-Fordism if not a change in working practice? Given their central significance to the flexibility debate, these practicalities, many of which stem directly from innovations in microelectronic technologies, have been described in some detail. Sabel for example, describes economic transition in terms reminiscent of the regulationists:

> Stable demand for large numbers of standard products is the cornerstone of Fordism. It makes possible long-term investment in product-specific machines.... Anything that unsettles prospects of manufacturing a certain product in a fixed way and selling it in predictably large numbers for a foreseeable price undermines the propensity to invest in the Fordist strategy.... Many signs suggest that the Fordist model of organization is being challenged by new forms of the division of labour. International competition and

overlapping domestic conflicts between producers and consumers, and between workers and capitalists, are driving many large firms out of mass markets for standardised goods. To survive this challenge manufacturers have no choice but to produce more-specialised, higher-quality products. (Sabel 1984, pp.194/95)

Within this analysis, the notion of 'flexible specialization' has been central. This model again draws on the transition from Fordist to post-Fordist methods of production. From the 'flexible specialization' perspective, industrial development is characterized by the emergence of a number of productive techniques which in the first instance tend to co-exist within the economy. Over time however, the craft-based techniques of the early industrial period were challenged and then overcome as automated mass production emerged during the twentieth century.[7] During the 1970s, stagnating demand for mass-produced goods, combined with growing industrial application of highly sophisticated computer-based technologies, signified the displacement of 'rigid' automated mass production by techniques of flexible specialization. In this context, 'flexibility' refers to:

> Labour market and labour process restructuring, to increased versatility in design and the greater adaptability of new technology in production. "Specialisation" relates to niche or custom marketing, the apparent end of Fordism, mass production and product standardisation. (Smith 1991, p.139)

Pollert has also summarized the main characteristics of flexible specialization in terms of differences between this and the earlier paradigm of 'inflexible' mass production:

> Mass production... is based on the special-purpose machine, organised on an assembly line, operated by a semi-skilled labour force, producing standardised products for a mass market.... Flexible specialisation is a new form of skilled craft production made easily adaptable by programmable technology to provide specialised goods which can supply an increasingly fragmented and volatile market. (Pollert 1991, p.17)

It should be emphasized, that although the transition towards flexible specialization has been enabled by technological advance - flexibility is a key characteristic of the technology itself - the turn towards flexible specialization is also attributed to changes in *the demand for goods* in the market. Piore and Sabel have argued for example, that it was the saturation of mass consumer markets during the 1960s and 1970s which provided the impetus for the switch from Fordism to post-Fordism. Sabel notes for example:

To the extent that consumers demand a particular good in order to distinguish themselves from those who do not have it, the good becomes less appealing as more of it is sold. Consumers will be increasingly willing to pay a premium for a variant of the good whose possession sets them off from the mass; and as the number of variants competing for attention and encouraging further differentiation of tastes increases, it becomes harder and harder to consolidate production of a standard product. (Sabel 1984, p.199)

In order to capture the idea that consumers have become much more active in their demands, McHugh *et al* develop the term 'prosumer':

Prosumers contribute by various degrees to the design of the product they request. They are proactive customers that work with the sellers to define the products and services they are buying.... Prosumerism and the demand for mass customization have become more than just business buzz words. Customers are demanding that they are treated as though they are the most important people. They want their requests treated as the driver of innovation in product, service and support. (McHugh *et al*. 1995, pp.15/197)

We can add to this that from a culturalist perspective prosumerism not only includes product choice, but also a more diverse range of self-perceptions about what it means to be a consumer.

— Looking more closely at the technological dimensions of flexible specialization, three factors can be singled out. Firstly, the introduction of advanced robotics and other types of computer-controlled machinery has made it possible not only to improve the design specification and quality of products, but to produce them more quickly and more cheaply than was possible with traditional Fordist techniques:

Instead of Fordism's specialised machinery producing standardised products, we now have flexible, all-purpose machinery producing a variety of products.... As a result, the economies of scale of mass production can now be achieved on much smaller runs, whether small batch engineering products, or clothes, shoes, furniture and even books. (Murray 1989(b), pp.56-7)

Secondly, the assignment of routine information and data-processing tasks to computer, has made it possible to displace the rigidly hierarchical and bureaucracy-bound management style of Fordism with much more responsive and fluid forms of lateral communication:

With the revision of Taylorism, a layer of management has been stripped away. Greater control has allowed the decentralisation of work. Day-to-day autonomy has been given to work groups and plant managers. Teams linking departments horizontally have replaced the rigid verticality of Fordist bureaucracies. (Murray 1989(a), p.46)

70

Thirdly, in combining flexibility of production with flexibility of organization and control, flexible specialization has also brought about radical changes in the co-ordination of activities within an individual firm, between one firm and another, and between producer and retailer:

> Product ranges are modified more quickly, and are more internally diversified than the classic forms of production for mass consumer markets. Modern information systems allow both finer tuning of product flows and mixes in relation to changing and segmented markets, and greater producer influence over consumer demand. (Rustin 1989, p.57)

Perhaps the best known application of flexible specification is in the motor vehicles industry, where the potential benefits of this level of integration in terms of productivity, quality and product flexibility have been amply demonstrated by the Japanese system of manufacture. As Jones has pointed out, in emphasizing the standardization of components (and therefore of products) to achieve maximum throughput, the Fordist philosophy 'tended to eliminate any opportunity for responsible involvement and initiative [since] it was assumed that the worker would not report on problems, would not repair his own machines and would take no initiative for spotting and correcting faults'. As a consequence: 'Large stocks of parts had to be held between each major production operation so that parts of the system could continue to operate, while problems in other parts of the system were being diagnosed and repaired, and to insulate the system from industrial relations or other problems in the supplier firms' (Jones 1985, p.139). Not only therefore, did the system have to take account of fluctuations in the supply of components, it also required a large number of production engineers and supervisors to oversee an army of alienated and apparently recalcitrant assembly workers, and had to spend time and resources in checking the quality of the product at the end of the production line.

In contrast, the Japanese approach sought to overcome these difficulties of supply, motivation and quality by introducing the now familiar 'just-in-time' and 'total quality control' systems. The Japanese system improved motivation by making the workforce directly responsible for their own tasks and machines. This increase in individual responsibility also solved the problem of quality control, since defects could be detected and corrected actually during production rather than in retrospect. Problems with fluctuations in the supply of components, and consequently with the problem of stockpiling were resolved by developing much more flexible relationships with materials and parts suppliers:

71

The operations of a multi-tiered structure of component suppliers are closely integrated with the final assembler. The interdependence of each link in the supply chain, built up over many years, serves to devolve the organization of the system while at the same time mobilising all the resources of each firm to improve the total system performance. (UNIDO, *Industry and Development Global Report* 1988, p.250)

(The Japanese system of subcontracting and inter-firm co-operation is described in more detail in chapter six below). As a direct consequence of these innovations, Japanese producers have been able both to develop much greater variety within established product ranges, and to introduce entirely new models much more quickly and efficiently than their Western competitors. The UNIDO report quoted above suggested for example that the new process 'has reduced the lead time for developing a new model from 5 to 3.5 years, using about one half the number of man-hours in design and engineering. Models are replaced after only four years in Japan, as compared with every eight years elsewhere' (UNIDO 1988, p.250).[8]

In summary, flexible specialization is seen as a response to the availability of new production methods combined with greater fluidity in likely consumer demand for non-mass produced goods. Given the apparent unsuitability of Fordist techniques for producing such a diverse range of products in limited numbers, a new technological paradigm has emerged based around the techniques of flexible specialization. There is a clear implication within this perspective, that the survival of capitalist enterprises producing consumer goods, will depend upon the extent to which they are able and willing to restructure their organization and production methods around the model of flexible specialization.

Core and Periphery

The third strand of debate centres around the issue of whether employers are adopting a deliberate strategy of dividing their operations between a highly-skilled 'core' and a 'periphery' of transiently employed workers. The core/periphery model can usefully be seen as the workforce dimension of the flexibility debate. The argument runs that if manufacturing firms adopt flexibility, this will inevitably require - and indeed cannot be achieved without - changes in the organization and activities of the workforce itself. Flexible production therefore conjures up the idea of the 'flexible firm':

The ideal typical flexible firm is one which has attempted to secure three sorts of economic flexibility. First, numerical flexibility: the ability to change the size of the workforce quickly and easily in response to changes in demand.

72

Second, functional flexibility: the ease with which workers can be redeployed to different tasks to meet changes in market demand, technology and company policy; and third: financial and pay flexibility to facilitate numerical, and especially, functional flexibility. (Gilbert *et al.* (eds.) 1992, p.4)

(Issues of recruitment and of financial and pay flexibility are discussed in more detail in the following chapter).

Following Penn (1992, pp.67-8), the ideal type core/periphery model of the flexible firm developed by Atkinson and Meager (1986) takes the form of a core of functionally flexible highly- and multi-skilled workers, surrounded by two or more groups of peripheral workers. The first peripheral group is made up of semi- and unskilled workers whose numbers can be increased or decreased to give the firm numerical flexibility. The second peripheral group, is made up of various temporary, part-time, casual and un- or semi-trained workers who can also be hired and fired according to fluctuations in demand. Beyond these groups, are various categories of workers, not directly employed by the firm, whose services can be bought-in on a contract basis.

The adoption of this strategy is seen as a response by employing organizations to particular changes and pressures within the economy. These include a combination of generic (and inevitable) factors, such as increasing competition in the market, uncertainty about future prospects, and continuing technological advance, and particular conjunctural factors (which may or may not be permanent) including high unemployment and weak trade unions.

Gough has summarized the likely characteristics of this segmented workforce as follows:

> The core workers use advanced reprogrammable machinery and they can move between tasks. Their production is therefore flexible with respect to product change, thus enabling the short-run production of varied products at relatively low cost. They have secure employment contracts. The peripheral workforce may or may not use advanced machinery, but, at any rate, they tend to be less skilled than the core workers. Their production includes both the "remaining" production of standardised products, and the overflows of production from the core during peaks in demand. Their employment contracts are insecure. (Gough 1992, pp.33-4)

In summary, the core/periphery dimension of the flexibility debate describes the employment consequences of transition towards flexible specialization in firms under conditions of post-Fordism. In its ideal type, the management of such firms would achieve numerical and functional flexibility by concentrating 'quality' employment (in terms of levels of skill, ability to move from one task to another, higher levels of pay and job security) at their core, while 'degraded' or 'down-graded' employment would be dispersed amongst a number of more heterogeneous groups of workers either at the margins of the firm or outside it. The employment of these latter groups would be characterized by lower levels of skill and pay, and by high levels of job insecurity. Their value to employers rests primarily in their 'willingness' to be available and yet largely 'dispensable'.

Inconclusive Evidence of Flexibility?

Having outlined the three main dimensions of the flexibility debate, it will be useful to consider briefly what evidence there is that these changes are actually taking place. Taking these three dimensions in reverse order, a number of authors have suggested that it is not at all clear whether firms are actually adapting themselves to the core/periphery model of the flexible firm. Discussing the implication that management can increase flexibility by developing and controlling a core of elite workers for example, Gough has argued that the development of transferable skills within the economy as a whole may make particular firms reluctant to take on the responsibility for training leading to 'underinvestment in training and under-supply of skilled labour':

> This can increase the bargaining power of skilled workers. Thus the highly socialised form of production implied by flexible integration gives workers strong potential points of resistance - in other words, inflexibility for capital. (Gough 1992, p.35)

Similarly, in discussing the employment situation of research and development staff, Whittington has suggested that this group 'on the face of it a classic core group', have seen their prospects diminish rather than increase:

> Demands for different types of flexibility have not been made on discrete employment groups; rather they have been deliberately combined, so that numerical flexibility has reinforced functional flexibility. In practice, managers do not respect Atkinson's boundaries. (Whittington 1991, p.102)

Discussing the suggestion that the consolidation of a skilled core at the electronics firm Lucas would lead to a general improvement in both skills and employer/employee relations, Elger and Fairbrother are less than convinced:

> There was little evidence that the changes in work relations involved any sustained shift towards multiskilled teamworking or more harmonious relations between workers and management, but rather more of greater work pressure associated with increased responsibilities. In this respect, [these

findings] also underline persistent diversity and unevenness in the patterns and processes of change. (Elger and Fairbrother 1992, p.105)

Although more decisive evidence has emerged regarding the expansion of an insecurely employed periphery (Pollert suggests for example, that: 'There is clear evidence of the growth of unemployment, and intermittent, non-permanent and vulnerable forms of work' (Pollert 1991, p.11)), numerous researchers have concluded that these forms of work are a long-standing rather than new-fangled means of organizing the labour process:

> The findings ... point to an increase in the use of insecure and indirect forms of employment. But such developments are by no means universal, being greater in some sectors than in others. The use of temporary contract, outworking and subcontractors are practices of long standing. In the majority of cases, workplaces using temporary contracts and subcontracting out service activities reported a continuation of existing practice. (Marginson 1991, p.44)

Leman has reached a similar conclusion about employment in the mail-order industry:

> Temporal flexibility is on the increase in the telephone ordering departments, and is associated with an extension of peripheral, part-time female employment. There is, however, little evidence of functional flexibility or multi-skilling. There is numerical flexibility but this is not new; employment in the industry has always been cyclical.... (Leman 1992, p.132)

It seems clear then, that although changes are taking place in the organization of work, it may be somewhat premature to deduce that these constitute a decisive shift towards the model of the flexible firm. Evidence of a concentration of skills, or of a broadening of multiskilling at the core is less than decisive, while activities within the periphery may reflect longer-term trends rather than a new direction. Even at the more general level of analysis, the basic tenets of the core/periphery model may fail: the evidence, Pollert suggests, implies that distinctions between such groups of workers are far from clear cut: 'Evidence on changes in the labour process lends more support to the concept of an "endangered core", and a broad dynamic of the core's expulsion from a central position, than to a picture of polarisation between a privileged elite and a periphery' (Pollert 1991, p.12). Walsh casts doubt on the whole idea that the core is some how more important than the periphery:

> It is a naive and erroneous simplification of the flexible-firm model that only "core" workers are indispensable to the company's operations.... part-timers and casuals are central to business operations..... Part-timers' and casuals' work may be undervalued, but it is by no means peripheral to either employer or employee. (Walsh 1991, p.114)

Since the model of the core and peripherally organized flexible firm presupposes the development of techniques of flexible specialization, it follows that the inconclusive (if not contradictory) evidence of the emergence of the former may cast some doubt on the transition towards the second strand of the flexibility debate, flexible specialization. Rainnie and Kraitham emphasize for example, that although the development of flexible specialization is seen as an inevitable response to the 'crisis' of mass production, this idea of managerial response assumes that management are in fact able to develop accurate strategies for the future. In reality however:

> Managerial tactics themselves (if not strategy) drawn up in one particular time frame can take an inordinate length of time to translate themselves into practical action at workplace level. By that time the external circumstances that "demanded" the shift in strategy, assumed to be timeless, can change. Thus what appears at one point to be rational can, by the time of implementation, be counterproductive. (Rainnie and Kraitham 1992, p.49)

Secondly, it has been suggested that in focusing on the technological dimensions of flexibility - on what the technology does or does not allow - exponents of flexible specialization tend to give the technology itself a determining influence over the organization of work and thus pay insufficient attention to its human dimensions. As Smith puts it, this 'technical determinism stems from the isolation of one factor, technological state or organisational form' from the overall situation in which capitalist investment and accumulation actually takes place. Advocates of the technology-driven move towards flexible specialization compound this difficulty by tending to assume that the organization of work and labour relations will inevitably be brought into line with the technology:

> The flexible specialisation thesis is premised on technological determinism not simply because... hardware was given unusual powers to shape work organization, but rather because its promoters have invested particular combinations of labour and capital with qualities to reconcile capitalist social contradictions. They have also invested particular production or technological systems with a completeness or totality which does not mirror the ongoing production diversity within capitalism as a whole. (Smith 1991, p.155)

By making such claims about a universal or paradigmatic shift from one regime of production to another, advocates of flexible specialization tend to assume: 'that it is possible to tame the market economy and that capitalist social relations are not inherently contradictory: it is possible to choose whether to continue on the old, declining path of mass production, or to reform through flexible specialisation' (Pollert 1991, pp.17-18).

Two important issues arise from this. In the first place, the model (especially as originally formulated by Sabel) assumes that recent developments will bring about a return to industrial harmony both between employers and employees and between one group of workers and another. It is extremely questionable however, whether capitalist industrialism ever has (or evil will) achieve such apparent harmony. It might be more realistic to accept that its inherent contradictions will inevitably cause deep divisions between these groups. Recent moves towards flexibility may in fact make matters worse rather than better:

> Against the background of economic restructuring and recession, employment legislation has increased the disadvantaged and unprotected workforce, and exacerbated the already existing polarisation between the legally protected workforce and the rest.... [Employment legislation] makes sense in terms of disciplining and disempowering the workforce; it is the opposite of what one would expect if state policy aimed to reinforce the employment and organisational rights of a core workforce. (Pollert 1991, p.15)

In the second place, it was noted above that Piore and Sabel emphasized that flexible specialization developed as a response to changes in consumer demand away from mass-produced towards individualized goods. As Pollert points out however, changes in consumer tastes might simply reflect changes in the types of goods which are available rather than being generated 'independently' or 'spontaneously' by consumers themselves: 'The cultivation of specific niches, whether for clothes, food or music, may become more sophisticated as competition intensifies, but this demonstrates no more than another manipulation of the mass market' (Pollert 1991, p.18).

Whilst acknowledging the logic of Pollert's comment on this point, it is worth noting that as standards of living improve, individual consumers are likely to have an increasing surplus income which can be disposed of in purchasing 'non-necessary' goods. Under these conditions, it would not be surprising if their wants for more diverse types of goods would also increase. Increased demand for product diversity is an effect of increasing affluence as much as it is an effect of 'manipulation'. Having said this, Sabel seems to contradict himself by suggesting that specialized production 'rests on the idea that, at the outset, customers' wants are vaguely defined and potentially diverse', that they have 'no precise need for a particular good': 'The job of the innovative firm is to find a technically and economically feasible way of satisfying this inchoate need, thus creating a new product and defining the customer's wants at the same time' (Sabel 1984, p.202). It is difficult to see how consumers or prosumers can play a leading role in product innovation and yet apparently have no clear idea of what they want.

Returning to the first strand of the debate over Fordism and post-Fordism, it should be clear that Marxist and other propositions about the true nature and implications of moves towards flexibility find some support in the preceding arguments. Firstly, and at the level of production itself, since evidence of the emergence of flexible specialization and the flexible firm point towards bits-and-pieces of change rather than towards a decisive split with the past, it is clearly necessary to see these developments as a continuation rather than transcendence of industrial capitalism. Post-Fordism is the latest phase of capitalist economic organization; it is not capitalism in an entirely different form.

Secondly, although liberal researchers like Sabel and others tend, very much in the manner of Bell, to represent post-Fordism in terms of the re-establishment of harmony - a revival of industrial democracy through enabling and skilful work - the present evidence points much more clearly towards a perpetuation of conflicts between employers and employees, and between one group of employees and another. To the extent that advocates of post-Fordism conduct their analysis at the level of 'industrial society' rather than at the level of industrial *capitalist* society, they may be guilty of putting forward an incomplete and possibly misleading picture both of the past and of the present.

Thirdly, the all-encompassing image of post-Fordism in its economic and political guises has also penetrated, and in some instances coerced, the ideological and cultural dimensions of people's orientation to work. It may well be that consumer tastes and lifestyles have changed, and that many individuals are seeking new ways of structuring and furnishing their 'private spaces', but the underlying logic of post-Fordism remains one of producing and selling goods at a profit. The fact that methods of production and patterns of consumption have continued to develop does not in itself provide evidence of a 'new society'. If individuals feel a need to seek security in a privatized and personalized world, what does this tell us about the public world from which they seek escape?

The Work Paradigm

Much controversy therefore surrounds the issue of whether the technological paradigm of flexibility is or is not being universally adopted as *the* new model for the labour process of the future. If we take a step back from these debates however, it is evident that despite their different points of departure, all parties acknowledge that a process of change *is* under way, and that the extremely dynamic technological paradigm of microelectronics is one of its star performers. Arguments over whether or not flexibility signifies the 'final' transcendence of Fordist capitalism, whether the ideal-typical flexible firm will entirely displace previous designs, and whether the workforce will be divided between core and periphery, are all arguments about the *pace, extent and scope* of change, rather than about whether such change is actually taking place. Even the most casual observation of the current state of affairs, let alone the fact that so many academics, policy makers and practitioners are devoting so much time to these issues, leaves one in no doubt at all that basic characteristics of the late-industrial labour process are quite different to those of the 1970s and 1980s, and may well be different again in the 2000s.

As our brief synopsis of post-Fordism/flexibility storyline has shown, this consensus arises from the fact that each of the variations on offer largely agree as to what the primary determinants of transition are: the role of technology within the productive process, and the availability of a socio-institutional framework which supports and legitimates the accumulation of capital. Technology and its impact on job security, levels of skill and managerial strategy will be the focus of discussion in the following chapter. For the remainder of this chapter we will concentrate on one of the most interesting aspects of the socio-institutional framework, its role in the maintenance of 'consensus' amongst the population.

As we have seen, it is widely accepted that the earlier paradigm of Fordism achieved growth and stability in the way that it did because of the parallel development of a suitable socio-institutional framework. In the UK in particular, this took the form of a Keynesian economic strategy and a proactive state bureaucracy, which brought key features of labour legislation, educational and welfare policies into line with the requirements of a mass production and mass consumption economic structure. The crisis of the 1970s was compounded by the inability of these institutions to offset the effects of falling living standards and increasing dependence on the state in the face of economic decline.

Apart form the immediate practical difficulties of finding work, it can be argued that the most significant threat to the sustainability of the labour process centred around the issue of whether people would continue to participate in it. If, as the discourse of industrialism discussed in the first chapter has indicated, we participate in the mechanisms of employment in order to meet various expectations, then any prolongation of not having them met is bound to undermine people's confidence in the practical expediency of that labour process. In this sense, the socio-institutional framework constitutes a set of mechanisms through which people's expectations of work can be reconciled with the realities of the economic structure as manifest by the prevailing organization of the productive forces.

If the mode of regulation is necessary in order to sustain capital accumulation, then it is *also* necessary as a means of enabling individuals to realise their ideas and expectations of work. This recognition of the *consensual dimension* of the mode of regulation has been widely acknowledged by participants in the flexibility debate. Some members of the regulation school for example, have referred to the necessary development of an 'hegemonic structure' which provides a linkage between the regime of accumulation and mode of regulation. Following Boyer and Mistral (1983), Esser and Hirsch explain that in their formulation:

> We use *hegemonic structure* to describe the concrete historical connection between the *mode of accumulation* and the *method of regulation*, which endows the economic form of capital reproduction (ensuring valorisation) and political-ideological (legitimation, force and consent) reproduction of the system as a whole under the domination of the ruling class(es), with relative durability. (Esser and Hirsch 1994, p.74, original emphasis)

Similarly, Jessop and Lipietz have added the concept of a 'mode of societalization' to the taxonomy of regulation, in order to capture the way in which the profitability of the economic system not only relies upon a sympathetic socio-institutional framework, but also upon the development of forms of socio-political interdependence and consent. In Amin's words:

> This concept refers to a series of political compromises, social alliances and hegemonic processes of domination which feed into a pattern of mass integration and social cohesion, thus serving to underwrite and stabilize a given development path. (Amin 1994, p.8)

In his analysis, Jessop defines 'mode of societalization' as the fourth referent for the terms Fordism and post-Fordism:

> A pattern of institutional integration and social cohesion which complements the dominant accumulation regime and its social mode of economic regulation and thereby secures the conditions for its dominance within the wider society. (Jessop 1994, p.252)

Although Jessop suggests that it is 'too soon' to anticipate what a post-Fordist mode of societalization would involve, he is clear that Fordist society is typically 'an urban-industrial, "middle class", wage-earning society' (Jessop 1994, p.254; see also Jessop 1992(a) and 1992(b)).

Taking this analysis a stage further, and partly drawing on Jenson 1989, Lipietz identifies the necessary development of a societal paradigm to describe 'a mode of structuration of the identities and legitimately defensible interests within the "universe of political discourses and representations"' (Lipietz 1994, p.340). This field of socio-political contest forms part of the mode of regulation made up of 'the set of norms (implicit or explicit) and institutions, which continuously adjust individual anticipations and behaviours to the general logic of the regime of accumulation...:

> We might say that the mode of regulation constitutes the "scenery", the practical world, the superficial "map" by which individual agents orient themselves so that the conditions necessary for balanced economic reproduction and accumulation are met in full. (Lipietz 1994, p.339)

For Lipietz, the success and sustainability of the prevailing paradigm is dependent upon the development of an hegemonic bloc which unites, in a particular socio-economic formation, the regime of accumulation and the mode of regulation. Crucially, hegemony is characterized as much in terms of political and social struggle, as it is in terms of competition between ascendant and descendent technological paradigms:

> The establishment of a mode of regulation, like its consolidation, largely depends upon the political sphere.... These struggles, armistices and compromises are the equivalent in the political domain of competition, labour conflict and the regime of accumulation in the economic sphere. Defined by their daily conditions of existence, and in particular by their place in economic relations, social groups do not engage in a struggle without end. *Social bloc* is the term to delineate a stable system of relations of domination, alliances and concessions between different social groups (dominant and subordinate). A social bloc is *hegemonic* when its interests correspond with those of a whole nation. In any hegemonic bloc the proportion of the nation whose interests are discounted has to be very small. (Lipietz 1994, pp.339-40)[9]

Applying this scheme to recent developments in capitalist society, Lipietz describes in familiar terms, how the Fordist or 'progressivist paradigm':

> Offered a conception of progress which itself rested upon three pillars: technical progress (conceived as technological progress unconditionally driven by "intellectual workers"); social progress (conceived as progress in purchasing power while respecting the constraint of full employment); and state progress (the state conceived as guarantor of the general interest against "encroachments" of individual interests). And this triple progress was supposed to weld society together, by advancing goals worthy of collective pursuit. (Lipietz 1994, p.342)

He goes on to suggest that the collapse of this paradigm during the 1970s - its loss of hegemonic solidarity - ushered in a new phase of 'economic liberalism' or 'liberal-productivism' founded upon 'the cult of the enterprise':

> The clarion call of the Western intelligentsia the first half of the 1980s was: we must be competitive! And to that end the initiative of entrepreneurs must be freed. And if the social consequences are unfavourable? Too bad. We must be competitive! To what end? Because free enterprise dictates that we be competitive. And so the story unfolded. (Lipietz 1994, p.343/4)

From this perspective then, the transition from Fordist to post-Fordist capitalism, corresponds to a breakdown in one form of socio-economic hegemony or social bloc, and attempts by the owners and controllers of the means of production to re-establish their hegemonic domination on a new footing.

Whilst accepting that this crisis of hegemony originates in, or at the very least, becomes a real possibility because of, practical developments in techniques of production and the organization of work, it *also* comes about as a result of a breakdown in the perceived legitimacy of the earlier paradigm. What unites these two factors, is that all those involved are seeking to protect their *economic interests*:

> The fit between "hegemonic bloc", "regime of accumulation" and "mode of regulation" becomes visible *as long as the interests constituting the consensus on which the hegemonic bloc is built and reproduced are economic interests.* (Lipietz 1994, p.340, emphasis added)

There is therefore strong support for the suggestion that a fully hegemonic economic structure crucially depends on a high degree of consent amongst the population. When a number of theorists speak of the 'adaption of many social institutions', of the need for a 'favourable institutional framework', of 'big changes in the conceptual framework', of 'a pattern of mass integration and social cohesion' of 'institutional integration and social cohesion', and of 'the set of norms which continuously adjust individual anticipations and behaviours to the general logic of the regime of accumulation', they are alerting us to the fact that participation in the mechanisms of employment is not simply 'automatic' or 'mechanical' but also depends upon the expression of belief and expectation.

Arguably, unless people feel, or come to feel more intensely, that their economic interests are under threat, then loss of hegemony is unlikely to occur. Neither a revolution in the means of production - in this instance the emergence of microelectronic technology - nor a change in the political philosophy of the dominant group (in effect the government or administration), *which had no detrimental effect* on standards of living, or on the prospect that these standards would gradually improve, would necessarily represent a significant challenge to societal hegemony. If either of these factors *did have* such an effect, then it is very likely that a significant challenge would emerge. If *both* the regime of accumulation *and* the mode of regulation suffer a loss of hegemonic legitimacy *at the same time*, there is a real possibility that the integrity of the socio-economic edifice would be strongly compromised.

Following the thrust of this analysis, we can usefully describe the necessary combination of a particular organization of work (regime of accumulation) with a corresponding set of ideas, beliefs and expectations of work (the ideational aspect of the mode of regulation), as a *work paradigm*. What we are getting at here, is that all historically identifiable manifestations of a particular way of organizing the productive process, are made up of a set of ideas about work (its conceptual dimension) and a set of techniques and types of organization for actually doing that work (its practical dimension).

If, as we have just seen, the mechanisms of employment, division of labour and so on do provide people with the practical means of meeting their expectations, then at least minimally the perceived legitimacy of the paradigm will be sustained. However, under circumstances where these material expectations are not being met, then this is likely to have a corrosive effect upon people's sense that those expectations are in fact achievable at all; people may loose faith in the mechanisms of employment and in the wider economic structure which surrounds it. In Durkheim's terms this amounts to an erosion of the role of the division of labour in providing people with a sense of belonging within society. Working is an expression of shared purpose and common meaning. Without it people feel lost and dismayed.

Although 'final crises' of this kind are quite rare (the Wall Street Crash and the depression which followed is perhaps as close as the Western economies have come this century), the need for there to be a 'correspondence' or 'balance' between the practical and ideational aspects of work strongly suggests that in the normal course of events a process of alternation and adjustment takes place between how people work and their ideas about work - we adapt our perceptions of work to keep them in line with current circumstances. Conversely, and assuming that the practical means for doing so are available, changes in our ideas about work can have an impact on how we work; the process of adjustment takes place in both directions. This is very much what Weber had in mind when he identified the 'affinity' between the Protestant 'ethic' and the 'spirit' of capitalism. Inspired by their desire for spiritual salvation the entrepreneurial bourgeoisie developed new kinds of business practice to begin 'saving'.

The significance of this process of balance and adjustment in our current analysis is that if, as evidently is the case, technologically-induced changes in the labour process will continue to have a profound effect on the practice of work, then it is inevitable that people's *perceptions* of what work will be like in the future *will also* be affected. In trying to understand what the future of work will be like, we not only have to be aware of practical changes, but also, and perhaps even more urgently, we need to understand what form new ideas about work, and new orientations towards work are taking.

It is already possible to list six of the ideas which have changed considerably during the last few years. First, the transfer of employment away from manufacturing to services, has dispelled the idea, always in part a myth, at 'proper' work involved 'real men' in the production of materials and manufactured commodities through muscular effort, 'blood, sweat and tears'.

Second, the passing of many large-scale primary industries such as coal mining and steel manufacture, has resulted in a severe decline in the idea of an occupational community which lay at the centre of many people's sense of what it meant to be 'a worker'. Third, the much more geographically fragmented and fluid nature of employment opportunity, has undermined the expectation of living and working in one locality more or less for life.

Fourth, work is no longer seen as a largely male preserve, but as an activity which involves at least as many women as it does men. Fifth, the emergence of part-time working, has displaced the idea that 'a proper job' meant full-time employment. Sixth, the shift towards various forms and combinations of temporary, contract-based, and periodic employment has superseded the idea of work as a single life-long activity - 'a job for life'.

The Flexi-Future of Work

Within the narrative of post-industrialism/post-Fordism the story of work changed from an epic to a soap opera. So many different story lines are now being followed, that one has to tune in two or three times a week just to keep in touch. The reason for this, is that although the main themes are easily identifiable - changes in the nature and organization of the labour process, the struggle between the established and the new, divisions between the winners and the losers - the accuracy of assessments about where present developments are leading is conditional upon both the level of generality of the analysis, and by the particular characteristics of the topic being investigated.

Although the theme of technological change and the concept of flexibility crop up in all areas of debate, different kinds of conclusions emerge depending on whether we are looking at the relationship between the economic structure and the wider society, the immediacies of day-to-day tasks within the labour process, or at likely changes in the distribution or segmentation of the workforce. Looking at the latter for example, the evidence we have considered in this chapter demonstrates that clear-cut messages about specific changes in particular contexts are difficult to come by. Whilst it is certainly the case that a number of important sectors of industry (particularly those which we would previously have labelled as 'mass production' industries) have adopted a flexible approach in organizing their productive activities ('just-in-time', 'total quality control', 'japanization'), there are many others which have not. Even within those which have, significant variations have been found in the extent to which they are or are not following the ideal-typical model described above. In looking at the research literature, one sometimes wonders whether it is just the labels that are applied to various activities which have changed rather than the activities themselves. Just because managers and supervisors are using a different jargon to describe what they are doing, it doesn't follow that they would see themselves as missionaries in the 'brave new world' of the flexi-future of work.

Similarly, evidence of a clear-cut and growing division between the so-called 'core' and a variety of 'peripheries' is by no means conclusive. Even if such a situation were clearly identified, then this could legitimately be seen as a reiteration of a typical characteristic of the industrial division of labour as such, rather than as something which has only emerged during the last few years. This unclarity is reminiscent of Bell's failure to distinguish properly between occupations and industries. If we are using the labels 'core' and 'periphery' to describe the characteristics of broad categories of *job*, then all we are really doing is repeating what we already know. As the narrative of industrialism has shown, changes in the types of job available will always fluctuate in accordance with the requirements of the employer. The names we give to the categories into which we place these jobs, and the nature of those jobs may change, but the basic explanation of *why* different kinds of jobs are available has not changed at all.

If on the other hand, we are using these labels to describe different categories of *employee*, then there is a stronger case for saying that employers are increasingly expecting some of their staff to be able to combine a number of particular skills into that one person. In this sense, a core employee is a highly-skilled utility player, while a peripheral worker is likely to have fewer and lower-level skills (we will return to this point in the following chapter).

Although 'peripheral' employees have lower skills and can therefore be replaced more easily than core workers, both are still *necessary* to the employer because obviously if a particular task did not need doing then nobody would be employed to do it.

The messages we can take away when operating at a higher level of generality are much clearer. First and least ambiguous, we know that whatever else it is, the industrial labour process of the future will be a *capitalist* labour process. Despite repeated and failed attempts by writers such as Bell and Sabel to sell the idea that recent changes sign the way towards a happy and prosperous future for all, the costs and benefits of change will not be equally distributed. However strong the counter-rationalities of anti-productivism may seem to be, and however deeply it has become submerged in both the academic and public consciousness, the underlying rationality of the future of work will be the production of commodities and services at a profit. Although in the 1990s this might sound like a distant echo from tales past, a vaguely remembered chorus from a Victorian nursery rhyme about the 'bad old days' of work, any other explanation takes us too far into the realms of future-fiction rather than future-fact.

Second, the labour process of the future will be an *industrial* labour process. Without denying the microelectronics-based technologies constitute a new 'technological paradigm' which has profoundly affected the nature and organization of work, and accepting that a significant and perhaps increasing proportion of the workforce will be concentrated in non-manual service-type occupations (issues we will be exploring in more detail in the following chapter), the predominant experience of work will be of participating in a complex division of labour important parts of which are dedicated to the automated production of commodities. There are no real grounds for deviating from the conclusion we reached after looking at the first-phase discourse of post-industrialism, that recent changes do not represent a complete break with the past. The direction and tone of industrialism have changed, but neither its basic characteristics nor its underlying dynamics have. If we do choose to use the prefix 'post', then we must be very clear that we are using it to mean 'following-on from' 'a later stage of' rather than to suggest that everything which comes after will be completely different from what went before.

A third clear message is that a general feature of the labour process of the future will be flexibility, meaning adaptability and openness to change. Whilst this approach will be most apparent in practical matters - how work is actually organized, the manner in which employees will be required to move between jobs, the responsiveness of producers to perceived/freshly created consumer demand - it will also be foregrounded in people's *perception* of work. In this sense, flexibility is as much an attitude of mind as it is a way of working. Following the arguments just put forward, the idea of flexibility will establish itself as a basic ingredient in the conceptual aspect of the new work paradigm. For people who are preparing to enter the labour process in the final years of the twentieth century, it will be part-and-parcel of their strategy for adapting to the new and much more changeable pattern of working life. A few years beyond that, flexibility will have become a feature of the taken-for-granted stereotype of work. In the same way that we might be amused to think that most people actually used to walk to work, academics will tell jokes about how people used to think that there was such a thing as a 'job for life'.

Fourthly, and emerging from these points, the message comes across loud and clear that questions over the rationality of late-industrialism still need to be resolved. As we shall see in the following chapters, it is extremely difficult to reconcile the rationalities of economic production with those of social consumption. Despite improvements in technique, greater efficiency, higher output, better quality products and so on, it is still much easier to settle for the 'formal' rationality of trying to find even better ways of doing these things than it is to get involved in a proper discussion about whether it is 'substantively' rational to do so. Under circumstances where access to, let alone sustainability of, formal paid employment is becoming more and more problematic, one of the greatest challenges facing the work paradigm of the future will be to look again at how access to work and the proceeds of production can be more evenly and equitably distributed.

3 The New Technological Paradigm

Following on from issues raised in the previous chapter, the purpose of this chapter is to look more closely at two of the most important strands of current debates about technological innovation; its likely impact on the types and levels of skills amongst the workforce, and its impact on managerial strategies in the context of increasing organizational complexity. To begin with though, it will be instructive to look briefly at the 'paradigmatic' nature of microelectronics-based technologies in order to understand why it is that they have had such a profound and rapid impact on the labour process - where does their transformative capacity come from?

The Technological Paradigm of Microelectronics

In order to capture the sense in which a particular technology or group of technologies can shift or transform the technical basis of the whole productive system, a number of researchers have invoked the idea of an industrial or technological 'paradigm':

> A new industrial paradigm is made up of a series of technically and economically interrelated radical innovations that have pervasive effects on the whole of economic life and involve major changes in the capital stock and skill profile of the population; the development of computers and communication technologies is a contemporary example. (Dunford 1989, p.114, note 1)

Using terms which will be familiar from the discussion in the previous chapter, Freeman (following Perez 1983,1985), defines the current paradigm of microelectronics as having the following characteristics:

> (i) The shift towards information-intensive rather than energy and materials-intensive products and processes... (ii) the change from relatively inflexible dedicated mass production systems, towards much more flexible systems, capable of manufacturing a diverse range of output as efficiently as a single homogeneous product... (iii) new patterns of business organization implying "systemation rather than automation". (Freeman (ed.) 1985, p.x)

One of the most influential attempts to explain the origins, and understand the pattern of development of the latest paradigm involves placing it in the context of previous clusters of innovation. This theory of cycles or 'long waves' of economic growth was first put forward by the Russian economist Nikolai Kondratiev during the 1920s (Kondratiev 1935), and has subsequently been developed by Joseph Schumpeter (Schumpeter 1989), and more recently by Christopher Freeman and other researchers at the Science Policy Research Unit (SPRU) at Sussex University (Freeman *et al.* 1982; Freeman and Perez 1988; Dosi *et al.* (eds.) 1988; and Cooper and Clark 1982). Figure 3.1 shows the dates of the five fifty-year waves and a number of the most salient features associated with them.

	1st wave	2nd wave	3rd wave	4th wave	5th wave
years	1787-1843*	1843-1896	1896-1949	1949-2003	2003-2056
peak	1814	1864	1920	1973	2030
power	manual steam	steam	steam electrical oil	oil electrical nuclear	electrical (+?)
key products	cotton textiles pig iron	coal, iron steel	manufactures chemicals automobiles	petro-chemicals plastics synthetics electronics	microelec-tronics IT
transport	horse rail	rail	combustion engine	petrol/ diesel engine jet turbine	petrol/ diesel (+?)
mode of prod-uction	factory	factory	conveyor/ flow line	continuous process/ mass production	flexible specializ-ation

* These dates are taken from Mager 1987.

Figure 3.1: Key features of the five Kondratiev waves

As Freeman puts it, Kondratiev sought to explain these long waves in terms of 'the replacement cycle of long-lasting infrastructural investments [such as buildings and transport] and the availability of loan capital for these very large investments' (Freeman 1984, p.106). Schumpeter developed these ideas further by suggesting that long waves were specifically associated with the diffusion of new technologies:

> In [Schumpeter's] theory the initiative of entrepreneurs, drawing upon the earlier discoveries and inventions of scientists and inventors, creates entirely new opportunities for investment, growth, and employment. The profits made from these innovations are then the decisive impulses for new surges of growth, acting as a signal to swarms of imitators. (Freeman 1984, p.108)

This momentum is cyclical in nature, since over time, factors such as market saturation, a slow down in productivity increases and gains from economies of scale, will result in reduced profits acting as a disincentive to investment.

A similar account of the relationship between investment and technological innovation is given by Mandel. He suggests that: 'Under the whip of competition and the constant quest for surplus-profits, efforts are continually made to lower the costs of production and cheapen the value of commodities by means of technical improvements.... The renewal of fixed capital thus implies *renewal at a higher level of technology...*' (Mandel 1975, pp.110-11, original emphasis). Most significantly, in order to achieve an increase in productivity which is sufficient to begin a 'new cycle of extended reproduction', and to achieve 'qualitative leaps forward in the organization of labour and forms of energy', there must be 'a *fundamental renewal* of productive technology, or of fixed capital, which induces a qualitative change in the productivity of labour' (Mandel 1975, p.112, original emphasis):

> Only the values set free for the purchase of additional fixed capital in *several* successive cycles enable the accumulation process to make a qualitative forward leap of this kind. The cyclical recurrence of periods of underinvestment fulfils the objective function of setting free the necessary capital for this kind of technological revolution.... It then becomes possible to achieve not only a partial and moderate, but a massive and universal revolution in production technology. This will ensue particularly if *several factors are simultaneously and cumulatively* contributing to a rise in the average rate of profit. (Mandel 1975, pp.114/115-16, original emphasis)

The validity of the association of new technology with periods of high investment and growth, therefore depends upon both the scale and pervasiveness of the technology and upon the timing of invention, innovation and investment. Applying these criteria to microelectronics-based technologies, the discourse of post-Fordism/flexibility discussed in the previous chapter certainly suggests that they do qualify as paradigmatic.

In tracing the historical impact of this paradigm, advocates of long-wave theory suggest that the levelling off of economic fortunes in the West during the 1970s, was closely associated with the maturation and subsequent decline of the mass-production oriented industrial paradigm of the fourth wave, and the emergence of the fifth wave based on microelectronics. The 1980s and 1990s therefore constitute a period of transition from one technological paradigm to the next. The considerable disruption of patterns of working currently being experienced by all the leading economies of the late-industrial period are seen as being a direct consequence of this transition.

Because the transition from one wave to the next is governed by the *rate* at which the new technological paradigm becomes established (some technologies are incorporated into the labour process more quickly than others), and because renewed stability within the labour process can only occur once the new paradigm *has become* fully established, it is extremely difficult to anticipate exactly how long and how deep the period of transitional disruption will be. If the development of the present wave follows the fifty-year pattern of previous waves we can anticipate that it will reach its peak around 2030. At the very least we can say that instability will be an ever-present feature of the labour process until well into the twenty-first century.

In addition to the technical/structural or techno-economic features of the paradigm (its physical properties and characteristics), Freeman and Perez suggest that one of the most important factors governing the rate at which the emerging paradigm becomes fully incorporated into the labour process, is the extent to which convivial social and institutional factors are also present. Although long-wave theorists do not use the same terms as the regulationists (regime of accumulation, mode of regulation), they reach very similar conclusions in suggesting that there has to be a satisfactory balance or alliance between the technical/structural aspects of the paradigm and the 'socio-institutional' context in which it develops. Following Perez, Freeman concludes that:

> The widespread generalization of the new technological paradigms, not only in the carrier branches of the upswing but also in many other branches of the economy, is possible only after a period of change and adaption of many social institutions to the requirements of the new technology. (Freeman 1984, p.109)

During the 1950s and 1970s for example, the combination of high output and increased productivity 'depended upon the good match which then existed between the low labour cost energy-intensive technological paradigm and the favourable institutional framework within which it was exploited' (Freeman 1984, p.109), i.e. between Fordist-style mass production techniques and continuous process industries and Keynesian economic policy. In contrast, despite continued technological innovation, the slow down in productivity during the 1970s and 1980s indicates 'some degree of "mis-match" between the new technological paradigm [of microelectronics] and the institutional and social framework' (Freeman 1984, p.110).

The suggestion here, is that during the 1980s and 1990s new techniques of production and work organization have tended to move forward more quickly than other social and political institutions, with the result that the latter now tend to inhibit or have a dragging effect on the former. Technical and economic progress are therefore being hindered not only by the practical problems of innovation, but also by reactionary attitudes and practices in the socio-institutional structure. Freeman has indicated some of the ways in which the latter will have to change if the braking effect is to be removed:

> It will involve big changes in the pattern of skills of the work-force and therefore in the education and training systems; in management and labour attitudes; in the pattern of industrial relations and worker participation; in working arrangements; in the pattern of consumer demand; in the conceptual framework of economists, accountants and governments, and in social, political, and legislative priorities. (Freeman 1984, p.120)

Although the techno-economic features of the paradigm set the limits of what the new world of work *could* be like, its *actual* form will be strongly influenced by choices which are made within the socio-institutional field. The final outcome will therefore be a product of a reflexive reordering of past and present practice rather than of direct and unnegotiated technological determinism:

> We are not making an argument for mere technological determinism. The variety of suitable environments is quite large, and whatever specific form is arrived at, from the wide range of viable options, will in turn determine the preferred ways in which the latent technological potential develops through strong 'feedback' selective action and gradual mutual adjustment. (Perez, 1985, p.445, quoted in Elam 1994, p.46)

Despite the coherence and intuitive appeal of long-wave theory, and despite attempts to exorcise the charge of technological determinism, a number of writers have persisted with this line of critique. Elam has commented for example, that: 'there is a predominant tendency to reduce significant qualitative changes within capitalism to "key factors" and very tangible technological content - the changing technological hardware of history' (Elam 1994, p.46). As a consequence he suggests that the social and human dimensions of these changes are either left to one side or neglected altogether:

> [Techno-economic paradigms make] insufficient room for the less tangible social innovations which always coexist alongside the more hard and fast technical ones.... In order to successfully take into account these social innovations, the neo-Schumpterian perspective will have to shift attention away from generic technologies and the most accessible facts of production, towards specific patterns of social relations and the more opaque bases of different productive paradigms which can only be brought to light through studies of individual workplaces in particular socio-cultural contexts. (Elam 1994, p.47)

Whilst it is certainly the case that any manifestation of 'technical' changes takes place in the context of various kinds of 'social innovations' and 'social relationships' (including those affected by gender, cultural and identity issues), and that getting a grip on these means making specific empirical studies of every case, one of the advantages of the long-wave/paradigm-shift approach is that it provides us with an analytical framework for understanding *why* the current period is transitional, *what* factors make it so, and *how long* it is likely to last. It is precisely *the generality, the common features* of the changes which are under way that makes a particular period transitional.

As the narratives of industrialism and post-industrialism have shown us, this is not the first time that the labour process has taken a decisive step forward as a consequence of technological change and it would seem ridiculous not to learn from what has gone before. The details are different and the context changed, but the underlying processes are a recurrent feature of what industrialism *is*.

More specifically, the long-wave/paradigm-shift approach identifies the importance of the relationship between the development of basic science and its incorporation into devices with practical application, and the need for large amounts of investment. Whilst it might seem rather obvious that the process of innovation and application costs money, it is *the concentration* of that investment which is decisive.

As we shall see in looking at debates over the globalized nature of modern economic activity in chapter six, one of the most powerful explanations about why the new paradigm developed much more quickly in the emerging Southeast Asian economies than in the established economies of the West, was precisely because the former had the necessary capital resources and were prepared to invest them in the new technology. The emergence of Britain as 'the workshop of the world' during the nineteenth century, and the emergence of the US as the leading industrialized economy at the turn of this century can be explained in the just same way (see Kenwood and Lougheed 1992, Hirst and Thompson 1996).

Large amounts of capital had been accumulated during the mature phase of the previous waves (steam-powered mechanization especially in textiles, and heavy manufacturing/factory production respectively) which was then invested in the new technologies of the day. This overlapping pattern of investment, innovation, accumulation and stagnation also sends a very clear signal that those economies which gain the most from one wave almost inevitably get left behind as the next wave develops. A British businessman in the 1860s and an American businessman in the 1960s would not have believed that the near-global economic domination of their countries was about to enter a period of serious decline.

Secondly, and looking again at which characteristics of the new technology give it the capacity to so thoroughly transform the labour process, we can note that whereas innovations during the third and fourth waves (the conveyor belt, continuous process, mass production) were essentially a physical extension of earlier systems of mechanization and were based upon well-established scientific/technical knowledge in metallurgy and engineering, the underlying science of microelectronic technologies (solid state physics) is entirely different (Braun and MacDonald 1982; Bessant *et al.* 1981; Soete (ed.) 1985; and Forester (ed.) 1980 and 1985).

This alerts us to an important distinction between the devices themselves and the uses to which they are put. Contemporary devices can be *seen as* evolutionary in that they are used to overcome age-old problems of increasing the efficiency and quality of production. In themselves however, they constitute a major *discontinuity* because they are based on a different kind of science. It is precisely because they are so different that they offer the potential for a comprehensive shifting up of the productive process onto a new level of sophistication. It is no longer a question of overcoming the limitations or of solving 'bottlenecks' in existing systems (Bell 1972, Coombs 1984, Walker 1989), but of finding new ways of exploiting the inherent flexibility of microelectronics.

Indeed it is not unreasonable to suggest that the current search for further innovations is not so much directed at overcoming any inherent limitations of the technology, than at trying to realize the full potential that it offers. The concept of flexibility and the debate which surrounds it is really just a catch-all phrase for this effort. One of the most interesting possibilities is that because the current paradigm is radically effective at the level of overall organization and control (rather than just at the level of its intermediate parts), industrial and business processes could be engineered to make them much more responsive to people's preferences about how they would *prefer* to work. To speak the unspeakable, human requirements might take precedence over the requirements of the system.

Finally, because the type of knowledge upon which the paradigm is based is heavily scientific, and because one of the primary characteristics of the late-modern period is precisely its capacity for scientific research (Bell's scientific/technical elite, Galbraith's technostructure, Giddens' expert systems), it is extremely likely that the rate of technological progress will continue apace. For example, the importance of basic science for recent developments of biotechnology - which is as different from solid-state physics as solid-state physics is from the science of steam power - has been noted by Sharpe:

> For the first time scientists have been released from the slow and uncertain techniques of trying to improve on nature by breeding mutant strains, and instead have at their fingertips techniques which enable them to do this with a surprising degree of certitude. The implications of these developments are enormous, not just for medicine, where to date most experiments have been concentrated, but for the chemical and fuel industries, the environment and, above all, food and agriculture. (Sharp 1989, pp.119-20)

Contemporary developments in artificial intelligence, fibre-optic and laser technology, and perhaps most dramatically in virtual reality are also likely to play a leading role in next (sixth) paradigm (see for example Marx 1989, Hall 1987, Kelly 1995).

The rapid commercial uptake of technological innovation, both in process and in product, illustrates the further point that innovation is no longer simply 'pushed' by science but is 'pulled' by consumer demand. Having developed a taste for, and dependence upon novel devices, the economics of innovation are at least as secure as the economics of many basic commodities like clothing and food. In this sense, the 'knowledge base' of the current paradigm not only responds to the 'scientific knowledge' of white-coated laboratory boffins, but to the 'high-street knowledge' of the commercial and domestic consumer.

The Question of Skill and Quality of Working Life

One of the most important and longest-running debates about the impact of technological change on the labour process relates to its impact on levels of skill. There are two principal reasons why this is of great concern to the future of work. First, and as indicated by the narrative of industrialism discussed in chapter one, levels of satisfaction are closely related to levels of skill at work. If jobs are monotonous and mundane then it is likely that individuals performing those tasks will experience work as dissatisfying and unfulfilling. In contrast, jobs with a higher skill-content are likely to provide much greater opportunities for autonomy and creativity and thus higher levels of reward and satisfaction (for summaries of empirical research see: Silverman 1970, Rose 1975, Thompson 1983, Grint 1991, and Ransome 1995).

Second is the issue of what kinds of skills-training need to be provided to ensure that employing organizations can find employees with qualification which are appropriate to their changing needs. The negative impact of lack of appropriate skills therefore seriously affects both employers, who will find it difficult to find employees to operate their businesses, and employees who may find that changes in the skill-demands of industry are rendering their earlier skills redundant. Clearly both of these issues have implications for the quality and availability of work in the future, and for core/periphery debate outlined in the previous chapter.

The first difficulty in reaching constructive conclusions about these issues is what do we mean when we talk about 'skill'? For analytical purposes, we can identify three related dimensions of the idea of skill (see Figure 3.2 below).[1] Firstly, and closely associated with the wave of critical labour process theory which emerged following the work of Harry Braverman and others adopting a Marxist approach during the 1970s,[2] 'skill' is essentially seen in terms of the degree to which the conceptual and practical aspects of an activity remain intact. If this necessary duality or 'conceptual integrity' is disrupted then this amounts to a 'loss of skill' because the individual is deprived of any real satisfaction in their work:

> The unity of thought and action, conception and execution, hand and mind, which capitalism threatened from its beginnings, is now attacked by a systematic dissolution employing all the resources of science and the various engineering disciplines based upon it. The subjective factor of the labor process is removed to a place among its inanimate objective factors. (Braverman 1974, p.171)

On this understanding, the progressive division and sub-division of tasks within the capitalist labour process is seen as inherently 'deskilling' because of its tendency to fragment work into ever smaller elements of production:

> A necessary consequence of the separation of conception and execution is that the labour process is now divided between separate sites and separate bodies of

workers. In one location, the physical processes of production are executed. In another are concentrated the design, planning, calculation, and record-keeping. The preconception of the process before it is set in motion, the visualization of each worker's activities before they have begun... have been removed from the shop floor to the management office. (Braverman 1974, p.125)

The designation 'capitalist' labour process is important here, as Braverman and others imply that although industrialism always requires an increasing specialization or individuation of tasks, the *capitalist* division of labour manipulates this process in order to further its own class interests:

Neither the... minute division of labour nor the development of the centralized organization that characterizes the factory system, took place for reasons of technical superiority. Rather than providing more output for the same inputs, these innovations were introduced so that the capitalist got himself a larger share of the pie at the expense of the worker. It is only the subsequent growth in the size of the pie that has obscured the class interest which was at the root of these innovations. (Marglin 1976, p.14)

	Three categories of skill		
Three dimensions of the idea of skill	*higher (graduate level)*	*intermediate (vocational training)*	*lower (basic skills)*
conceptual integrity (conception and execution)	increasing - expectations might gain momentum quite rapidly	increasing	always have been low, but no sign of improvement
qualitative/subjective (personal/professional satisfaction)	increasing	increasing	improved working conditions only
practical skill (the task itself)	increasing	increasing	falling/no change

Figure 3.2: Future impact of technology on levels of skill and degree of satisfaction along the three dimensions and across the three categories of skill

Despite research carried out by Zimbalist (1979), the Brighton Labour Process Group (1977), and Crompton and Jones (1984) which broadly confirmed Braverman's deskilling hypothesis, other researchers have stressed that there is little conclusive evidence of deskilling, at least of the universal or industry-wide dimensions implied by Braverman. Bringing together examples in a number of industries Wood concluded: 'The implication is that the quest for general trends, such as a progressive deskilling of the work force, or general conclusions about the impact of new technologies are likely to be both theoretically and practically in vain.' (Wood (ed.) 1982, p.18)

A similar view was expressed by Francis who concluded that although 'the introduction of new technology creates the opportunity for a wide range of choices to be made about how work should be organised', 'there is no general trend, either towards or away from de-skilling' (Francis 1986, p.78). More recently still, and drawing on studies carried out during the late-1980s (Daniel 1987, Gallie 1991, Penn *et al.* 1994), Gallie is quite clear that 'by far the strongest tendency was for a marked rise in the skill requirements of jobs' (Gallie 1996, p.135).

Raising issues which we will be looking at shortly, some critics attribute this lack of confirmation to the fact that Braverman's account overestimates the extent to which managements have a free hand in imposing lower levels of skill on the workforce. Wary of its technological determinist flavour for example, Penn suggests that such an account is: 'highly misleading since it leaves out of the model the crucial factor mediating the relationships between technological development and skill in the labour process, namely, organized resistance by occupational groupings within the manual working class' (Penn 1982, p.104). Similarly, Giddens and Mackenzie have argued that 'what is lacking' from Braverman's account 'is an adequate discussion of the reaction of workers, as themselves knowledgeable and capable agents, to the technical division of labour and Taylorism' (Giddens and Mackenzie 1982, p.40).

Rather then, than being systematically down-graded, the possession of skill can be seen as one means by which workers can in fact maintain their autonomy: 'It remains important to recognize the residual forms of expertise and skill and the condition in which they may constitute effective obstacles to capitalist initiatives' (Wood 1982, p.38).

Although Braverman has been further criticized for 'conflating the acquisition of knowledge with its monopoly' (Wood (ed.) 1982, p.79), i.e. of assuming that any loss of conceptual knowledge on the part of the worker automatically results in absolute knowledge on the part of management, for being insufficiently precise in his definition of skill, and for tending to equate skill with a somewhat romanticized ideal of pre-industrial or at least prefactory 'craft production' (see Beechey 1982, pp.62-7), this first dimension of the idea of skill as conceptual integrity remains useful as it emphasizes that skills are relative rather than absolute. Since it is extremely difficult to compare one particular skill with another, let alone to compare skills of an earlier historical period with those of the present, it is helpful to retain the idea that part of what skill is, is simply the expectation that work provides opportunities for people to realize their ideas through creative and productive activity.

The second dimension of the idea of skill refers to the more qualitative and subjective aspects of working activity. On this understanding, if a particular task brings satisfaction then it can be regarded as 'skilful' even if objectively it might appear not to be so. This dimension is useful as it allows for the wide discrepancy which exists between individuals in their actual experience of work. It would seem highly problematic for example, to presume that simply because two or twenty individuals are performing largely identical tasks, that they are experiencing identical levels of satisfaction, or indeed that their feelings of what satisfaction is are the same.

Similarly, although an observer might regard a menial and unskilled task as dissatisfying or undesirable, it does not necessarily follow that the worker sees it that way or would prefer to be occupied in something more meaningful. As Gallie reminds us, the quality of the subjective or experiential aspects of skill are often associated with the degree of autonomy or 'control' an individual has over the work that they do. The more highly skilled the job, the greater the degree of discretion and thus the higher the level of satisfaction which might be experienced (Gallie 1996, p.134). We will discuss this point under the heading of 'control' later in this chapter.

Although more difficult to assess, we can also locate the kinds of satisfaction associated with the fulfilment of 'identity' and 'cultural' expectations within this dimension. The third dimension of skill we can identify refers to the practical skill or 'craft' required to perform the task itself. Although still problematic, this is perhaps the easiest dimension along which to measure and compare the skill-content of particular tasks, and is the dimension which was most often used in empirical investigations of the skill debate during the 1980s (e.g. Crompton and Jones 1984).

Immediately we can see that any answer to the question of whether technological change affects levels of skill is likely to vary according to which of these three aspects of skill are being referred to. It could be argued for example, that whilst word-processors are ostensibly more complex than manual typewriters, the practical skills needed to operate the former are of the same order as those required to operate the latter. The introduction of word-processors constitutes an improvement in technology, but without requiring any significant raising or lowering of practical skill. At the same time, if the organization of the work remains the same, and if the substance of what is being typed is relatively mundane, a move towards working with these devices may have little or no discernible impact upon levels of subjective satisfaction or conceptual integrity.

If however, the capacity of the technology for increasing the scope and complexity of information-handling tasks were reflected in a positive raising of interest and responsibility, perhaps accompanied by a reorganization of how the office was run, then the technology could be seen as having a skill-enhancing effect on those involved. In an early study of the possible deskilling effects in clerical work, Crompton and Reid conclude for example, that: 'The introduction of on-line or distributed-processing computer systems... may provide the opportunity or impetus to reverse the deskilling of clerical work' (Crompton and Reid 1982, p.177). In a more recent study of computerization in the insurance industry, Appelbaum and Albin conclude that: 'Whilst no simple answer to the question of the effect of new technology on the skills of the workers employed by insurance companies emerges from this analysis, it should not then be concluded that at some stage the determinants of the choices cannot be specified' (Appelbaum and Albin 1989, p.265). We can also note the possibility of a knock-on effect where positive benefits might accrue to individuals in the organization who do not themselves use word-processors, because of a reorganization of work amongst those who do.

As we have found to be the case with important aspects of the post-Fordism/flexibility debate, questions about the specific impact of technology can only really be answered in the context of particular tasks in particular working contexts. We should also note that an almost obsessive fixation with trying to prove or disprove the deskilling hypothesis during the 1980s gave rise to a heavily zero-sum notion of skill; jobs were either as skilled as previously, or they were less skilled. Now that things have moved on, we can see that the real issue is not so much about passing judgement on whether absolute levels are moving up or down, but of understanding how technological innovation generates changes in *the types of work* that people do and the *new ways* in which they can be organized. What advantage is to be gained for example, by a highly-skilled engineer if he or she cannot find an employer who needs those skills? We have to look more carefully at the dynamics of the relationship between having *appropriate skills* and opportunities for employment.

In looking at how future trends in the demand and distribution of skill will vary according to the type of activity involved, it will be useful to break the discussion down by looking at the three categories of higher, intermediate and lower-level skills (see Figure 3.2 above). Broadly, the first level typically includes people educated to graduate level, the second includes people with school-leaving and vocational qualifications, and the third includes people who may have only basic numeracy and literacy skills. Whilst many would assume that these latter skills are now universal, Ducatel quotes evidence which suggests that: 'there may be as many as six million adults in the UK who experience basic numeracy, reading and writing difficulties. The number with severe difficulties is lower; nevertheless the estimates indicate that around 600,000 are illiterate, that is unable to read or write at all, with many more unable to do simple sums' (Ducatel 1995, p.77, referring to Holmes 1989). More recently the Adult Literacy and Basic Skills Unit has reported that of its sample of 21 year-olds, over 40 per cent reported difficulty with writing and spelling, and a further 24 per cent had difficulties with numeracy (*Social Trends* no.25, 1995, table 3.25).

Whilst it is evident that most employing organizations will require individuals in each of these categories, these divisions will help to clarify the variable rather than universal way in which technological change has affected patterns of skill-level and skill-demand in the past and is thus likely to do so in the future.

Looking at the situation in the engineering industry, Campbell and Warner conclude that the demand for highly-skilled employees will remain strong while the demand for the less-skilled will decrease: 'Not only will fewer people be employed in manufacturing, but those who are will be different in kind than hitherto. Within the electronics and computer-related sectors, we are already moving towards a '"white-collar" labour-force profile' (Campbell and Warner 1992, p.15). The same conclusion is reached by Christie *et al.*:

> Where job gains have been caused by the use of new technology, they appear to be concentrated among skilled electrical craftsmen, technicians and engineers with electronics or electro-mechanical skills. Moreover, these types of worker have been replacing the 'traditional' mechanical tradesmen as the latter have retired, moved or been displaced. (Christie *et al.* 1990, p.62)

Within the highly-skilled category, and aside from a decline in the need for mechanics and craftsmen having traditional engineering skills, we can include electronics, control, systems, software and design engineers with microelectronics expertise; together with data processing staff and electronics and instrumentation technicians.[3] Within the lower-skills category these authors reach the conclusion that: 'the decrease in shop floor jobs has been substantially more than the decrease in non-shop floor jobs; and the decrease in unskilled shop floor jobs has so far been more than ten times as great as the decreases in skilled shop floor jobs' (Christie *et al.* 1990, p.160).

Picking up on the point that those in manufacturing 'will be different in kind than hitherto', these authors suggest that there will be an increasing 'hybridisation' of skills, particularly at the level of intermediate skills, as employees are increasingly expected to have a range of appropriate skills rather than specializing in a single task or groups of tasks:

> It is clear that, given rapid technological change, there will be 'hybridisation' of skills. Boundaries between craftsmen and technician's work could blur with a need for more broadly trained engineers who are able to adopt a systems approach to implementing the new technology. Rather than the trend to specialisation of function continuing to a higher degree as was the case with industrialisation and technological change in the past, the application of microelectronics seems to imply the reverse. (Campbell and Warner 1992, p.16)[4]

The hybridisation of skills and changes in the skills mix are likely to generate two further changes in patterns of skill-demand. *Within* the three *categories* of skill (higher, intermediate and lower), and accepting that 'the average level of skills of those remaining in employment may rise', these changes are likely to result in an increasing homogenisation of skills: 'There will be a lesser division of labour due to the eventual emergence of the 'hybrid-skills' phenomenon and therefore by implication an increase in the level of skill integration across-the-board in the enterprise' (Campbell and Warner 1992, pp.22-3). *Between the different groups of people* having those skills however, hybridisation and changes in the skills mix are likely to lead to an increasing polarization of the workforce between those with core skills and those without: 'Although there was a widespread tendency to remove demarcations between different crafts, there was little sign of attempts to break down barriers between craftsmen and production workers' (Christie *et al.* 1990, p.88). There is therefore a clear and direct connection between employment security and the level of skill that a person can offer. Whilst those with essential and highly-sought-after core skills are relatively secure, those with intermediate and lower skills are not:

> Whereas those possessing basic and intermediate skills may suffer periods of cyclical unemployment, they are less likely to be permanently unemployed through technology and structural factors, since the breadth of their skills enables them to adapt.... The unskilled on the other hand, whose work is more tied to routines, are likely to be swept out of all but the most menial tasks by increasingly cheap information technology. (Campbell and Warner 1992, p.6)

102

Further evidence of the increasing polarization of skills is provided by Gallie in his summary of recent survey data on how respondents assess changes in the levels of skill they use at work.[5] Having shown that 'there was a clear increase over the period in the level of qualifications required for jobs... [and that] a very similar pattern emerges with respect to training and on-the-job experience', Gallie notes that the trend towards increasing levels of skill is much more marked within the higher and intermediate skills categories than within the lower skills category:

> A majority of employees at all job levels experienced an increase in their skills, with the exception of semi- and non-skilled manual workers. The increase was particularly marked among professional and managerial workers (74 per cent [experiencing an increase]), technicians and supervisors (73 per cent) and lower non-manual workers (70 per cent). But it was also the case that 64 per cent of skilled manual workers thought that the skills involved in their work had increased. Moreover, even semi- and non-skilled manual workers were much more likely to have experienced an increase than a decrease in their skills (45 per cent compared with 15 per cent). (Gallie 1996, pp.136/137)

Whilst accepting these findings, it is important to note that, at the very least, unskilled workers, and particularly unskilled manual workers have experienced a far less dramatic increase in skill than have other categories of workers. The fact that less than half (45 per cent) of semi- and non-skilled workers reported that their jobs had become more skilful is certainly a matter of great concern. One wonders what the figure would have been amongst non-skilled workers alone. This evidence would certainly seem to continue to support Gallie's earlier conclusion that:

> The argument that is best supported is that of a polarization of skill experiences between classes. The already major skill differentials between the intermediary (let alone the service class) and the non-skilled manual class appear to have been accentuated in the 1980s. Those that already had relatively higher levels of skill witnessed an increase in their skill levels, while those with low levels of skill saw their skills stagnate. (Gallie 1991, p.349)

This evidence confirms the close relationship between employability and skills-demand. The effect of the technology is not just upon overall levels of demand in particular areas (fewer mechanical engineers, more electronics experts), but tends to re-shape the profile of skills both *within* different categories of skill (engineers with multiple skills, flexibly-skilled production workers), and *between* one category and another (semi-skilled *versus* those with lower skills). The dynamic nature of these relationships inevitably tends to multiply the extent of job insecurity because technological innovation not only eliminates areas of skill, and thus areas of employment in a direct way, but *also* affects the skills required of those in work, *and* varies the entry qualifications required of people trying to find work.

An individual may therefore become 'peripheralized' or pushed towards the margins of employment not because he or she doesn't have any skills at all, nor because he or she doesn't have the capacity and desire to acquire higher-level skills, but because it has become extremely difficult to keep track of which skills are required by prospective employers. Core workers are in a much stronger position because once in work, they are likely to be able to keep ahead of the game. We will return to this point shortly.

Turning from skill in terms of the task itself (the third dimension of the idea of skill outlined above), to recent developments in the subjective notion of skill (the second dimension), available evidence is inconclusive as to whether low-skill production jobs are becoming more or less satisfying under the influence of technological change. Christie *et al.* report that although the nature of these jobs had changed to include less physically-demanding tasks like process monitoring and machine supervision, and had generally become more monotonous, these were seen as being off-set by improvements in working conditions and in some cases by improvements in pay through increased productivity: 'In general, then, respondents did not think that job content had suffered because of use of new technology as far as process operators and production line operators were concerned.... Overall new technology seems to have changed job content in a number of ways which on balance do not amount either to degradation of work or to dramatic enhancement' (Christie *et al.* 1990, p.78). It should of course be remembered, that such judgements are relative, since the 'old' jobs may not have been very fulfilling anyway.

In the intermediate and higher-level categories of skill, technological innovation was generally seen, not unsurprisingly, as improving levels of satisfaction and interest in the work. In terms of the wider deskilling debate discussed above, Christie *et al.* are quite clear that although 'there is indeed some evidence of de-skilling' their findings and those of others 'do not support the view that automation leads to de-skilling and degradation of work':

> Changes due to the introduction of new technology may remove or reduce the need for some 'traditional' skills, but they can also involve the development of new skills and responsibilities. Some jobs may decline in quality; some may gain; others may simply be *different*, with no clear tendency towards de-skilling or up-skilling. The same technology may be thought to de-skill in one

plant and increase skills in another. Much depends on policy on job design and devolution of control by managers: simplistic notions of inevitable technology-driven de-skilling and degradation of job quality are not supported by the case studies or by other examples of recent research. (Christie *et al.* 1990, p.110)

Gallie's findings also provide clear evidence of the strong link between increases in intrinsic satisfaction and increases in job complexity and task discretion. Once again however, it is clear that these improvements have been far less marked amongst the many people who are still doing repetitive and unrewarding tasks: 'While 84 per cent of those in jobs where skills had increased had also experienced an increase in the variety of work, this was the case for only 39 per cent of those in jobs where the skill level had remained unchanged and for 28 per cent of those whose skills had decreased' (Gallie 1996, p.143).

As far as the future of work is concerned (see Figure 3.2 on p.97), both theory and empirical research confirm that the impact of technological innovation on skill varies both in relation to which dimension of skill (conceptual integrity, qualitative/subjective, task-specific) and to which category of skill (higher, intermediate, lower) is being discussed.

Broadly speaking, technological innovation is likely to continue to have a skill-enhancing effect across all three dimensions of skill for higher and intermediate categories, although the effects on 'traditional' skills and trades in the latter category is likely to be somewhat disruptive as the need for retraining continues. Along the dimension of conceptual integrity, we can suggest that as technological innovation allows the creative potential of employees to be increasingly realized in practice, they may begin to expect even higher levels of satisfaction in their work. There may be a significant escalation in the expectations which people have of the work that they do. If employers wish to retain such employees they may be obliged to introduce organizational and other changes in order to meet these rising expectations. Within the category of lower-level skills the situation will be more ambiguous because it is difficult to evaluate the impact of detailed changes in the work done upon people's level of satisfaction. A cleaner, safer and less physical working environment is no doubt beneficial, but it remains an open question as to whether these improvements actually overcome the problems of repetitive, monotonous and uninteresting work.

These conclusions have an important bearing on the question of how people can get the training they need in order to acquire the skills which employers demand, and what will happen if the current shortfall in appropriate skills - the 'skills shortage' - is not met, or the 'skills gap' (where the wrong kind of skills are being offered) is not bridged. From the employers' point of view, and surveying the large research literature on current trends in training (for an introduction see Metcalf (ed.) 1995), Campbell and Warner conclude that the skills shortage is having a negative effect on the ability of employing organization to continue to innovate: '[There is] a genuine and absolute shortage of engineers and scientists of graduate level. The shortage of these, we have found, is restricting the possibilities open to all but the largest, most prestigious and most technically advanced companies in engineering' (Campbell and Warner 1992, p.58). Paradoxically therefore, a lack of potential employees with appropriate skills is hindering the expansion of precisely those hi-tech enterprises which are most likely to increase levels of employment:

> Given the exclusion, if present trends continue, of so many from the manufacturing labour-force (or from employment generally), because of the lack of skills... it becomes imperative to expand the training programmes available to those excluded on a massive scale. This may be justified on economic as well as social grounds, as if anything the relative short-fall in competence is increasing faster then the growth in technical sophistication. (Campbell and Warner 1992, p.24)

Further still, because increasing competition between employers for suitably-qualified employees has given rise to much poaching and head-hunting, and because the level of training itself is time-consuming and expensive, employers are likely to become *more* rather than *less* particular about who they recruit:

> As training requires greater investment by employing organisations... they will be more selective in recruitment to find employees with the most appropriate prior qualifications and aptitudes, and to minimise the risks of selecting those who will not be a good long-term 'training investment'.... If firms begin to look increasingly closely at new trainees for long-term employment in the 'core' labour-force, they will be more likely to only take on the minimum they need, particularly as the costs of training grow for the reasons addressed earlier. (Campbell and Warner 1992, pp.20-1)

Taken together with other factors such as an over-emphasis on higher-level compared with lower-level skills, and a tendency to disregard the need for people with intermediate-level skills,[6] these researchers suggest that the 'skills gap' ('between the demand for highly skilled labour, and the supply of indiscriminately qualified labour') is one of if not the major problem which faces employing organizations, and that this situation is getting worse rather than better: 'There is little evidence that the gap is being bridged, or that the situation, at least in Britain, is improving in spite of the lengthening dole queues' (Campbell and Warner 1992, pp.22-3).

Three categories of skill		
core employees		peripheral employees
higher (graduate level)	intermediate (vocational training)	lower (basic skills)
increasing demand especially for those with graduate-level electronics/computer/IT-related skills, and experience	demand for those with traditional skills very low; demand for those with hybrid/mixed skills increasing rapidly. Emphasis on being 'flexibly skilled'	demand for people who can work flexible hours growing, but low expectation/low demand of skills being offered/required
general homogenization of skills within the core; traditional demarcations between 'trades'/'professions' collapsing rapidly	core/periphery boundary more and more visible	prospects of moving out of the periphery for those in the 'skills underclass' are not increasing

Figure 3.3: Future impact of technology on patterns of employers' demands for people with particular skills

From the employees point to view (see Figure 3.3), and as already noted, the raising of skill-demands will tend to raise the threshold of qualification required of prospective employees. This could contribute to maintaining *and increasing* the degree of polarization which persists between core employees and peripheral workers, because the latter may effectively become trapped in menial jobs through lack of appropriate qualifications:

> The key question is whether the lower-skilled work being created... actually represents a long-term option for a self-supporting lifestyle, or is it a long-term trap from which escape can only be made through high qualifications and skill. Moreover, as long as the middle ground between professionalised roles and lower-skilled roles continues to disappear, the chances of gaining promotion from a lower-skilled job inevitably become lower and lower. (Ducatel 1995, p.74)

If, as seems likely, the 'skills underclass' continues to grow thus providing a pool of largely unqualified labour (see Meager and Williams 1994, and Mingione 1991), employers might take advantage of the reorganizational potential offered by the technology to deliberately engineer large numbers of very low-quality jobs. This raises 'serious concerns about whether job opportunities for people with lower skills provide a satisfying work experience or are adequate to sustain family life':

> One big question mark over the future of lower-skilled employment, therefore, is less about its position numerically, but more about its viability for the workers concerned. In the absence of bargaining power (with continuing high levels of unemployment and job insecurity) the danger is that the wages of such workers will be driven down to uneconomic levels. (Ducatel 1995, pp.69/72)

The incentive of being able to employ cheap labour may therefore override any wider humanitarian desire to use the technology to improve the quality of jobs. Savings at the lower level would then be used to retain essential core employees. As a complete reverse of increasing satisfaction amongst higher level employees, the experience of menial work within the periphery may become a self-fulfilling prophecy; these employees may more or less completely abandon any realistic expectation of increased satisfaction in the future. Having a job at all becomes much more important than what the job actually is.

To the extent that the state plays a highly significant social role in providing the necessary training and re-training (directly through publicly-funded training schemes, and less directly through further and higher education), we have a clear example of why the satisfactory emergence of the new paradigm is partly dependent on a suitable socio-institutional framework. With clear frustration, Campbell and Warner open their account of the skills debate with a severe critique of trends in the UK:

> There are two fundamental problems with the strategy [of training] currently adopted nationally. First, there has been a degree of bureaucratic and ideological confusion over what successive training initiatives are intended to achieve, leading to some incoherence. Some initiatives - the Youth Training Scheme (YTS) and Employment Training (ET) are examples - have appeared to have the primary aim of reducing youth unemployment rather than improving economic performance. Others such as the Technical, Vocational and Educational Initiative (TVEI) were loosely based on German models, but insufficiently well thought-through to have a significant effect. (Campbell and Warner 1992, p.2).

In a similar critique Marsden and Ryan highlight a direct connection between lack of training and the ideological position of the UK government during the 1980s and 1990s:

> A central problem with public policy towards initial training in Britain lies in its neglect of the institutional context which is required to make it viable. The belief that deregulation will mean the creation of free markets and that free markets can solve training problems has been associated with the neglect of institutions, including internal and occupational structures in the labour market.... The result is the resurgence of skill shortages, both quantitative and qualitative. (Marsden and Ryan 1989, pp.17-19, quoted in Campbell and Warner 1992, p.3. See also Ainley and Corney 1990, Keep and Mayhew 1995)

A point which is repeatedly made about the impact of innovation on skill levels and levels of satisfaction at work, is that much depends on the skill of managers in introducing these changes. In practical terms, this means that managers have to know what they are doing: 'almost everything depends on how the process of change is managed', 'much depended on management choices on job design', 'the level of variety an autonomy in the work depended to a large extent on choices made about job design and devolution of responsibilities' (Christie *et al.* 1990, pp.81/110/114). Perhaps ironically then, one of the most important areas of skill affected by innovation is that of developing appropriate *managerial* skills for the organization and control of the enterprise. This is very much in line with one of our earlier observations about the general characteristics of the new paradigm, namely that it is causing employing organizations to turn their attention very much towards realizing the full potential of the technology. We will address this important issue next.

Management, Organization and Control

In addressing the issue of what impact the new paradigm is likely to have on managerial approaches to the organization and control of the labour process, we are confronted again by the definitional problem of deciding what exactly it means to have 'control'. As is the case with the concept of skill, we can usefully identify three *levels* of control level (see Figure 3.4). Although it is important not to press too far the analytical symmetry between these levels and the dimensions/categories of skills just discussed, there are interesting points of correspondence between them. At the most general level and clearly showing their Marxist and Bravermanian ancestry, a number of researchers emphasize that 'absolute' control ultimately rests with the owners of the means of production and the managerial agents who organize and direct the labour process on their behalf. The remaining majority of the workforce are obliged to tolerate loss of control in return for opportunities for employment (Braverman 1974, Baran and Sweezy 1968, Burawoy 1979 and Gorz (ed.) 1976).

	From the employer's point of view	*From the employee's point of view*
general level (ownership/control of the enterprise as a whole)	absolute control	minimal control
functional level (operational integration)	relative control	relative control
practical level (the task itself)	minimal control	'absolute' control

Figure 3.4: The three levels of control at work

In terms of the competition or struggle for overall control, radical strategies draw on the story of work as told by Marx. Once the workers have reached the end of their tether, they will wrestle control away from the capitalist class by directly taking possession of the means of production. Thus will begin a new age of work wherein the workers will themselves control the labour process and all its proceeds. More moderate strategies adopt a gradualist approach in the expectation that by establishing representative organizations of their own (trade unions and socialist political parties) the workforce will be able to improve its working conditions, levels of pay and so on through negotiation and compromise rather than through direct and violent confrontation.

Although not a fully-paid-up socialist himself, this is what Durkheim had in mind when he suggested that the anomic tendencies of the industrial division of labour could be avoided once trade unions, trade associations and corporations, and employers organizations had become fully developed. The total overthrow of the capitalist system does not form part of this reformist agenda. Both these characterizations of capitalist ills and their remedies tend to assume a zero-sum notion of control, meaning that there is a fixed amount of control available within the industrial organization, and that the workers' struggle is about redressing the balance in their favour.

As a number of writers have pointed out however, within the organizations of the labour process, 'control' is a much more complex and variable phenomenon which operates in a number of different ways.[7] Summarizing comments by Friedman for example, Thompson suggests that a distinction should be drawn between the idea of 'control' used in an absolute sense 'to identify those "in control"' of the overall labour process, and 'control' 'in a relative sense to signify the degree of power people have to direct work', meaning the knowledge and skill that particular individuals have over a specific working activity (Thompson 1983, p.124; Friedman 1977, p.45). In this latter sense, employers' control cannot be absolute since they themselves don't have the skills which they are paying others to provide.

For Friedman, control is therefore negotiated between employers and employees rather than being imposed unchallenged by management: 'to treat worker resistance... as a secondary and primitive form of resistance because it is relatively ineffective for overthrowing capitalism, is to miss significant developments in capitalist productive activity during the past hundred years.' (Friedman 1977, p.50) In addition then, to the idea of absolute control at the general level, we can identify a second form of 'practical' control which operates at the much more specific level of the particular task or working activity. In this sense, practical control refers to the necessary skills and expertise which an individual must possess in order to be able to work at all. To the extent that employers themselves do not have these practical skills, the control employers have over the work in hand is likely to be relatively minimal.

Between the overall level and the specific level we can identify a third or intermediate level of 'functional' control which concerns the ways in which employing enterprises and institutions are internally organized. At this level, control is manifest within the procedures and mechanisms of planning, decision-making and organization through which the day-to-day running of the business is achieved. Although it can certainly be argued that the expression of this functional control within capitalist enterprises is likely to have a particular character by virtue of the fact the authority of those who occupy key decision-making positions within the management hierarchy is underpinned by the kind of coercive general control noted above,[8] functional control is more to do *with making the organization work* than with the exercise of power for its own sake. After all, efficient control of the enterprise is just as important in non-capitalist organizations as it is in capitalist ones.

From an owner's or manager's point of view, as one moves down the spectrum from (absolute) general control through (relative) functional control and towards (minimal) practical control over particular tasks, he or she has a reducing amount of control over what is going on. He or she may own the firm and thus have 'absolute' control over it in a general sense, but is very unlikely to have full control over every detail of what each employee is doing in practice. From the employee's point of view, the degree of control operates in the opposite direction with high levels of control over the task and very likely minimal control over the firm as a whole.

Whilst accepting that control at the practical level may not amount to very much if the task one is doing is relatively menial and repetitive, and accepting Gorz's point that: 'it is impossible to see the overall process in its entirety and to get the overall goal that is built into the workings of this gigantic machinery internalised by each individual and reflected in everyone's work' (Gorz 1982, pp.30-1), this interpretation draws attention to the fact that the autonomy and degree of influence of the worker within the enterprise is effectively dependent upon *the kind of tasks* which he or she carries out and therefore upon their *position* within the organization. For example, a skilled engineer in a nuclear power station has much greater influence within the employing organization than the person who does the washing up in the canteen. The engineer has this influence quite irrespective of any other personal skills he or she may have - the washer-upper may be a nicer person but this is beside the point.

On this understanding, the degree of control exercised/experienced at work depends on how important and unique are the skills of the individual worker. If those skills are crucial to the operation of the enterprise, and if people holding those skills are in short supply, then it is likely that their opinions will be recognized by management and attempts made to retain individuals having those skills. If on the other hand their skills are limited and easy to acquire, they may have no real control at all and management will probably not care very much whether it is this or that person who is employed.

We can say then, that one aspect of what it means to be a core worker has to do with the degree of control one has within the employing organization. The closeness of the fit between the possession of necessary and especially of higher-level skills, the higher levels of autonomy generally associated with that category of skills, and the concomitant desire of the employer to retain employees having those skills, shows that the relative security of core jobs/core employees is made up of a bundle of mutually supporting characteristics. The relative, and in some cases severe insecurity of peripheral employees is caused by the same factors but this time working against rather than in favour of the employee. Obviously those employees who want to move from the periphery to the core are in a very difficult position because the hurdles they need to jump are plural rather than singular.

Having sketched out, from the employer's point of view, a three-fold definition of absolute control at general level, relative control level of the internal operation of the enterprise, and minimal practical control at the specific level of the particular working activity, and having explored briefly some of the factors which might affect the balance of control within the employing organization, we can now look in more detail at how these issues have been explored in practice.

Historically, and beginning with F.W.Taylor's now infamous suggestion that management was in fact a science,[9] a major emphasis in research into the labour process has always been to provide managers with information on how they can improve the efficiency and productivity of their organizations. Accepting the dynamic character of control, Friedman argues that different forms of control correspond with developments in the labour process itself; like everything else in the world of work things don't happen just for the sake of it. He suggests that over time, 'direct control' which 'tries to limit the scope for labour power to vary by coercive threats, close supervision and minimizing individual worker responsibility' has been supplemented by a 'responsible autonomy' strategy which 'attempts to harness the adaptability of labour power by giving workers leeway and encouraging them to adapt to changing situations in a manner beneficial to the firm' (Friedman 1977, p.50).

Also concentrating on the relationship between changes in the nature of work and managerial strategy over time, Edwards has explored the idea that forms of control are closely related to 'structural' features of the workplace. Beginning with 'simple' control, he suggests that the entrepreneurial firm characterized by geographical centrality and small-scale and intimate workplaces, meant that 'the personal power and authority of the capitalist constituted the primary mechanism for control'. Even the increasing use of managers did not present a problem since 'the group of managers was small enough for each to be effectively directed, motivated, and supervised by the capitalist' (Edwards 1979, pp.25-6).

With the increasing size and complexity of operation and the resulting 'separation of the entrepreneur and his top managers from the daily activities of the workers', simple control gave way to 'hierarchical control' involving a vertical command and communications structure linking production workers to management via new strata of supervisors and foremen (Friedman 1977, pp.30-3). Most significantly, within these new forms of structural control - determined on the one hand by the growing need for bureaucracy, and on the other by technical developments in the way that work is carried out - the

113

exercise of power could be 'made invisible' as it was now 'embedded in the technological structure of the firm, or it could be embedded in the firm's social-organizational structure' (Edwards 1979, p.110). The exercise of hierarchical control thus becomes institutionalized within the labour process and represents a shift towards much more systematic approaches to management. We can recall that Galbraith's account of the demise of the 'entrepreneurial' corporation and the rise of the 'modern' corporation is based on a very similar reading of events.

Although both Friedman's and Edwards' typologies have been criticized for tending to simplify the nature of relationships between employers and employees, for underestimating the capacity of the latter to resist the imposition of control 'from above', and for implying that earlier forms of control are being completely displaced rather than supplemented by more recent forms (see Thompson 1983, pp.122-52 and Wood (ed.) 1982, pp.11-22) their accounts do illustrate a number of important points which continue to have a direct bearing on the organization and control of complex enterprises.

Firstly, the emergence of management is an integral feature of the development of industrialism itself. The displacement of simple or direct control by hierarchical or other 'complex' systems such as responsible autonomy implemented by professional managers is as much a requirement of industrial evolution as is the division of labour more generally. We should not therefore be in the least bit surprised to discover that the different requirements of the new paradigm will give rise in a very direct way to the development of revised managerial strategies.

Secondly, and given that organizations are inherently heterogeneous, it is likely that different forms of simple or complex control can coexist not only across firms but within a single firm. For example, a system of hierarchical control can be used to integrate the activities of the overall firm, whilst more simple or direct forms of control can be used to direct the activities of particular workers. As we shall see, and given earlier comments about the need for managers to retain core employees, it is likely that the latter will be managed in a much more convivial way than peripheral workers.

Thirdly, they have drawn attention to the fact that however much management gurus insist that strategies of control are primarily to do with technical and other changes in the labour process (control at the functional and practical levels), the particular choices which managers make about *how* work should be organized and *which* strategy should be adopted, will certainly be influenced by their desire to maintain absolute control at the general level. As Edwards puts it, new techniques of control 'must nearly always be understood as the result of the *particular* (capitalist) design of the technology and not an inherent characteristic of the machinery *in general'* (Edwards 1979, p.112, original emphasis). Similarly, in his analysis of why managements choose to develop one strategy of control rather than another, Marglin asks: 'But is work organization determined by technology or by society? Is hierarchical authority really necessary to high levels of production, or is material prosperity compatible with nonhierarchical organization of production?.' (Marglin 1982, in Giddens and Held (eds.) 1982, p.285).

Bearing these issues and debates in mind, we can now turn our attention to the latest twist in the tale of managerial strategy which goes under the name of human resource management or HRM. This approach represents a concerted effort to overcome the conflictual 'us and them' approach often associated with industrial relations during the 1970s, and to replace it with one in which 'employees are viewed as a valuable resource... which:

> if managed, rather than administered, effectively from the strategic point of view, will contribute significantly, *ceteris paribus*, to organizational effectiveness, and thus will be a source of competitive advantage to the organization concerned.... The leading advocates of human resource management, who are typically behavioural scientists in the USA, see it essentially as an organization-wide 'philosophy' which is much broader, more oriented to the long run and less problem-centred than personnel administration. (Beaumont 1993, pp.10-11)

A central theme here is that the successful management of working relationships should be seen as an integral part of the production process rather than as a separate or distinct realm of activity:

> The key messages or terms in the human resource management literature are a strategic focus, the need for human resource policies and practice to be consistent with overall business strategy, and the need for individual components of a human resource management package to reinforce each other, while the individual components of the package should particularly emphasize team work, flexibility, employee involvement and organizational commitment. (Beaumont 1993, p.25)

This new holistic approach shares a number of features with a related trend towards highlighting the importance of developing an 'organizational culture'. Although Grint is somewhat sceptical about the cogency of the 'organizational culture school', suggesting for example that they tend to adopt an overtly technocratic-determinist approach in which an investigation of the 'culture' of the firm 'is intended not so much to explain what the contemporary culture of an organization *is* but what it *should be'* (Grint

1991, p.131), the liberal softly-softly approach of managerial prophets such as Charles Handy (Handy 1976 ch.7, and 1989) can be seen as acknowledging features which Galbraith had earlier identified as part of the 'motivating system' of the organization:

> It can reasonably be concluded that identification - the voluntary exchange of one's goals for the preferable ones of organization - and adaptation - the association with organization in the hope of influencing its goals to accord more closely with one's own - are strong motivating forces in the technostructure and become increasingly so in the inner circles. (Galbraith 1972, p.158)[10]

Although Galbraith is analyzing the motivational psychology of American technocrats during the 1960s, we can still take the general point that the motivational aspects of working within complex organizations are likely to be enhanced if individuals feel that they are exercising some form of shared interest with other members of the organization:

> There is no denying that the subject of organizational culture was one of the 'hot' management areas of the 1980s [and figures] prominently in the strategic human resource management literature. In essence it is argued that an organization's external competitive strategy needs to be complemented and reinforced by an appropriate organizational culture which is itself shaped by and consistent with a coherent mix of human resource management policies. (Beaumont 1993, p.34)

This sense of mutuality is articulated within the HRM strategy through a number of personnel practices aimed at removing or reducing the extent to which employees feel that they are being treated devisively. Distinctions between blue- and white-collar-workers for example, are replaced by 'common all-employee coverage':

> This can manifest itself in a number of ways such as the introduction of single status or harmonized terms and conditions of employment, the spreading of performance appraisal arrangements to blue collar workers or the recruitment of production workers on the grounds of not so much their immediate employment skills, as their trainability and flexibility, and hence potential for longer-term development. (Beaumont 1993, p.16)

In addition to attempts to move away from collective agreements towards individual contracts about matters of pay, working conditions and structures of promotion or 'career enhancement', employee involvement has also been a guiding principle behind the development of new forms of direct financial participation or commitment by employees towards their employers. These include profit-related pay, profit-sharing and share-option schemes, worker

116

and worker/management buyouts, and pension and wage-earner funds (Schuller 1991). Whether one chooses to interpret these developments as evidence of a deliberate move towards 'responsible autonomy', 'role enhancement' or 'organizational culture', the overall thrust is towards improving employee commitment by replacing bureaucratic hierarchical management structures with a variety of 'soft' or 'open' management techniques including new forms of group- and team-working and 'quality circles', underpinned by a willingness to include a much greater proportion of the workforce in the decision-making process.

Internal and External Constraints on the Introduction of HRM Strategies

Whilst the recognition within HRM of the need for more enlightened and progressive approaches to working relationships can be seen as a good thing in its own right (reformist strategists and Durkheimian moralists would certainly regard them as a step in the right direction), we need to recognize that, in common with all previous developments in managerial strategy, both the *form* that HRM-type strategies take in practice, and the *extent* to which they are likely to be adopted across the labour process as a whole, are subject to a number of constraints which in varying degrees act internally and externally upon the employing organization. By using the analytical distinctions described above, we can understand better both the nature of those constraints, and, more importantly, get a grip on the patterns of constraint involved. It is easy enough to *say* that managements don't have a free hand in developing and applying new strategies of control and organization, what we really need to know is *why don't they?*

One set of constraints derive from the technical and organizational 'demands' of the technology. In line with issues discussed in the previous chapter, HRM strategies have to accommodate various kinds of 'flexibility'. In terms of the skills and size of the workforces they employ for example, organizations are having to alter their recruitment policies in order to ensure that they have sufficient people with appropriate skills to meet their skills-needs. Increasingly, and given what we have already noted about the falling demand for people with 'traditional' task-specific skills, prospective employees are now being assessed in terms of more generic skills such as the ability to work in groups, to adapt to new situations and as having the capacity to acquire new skills as the need arises. Under conditions of flexibility, employees are assessed at least as much in terms of their potential future capacity as they are in terms of the practical skills they have already acquired:

The HRM literature emphasizes the need for a multi-skilled, flexible workforce in which team working arrangements are particularly prominent. This has meant that the selection decision is less about matching an individual employee to the fixed requirements of an individual job at a single point in time. As a consequence, immediate skills and employment background are of rather less importance relative to willingness to learn adaptability and willingness/ability to work as part of a team. (Beaumont 1993, p.56)

Further, and touching on issues we will be looking at in more detail in a later chapter, the increasingly globalized nature of commercial activity means that patterns of recruitment and the way in which the different functions of the firm are organized have to accommodate divisions of labour at the international level. Beaumont notes for example, that 'if *strategic* human resource management was very much the phrase of the 1980s then it is a reasonably safe bet that *international* human resource management will be the term of the 1990s':

> The subject matter if international HRM will revolve around issues associated with the cross-national transfer and management of human resources... the cross-national interaction of human resources... and comparative HRM [practices].... Such issues will raise questions such as whether there is increasing divergence (convergence) across national systems, whether practices are culturally determined and to what extent practices in one system can usefully be adopted and modified in other systems. (Beaumont 1993, p.210)

He goes on to note that although this process is likely to be problematic (not least because different national approaches to managerial strategy are heavily influenced by differences in 'national culture'), the need for developing new types of 'competitive strategy' and for opening up the organization 'to forge linkages with organizations in other countries' through for example 'licensing agreements, technology transfer arrangements, bidding consortiums and international joint ventures' (Beaumont 1993, p.211), will clearly have an important impact on working relationships between individuals in domestic and overseas parts of the enterprise, and on the transfer of necessary skills and expertise:

> The increasing number of international joint ventures, together with the publicity of 'organizational incompatibility' problems, is likely to cause human resource management researchers in the 1990s increasingly to switch their attention away from wholly owned, foreign subsidiaries to international joint venture operations. (Beaumont 1993, p.213)

Managements also have to be flexible in their awareness of the new organizational possibilities offered by the technology itself. The most recent example of this has been labelled business process reengineering or BPR and constitutes a further move beyond the various combinations of team and group-working associated with the earlier phase of HRM. A first tenet of this approach, is that the central task of management is to identify and concentrate upon the 'core business processes' in an attempt to raise its capacity to add maximum value in meeting its customers' needs:

> By core business processes, we mean the handful of processes central to a company's operations that "creates" value for external stakeholders in the business. Core business processes create value for the customer, the shareholder or the regulator and are critical to get right. Companies usually have about half a dozen or so core business processes. They are the processes that the business's strategic thinking has identified as critical to excel at to meet or beat the competition. They make up part of the company's set of core competencies. A core competence may be a business process, a management skill, a "new" asset or an applied technology. (McHugh *et al.* 1995, p.52)

Whilst BPR may be undertaken to reduce costs through the now familiar practices of 'process improvement', outsourcing and subcontracting, and to become more competitive by reaching 'best-in-class status', it may also try to achieve 'break-point reengineering' by 'rewriting in its favour the rules of competition in its industry or segment. Here change will influence the whole business, resulting in a major shift in market dynamics' (McHugh *et al.* 1995, pp.59-60). The development of compact disc technology is a recent example of a product which established a 'break-point' by moving completely beyond the limitations of vinyl recordings, while the introduction of various kinds of 'direct line' telephone services in banking and insurance represent a break-point in how these kinds of services can be provided.

A second tenet of BPR is a shift towards seeing the networks and connections between the various parts of the enterprise, and between one enterprise and another, as being much more important than the physical or geographical components which make up the business. Although the idea of 'networking' became well established especially in the banking industry during the 1980s (De La Monthe 1986),[11] BPR contains a much more radical view of networks and how they can be used. Once these core processes have been identified and integrated into the strategic planning of the enterprise, the next step could be towards developing what McHugh *et al.* have labelled an 'holonic network' where the various providers of these core processes or functions come together to form a 'virtual company':

> A holonic network is a set of companies that acts integratedly and organically; it is constantly re-configured to manage each business opportunity a customer presents. Each company in the network provides a different process capability and is called a holon. Each configuration of process capabilities within the holonic network is called a virtual company. By combining the core competencies of many individual companies within the network, each virtual company is more powerful and flexible than the participating members alone could be. Each company in a virtual company is chosen because of its process excellence. (McHugh *et al.* 1995, p.4)

Although these authors develop the idea of the holonic network specifically as the basis for virtual companies, and see such companies as having a number of advantages over other 'large companies' (by being more organically interactive with the business environment, more flexible and more easily able to avoid the dead-weight of established 'large-scale' practice (McHugh *et al.* 1995, p.80), the principle of holonic networking can be seen as pointing towards a 'higher stage' of organizational development, and one which would fit very comfortably with the move towards globalizing the structure of the enterprise and its co-operative relationships up and down the sub-contracting hierarchy. The emergence of this kind of imaginative *thinking* about how things *could be* organized is a clear example how changes in the conceptual and ideational aspects of the work paradigm can make a very significant difference to the future form of the industrial labour process. Before the development and adoption of powerful information technologies these possibilities simply did not exist.[12]

A second bundle of constraints which have to be accommodated by management, relate to that other pillar of flexibility, the changing demands and prevailing sensitivities of customers and consumers. As we saw in the previous chapter, one of the underlying reasons for a shift away from mass production towards flexible specialization has been the commercial need to accommodate much more variable consumer demand for products and services. As consumers become ever more skilled in the art of consumption, enterprises which respond quickest are likely to be the most successful. The idea of holonic networks thus matches the idea of the pro-active consumer or 'prosumer' (both as high-street customer and as industrial and business purchasers of capital goods and support services), who 'contribute by various degrees to the design of the product they request':

> Through the design process, the customer forces the network to configure itself to provide the optimum processes to meet his needs. In this way holonic networks go far beyond [BPR] in that they define for the first time how to sell

customer-specific products while realizing economies of scale. (McHugh *et al.* 1995, p.15)

Alongside this increasingly variable and volatile demand for products, producers are also having to be more flexible in their assumptions about what exactly they are offering their customers. Whereas 'production' used to be seen largely in terms of the tangible commodity itself, businesses are now having to look much more closely at customers' demands for 'intangibles' such as delivery times, before- and after-sales service, product guarantees and longer-term reliability:

> The productive performance of a firm or an industry is compounded of its productivity and of various other factors that tend to be ignored in most economic statistics, like quality, timeliness of service, flexibility, speed of innovation, and command of strategic technologies. (Dertonzos *et al.* 1989, pp.32-3, quoted in Beaumont 1993, p.24)

A third bundle of constraints concern the willingness of the workforce to accept the new practices. It is evident that the introduction of new modes of organization and working practices is much more likely to succeed within organizations where the need for innovative flexibility has already been recognized: 'The American literature [observes]... that the need for flexibility, team working, motivation, participation, etc. is more compatible with... a competitive strategy that emphasizes product innovation and/or product quality' (Beaumont 1993, pp.25-6). In contrast, less innovative established industries may be much more reluctant to convert to HRM:

> Individual organizations which are embedded in national systems characterized by the extensive use of a low-wage competitive strategy, relatively decentralized labour-management systems, and strong financial pressures and influences which place a premium on short-run operating results seem the least likely to move (if at all) rapidly along these lies. (Beaumont 1993, p.6)

Not surprisingly then, resistance to change is much more easily avoided on so-called green-field sites where new practices can be introduced at the outset:

> The combination of a competitive strategy based on product innovation or quality enhancement with a new, greenfield site operation is a very powerful one, which is frequently associated with a relatively high priority being given to human resource management and a conscious attempt to establish (and maintain) a particular organizational culture. It is in such organizations that one is most likely to find... a comprehensive and coherent human resource management package. (Beaumont 1993, p.47)

Finally, if one of the central tenets of HRM strategies is to move away from a collective to an individual basis for negotiating recruitment and terms and conditions of employment, the speed with which this can be achieved depends in part upon the degree to which unions are prepared to abandon collective bargaining and/or the extent to which employees feel that they can negotiate without union support. Whilst acknowledging that union membership varies quite considerably from one group of workers to another, and that this variation is itself being affected by technologically-induced changes in the distribution of the workforce and patterns of working,[13] the way in which management negotiates the introduction of new strategies is bound to have implications for the core/periphery divide discussed above.

Whilst as Storey and Sisson observe, 'concerted strategic moves to deunionize are so far confined to particular marginal groups' while other [employers] might act 'as though unions might just go away if ignored for long enough' (Storey and Sisson 1991 p.170), and whilst managers themselves might not be very enthusiastic about some aspects of HRM,[14] the opportunity certainly exists for managers to reserve responsible autonomy and other 'quality' approaches to personnel management for their essential 'core' employees, whilst persevering with a low-quality coercive attitude towards their 'peripheral' workers. Gorz has argued for example, that serious divisions might arise between unions representing skilled, semi-skilled and unskilled workers respectively. He suggests that if 'trade unionism is particularly strong amongst semi-skilled workers':

> Then the unions find themselves in the dangerous position of having strong support among a declining category of workers and weak backing from the two categories which are in rapid expansion: the mass of temporary workers... the unemployed and 'odd jobbers'; and the new elite of 'reprofessionalized' workers, characterized by a marked tendency to defend their own specific interest by forming company unions or small craft unions. (Gorz 1989, p.69)

Alternatively, unions 'dominated by elites of privileged workers, will display a dangerous tendency to disregard peripheral workers... and - consciously or unconsciously - form an ideological alliance with the employers of the "successful" and the "able" against the "incapable" and the "idle"' (Gorz 1989, p.69).

Given increasing financial and market pressures, it is possible that managers will regard such divisions as very much to their own advantage. Beaumont suggests for example, that the fragmentation of interests between different groups of workers could create a kind of 'demonstration effect' where employers feel that by learning the lessons of innovative firms, they too can dispense with union representation:

> Management in the unionized sector, in order to try and compete effectively with non-union organizations, will increasingly seek to emulate and introduce the human resource management practices which have been pioneered in the non-union sector. And here the concern in some unions circles is that human resource management practices, with their emphasis on team-work, flexibility and individual employee commitment, will increasingly 'individualize' industrial relations, and drive a wedge between the union and its membership. (Beaumont 1993, pp.207-8)

Rather then, than following through fully on the general HRM principle that proper communication and cooperation with employees and their representative are essential if changes are to be implemented successfully, HRM strategies are actually designed to *replace* the need for union participation at all: 'In many cases there are individual contracts and no collective arrangements. There is either no role for trade unions or at best a limited one where unions are allowed to operate but only on management's terms' (Guest 1991, pp.50-1). Beaumont makes the same point: a concern 'of both industrial relations researchers and trade unionists is whether the introduction and diffusion of human resource management practices will increasingly 'substitute' for the union role, and thus help to maintain and increase the size of the non-union employment sector' (Beaumont 1993, p.207, for further discussion see Millward 1994, Rubery and Wilkinson 1994, Taylor 1994, Ackers *et al.* (eds.) 1996), Gallie *et al.* (eds.) 1996).

In light of these constraints, and compelling though the theory of HRM is, we need to dispel the myth that new innovations such as HRM and BPR are being adopted unproblematically in equal measure and across all types of employing organizations at the same time. HRM is not one thing, but is made up of a wide range of 'new wave' strategies which may or may not be appropriate to the operational needs of particular organizations. This being the case, it is likely that steps taken towards new strategies in the future will be characterized by a 'pick-and-mix' approach where organizations may choose to adopt some components of HRM without necessarily wishing to accommodate the whole philosophy. As competitive pressure increases, and as the rate of technical advance continues to accelerate, the basis on which these choices are made is likely to be extremely pragmatic and focused on immediate short-term needs.

In these respects, new-wave managerial strategies suffer from the same defects which have been exposed within the discourse of post-

Fordism/flexibility, namely that although something sounds like a good idea, and although a number of organizations have taken it on board, this does not mean that it will become the model for all organizations. Given these variations in the extent to which HRM strategies can or will be adopted, we should not be surprised to find that their introduction 'is essentially limited to a relatively small, unrepresentative sub-set of individual organizations' (Beaumont 1993, p.204), and that 'the organization introducing [HRM] initiatives could very well be the exceptions rather than the rule' (Storey and Sisson 1991, p.170):

> The overriding impression to be gained from studying what is happening (as opposed to what should be happening) is that, despite the powerful advocacy of the 'excellence' literature... there is little evidence of a strategic approach to human resource management being adopted in most organizations. (Storey and Sisson 1991, p.172)

Legge even goes so far as to question whether HRM is in fact a new approach at all:

> There is little real difference between normative HRM and personnel-management models and, in practice, it is probable that managing employee relations in the vast majority of companies remains a pragmatic activity, whether labelled personnel management or HRM. Furthermore, many of the techniques of HRM can be found in any personnel management textbook of a decade ago. (Legge 1991, p.40)

Returning to the typology of control developed at the start of this section (see Figure 3.5), we can take away a number of messages about how the new paradigm will affect control within the labour process in the immediate future. At the level of general control, it remains the case that managers (the overwhelming majority of which are themselves employees) are not only having to reengineer their strategies as a result of the internal pressure of technological change, but also, and increasingly urgently, they are having to respond to external forces which lie largely *beyond their control*. Now that international competitive pressures have become fully established at a global level, the question arises at to whether *any* organization is capable of exerting absolute overall control. Arguably, and although it might not be immediately apparent, the chief site of the struggle for economic control is between the declining economies of the West, and the rising 'tiger economies' of Southeast Asia rather than between capital and labour within any particular domestic economy (we will pursue this aspect of the globalization debate in chapter six).

General Level	(i) decline in managers exercising proprietorial control
	(ii) pressures of globalization making 'absolute' control much more relative
	(iii) 'control' becoming embedded within the organizational structure itself
Functional Level	(i) a merging of the demands of the system with managerial priorities, is concentrating attention at this level rather than at the general level
	(ii) general need to incorporate/integrate specific functions into the overall structure
	(iii) managers focusing on maintaining and increasing the fluidity of the production/business process
Practical Level	(i) the heavy emphasis on hybrid/mixed skills which can be flexibly applied further reduces managerial control over specific tasks
	(ii) 'expert knowledge' increasingly concentrated in the employee rather than the manager/supervisor
	(iii) functions much more fluid and flexible as old demarcations collapse

Figure 3.5: The exercise of control in the future of work

A notch or two below this battle of the titans, an important feature of these new approaches is that they have become systematically embedded within the organizational structure of the firm itself. From the point of view of how the control function is exercised, it therefore becomes increasingly difficult to separate out the demands of the productive or business system from the priorities of management. On the one hand it can be argued that management develops in the way that it does as a more or less direct and neutral response to systemic requirements. Viewed from a more critical employee-oriented perspective, evidence suggests that the particular choices made by management continue to reflect their desire to maintain overall control at the general level.

Whilst recent HRM strategies can be seen as positive in that they acknowledge the need to involve a much greater proportion of the workforce in the decision-making process, to improve communication, and to be more sensitive to the creative aspirations of all employees within the organization, it remains the case that managers continue to regard worker-participation with suspicion. If we take the position of the trade unions as indicative of whether HRM has or has not overcome perceptions of 'us and them', evidence suggests that many employing organizations may continue to take advantage of, and in some cases exacerbate, the potential conflict of interests between different groups of workers and their trade union representatives.

A further implication of the synergy between technology and strategies of overall control, is that as the pressure to innovate increases, and as the organizational demands of the technology become more pressing, managers may be obliged to concentrate their efforts at the intermediate and specific levels rather than at the general level.

At the level of functional control (how the day-to-day running of the enterprise is organized), the hierarchical direct-control approach is rapidly disappearing along with the clear-cut skill demarcations of the Fordist period upon which it was based. Under circumstances where flexibility of organization is the name of the game, and where the skills required are multiple and hybrid, new systems of functional control are bound to develop. Evidence for these trends emerges from Gallie's research on skill as he is able to show that although, as might be expected, 'task discretion' and 'degree of self-determination' were much higher amongst professionals and managers than amongst other categories of workers, between the late-1980s and early-1990s, *the most marked increases in task discretion are amongst manual workers and technicians/supervisors*. Further still, where people were being required to take on new tasks (as opposed to the normal tasks they had been doing for some time) it was (skilled) manual workers rather than technicians and supervisors who 'increased their discretion substantially'. Meanwhile, rather than consolidating their ability to exercise functional control, 'professionals and managers appear to have seen increased *constraints* on their ability to take everyday decisions' (Gallie 1996, p.142, emphasis added). He concludes:

> Overall, the pattern suggests that the second half of the 1980s and the early 1990s saw a marked decentralisation of decision-making within organisations. This is consistent with the view that it was a period characterised by significant de-layering in which employers were reducing the numbers of middle level managers, and devolving responsibilities. (Gallie 1996, p.142)

Although these changes can partly be accounted for in terms of changing attitudes towards how production and business processes can be organized, many of them are heavily determined by technical change.

The same process of change is also underway at the level of practical control (the job itself). Given that many tasks are now characterized by ever more complex communications, data and information-handling activities, and given that these activities require higher levels of trust, exchange and operational co-operation, the employee-manager employee-worker distinction becomes less clear cut. This tendency towards the necessity for co-operation rather than conflict is clearer still in the area of personal welfare and social services, where expert knowledge takes on a more universal form and cannot realistically be 'owned' or 'controlled' by managers alone. Outside the core however, where employees are not required to have these skills (or at least if they have them, not to use them), there is far less pressure to change things very much at all. In fact having made a virtue out of numerical flexibility, the situation might get worse rather than better. The question remains as to whether managers can legitimately persist in treating these various groups in different ways if they really do want to overcome the conflictual undercurrent which has characterized the struggle for control at work throughout the industrial period.

4 Feminist Perspectives and the Future of Work

One of the most important contributions to understanding what the future of work will be like comes from feminist perspectives. In order to gain a full appreciation of the issues they have raised we not only have to describe the likely position of women in the future of work, but also to understand what the future of work looks like from a feminist perspective. This places us in a much stronger position from which to capture what feminist perspectives have to offer than would be the case if we simply applied a 'feminist critique' to the kinds of labour-process-oriented arguments we have been looking at in previous chapters.

This is not to say that this critique is not important because it certainly is,[1] but rather to emphasize that by looking at the world of work through a different kind of theoretical and analytical lens, the feminist perspective provides a number of insights which have been left invisible or unrefracted within non-feminist 'malestream' accounts (Dex 1985; Crompton and Sanderson 1990, and Walby 1990). Throughout this chapter, the emphasis will be on trying to understand *why* it is that women generally occupy, or are seen as occupying different kinds of position within the productive and reproductive processes of society than those occupied by men. Clearly it is not possible to cover all the intricacies of feminist discourses which have a bearing on the future of work in a single short chapter. What we can do however, is to review a number of the leading theoretical positions which underlie the feminist approach, and to see how usefully they explain practical evidence of the disadvantages and inequalities faced by women in the world of work both now and in the future.

The basis of all feminist discourses is to expose the fact that women suffer from various manifestations of gender inequality because men seek to reserve for themselves a leading role in those activities which attract the highest levels of economic power and social prestige. Thus, within contemporary capitalist societies, the 'private' unpaid activities of bearing and raising children, of performing domestic tasks, and of maintaining the welfare of the household are typically attributed a lower economic and social status than are the 'public' activities of earning a living through participation in the mechanisms of formal paid employment.

Three important sets of questions arise from this: who it is that is making these attributions; why is it that they are making them, and what are the practical and ideological mechanisms through which they are made and maintained. The various strands of feminist accounts offer different kinds of explanatory answers to these questions, some placing the emphasis on one variable and some on another. Clearly the practical steps which might be taken in trying to rectify the situation depend upon which interpretation is adopted.

Patriarchy

A first and highly influential approach to answering these three sets of questions places particular emphasis on the concept of 'patriarchy' variously defined as 'the dominance of all men over all women or the dominance of older men over women and younger men' (Charles 1993, p.88 following Beechey 1979 and Barrett 1980), or as 'a system of social structures and practices in which men dominate, oppress and exploit women' (Walby 1990). From this perspective (see for example Walby 1986, 1990; Hartmann 1979 and 1981, Delphy 1984, and Scott 1988), it is men who construct and apply different levels of worth and value to different types of activity in order to ensure that the activities which they typically spend most of their time doing are categorized in the first division, while the activities of women are relegated to the second division. For as long as men are able to control this agenda, the attributions they make tend to become self sustaining; the activities of men are more important and prestigious than those of women because it is men that do them.

In terms of questions about the mechanisms through which men are able to do this, and concentrating for the time being on the practical aspects of these questions (the ideological aspects of these mechanisms are discussed later in this chapter), this perspective suggests that during the period of industrialization in the nineteenth century, men consistently took practical steps to exclude women from formal paid employment. For Hartmann, this was done in order that men could maintain control over women's 'labour power' meaning their ability to be economically self-reliant, and thus to occupy positions within society independently of men:

> The material base upon which patriarchy rests lies most fundamentally in men's control over women's labour power. Men maintain this control by excluding women from access to some essential productive resources (in capitalist societies, for example, jobs that pay living wages) and by restricting women's sexuality. (Hartmann 1981, p.15)

This reference to women's sexuality draws attention to the fact that there is a strong correspondence within the strategy of exclusion operated by men between the world of work and the domestic realm. In restricting women to monogamous relationships, and in enforcing strong legal and moral deterrents against having children outside marriage, men simultaneously protect their property (the accumulate of economic power) under the law, fill their wife's time with child-bearing and child-rearing responsibilities, and thus reinforce their own advantage over paid employment:

> For most men, then, the development of family wages, secured the material base of male domination in two ways. First, men have the better jobs in the labour market and earn higher wages than women. The lower pay women receive in the labour market, both perpetuates men's material advantage over women and encourages women to choose wifery as a career. Second, then, women do housework, childcare, and perform other services at home which benefit men directly. Women's home responsibilities in turn reinforce their inferior labour market position. (Hartmann 1981, p.22)

This strategy of excluding women from the paid workforce was sanctioned by the political and legislative institutions of the State within which men had established a monopoly of power and authority (Walby 1986, Hartmann 1981). This had the effect of reinforcing the apparently higher status of paid employment (and thus the personal status of those who do it i.e. men), and conversely of undermining the status of unpaid domestic work within the home and those who do it, i.e. women.

Because they were so thoroughly excluded from the public world of paid work at this time, the argument runs that women inevitably become responsible for, and were identified with, reproductive activities within the household, activities which cannot be left undone, since the welfare of the household depends on their being done. Worse still, because the State within capitalist societies is unwilling to provide the resources necessary for meeting the additional 'social' needs which people living in such societies have to cope with, households have no choice but to generate these labour-resources for themselves.

The State's effective denial that such needs exist, or if they do exist, that they have a low priority (compared for example, to the need for national

130

defence), implies that those people who are providing for these needs i.e. women, are not engaged in anything which matters very much; the greater the State's default, the more dismissive it becomes, and thus the lower is the social prestige which is attached to such tasks: 'The denigration of these activities obscures capital's inability to meet socially determined need at the same time that it degrades women in the eyes of men, providing a rationale for male dominance' (Hartmann 1981, p.29).

Given the interconnectedness of the household with the realm of paid work, and given that opportunities for employment do not remain the same over time, it is to be expected that patriarchal strategies will also operate at different levels and vary over time. Conscious of the need to theorize patriarchy as dynamic rather than static, and thus to avoid the charge that a theory of patriarchy tends to be reductionist and essentialist - meaning that patriarchy provides *the* explanatory concept for understanding relationships between men and women - Walby (1990) has developed a somewhat complex typology of patriarchy.

At the most abstract level patriarchy 'exists as a system of social relations' which is in articulation with 'the major systems of capitalism and racism'. At a slightly more concrete level 'patriarchy is composed of six *structures*'. In addition to the patriarchal 'mode of production', and the patriarchal 'relations in paid work' and 'in the state' which we have already touched upon, and which play the leading role in her analysis, she lists the three further structures of patriarchal relations in 'sexuality', 'male violence' and 'cultural institutions' (this list of six is not intended to be exhaustive since other structures might be identified).

At the more immediate level of day-to-day experience, each of these structures is associated with a number of 'patriarchal *practices*'. The relationships between these structures and practices, and between one set of structures/practices and another set of structures/practices is dynamic since although each is partly autonomous and can be conceptualized and analyzed as such, they have 'causal effects upon each other, both reinforcing and blocking' (Walby 1990, p.20, emphasis added).

Although therefore structured patriarchal relations within the household are reinforced by, and interact with, structured patriarchal relations within the world of paid employment, each of these structures and the practices to which they give rise have identifiable characteristics all their own. Applying these concepts to, for example, the practice of sexual harassment at work, we can see that this practice makes manifest, and cuts across, aspects of 'the more deeply sedimented' patriarchal structures of gender relations in paid work, of male violence towards women, and of gendered relations of sexuality. More abstractly still, this practice is also a manifestation of the articulation of the even more deeply sedimented systems of patriarchy with systems of capitalism and racism.

Next, Walby introduces a further distinction by suggesting that 'there have been changes in both the *degree* [intensity] and *form* of patriarchy in Britain over the last century' (ibid p.23). Reductions in degree or intensity might include greater equality of pay and access to higher education, while increases in intensity might include growing instances of violence towards women. Most importantly however, she argues that during the twentieth century there has been a shift in the balance between the 'public' and 'private' *forms* of patriarchy:

> Private patriarchy is based upon household production as the main site of women's oppression. Public patriarchy is based principally in public sites such as employment and the state. The household does not cease to be a patriarchal structure in the public form [i.e. once the public form holds sway] but it is no longer the chief site. In private patriarchy the expropriation of women's labour takes place primarily by individual patriarchs within the household [its institutional form is individualistic], while in the public form it is a more collective appropriation [its institutional form is collectivistic]. In private patriarchy the principle patriarchal strategy is exclusionary; in the public it is segregationist and subordinating. (Walby 1990, p.24)

Relating this to the notions of patriarchal structure and practice already identified, Walby argues that although both private and public forms of patriarchy are present in society at any given time, there has been a gradual but marked shift from the private to the public form within each of the structures during the twentieth century; the public form with its segregationist/subordinationist strategy is thus becoming the dominant form of patriarchy in contemporary society. The fact that this shift is particularly evident within the patriarchal structures/practices of paid employment and the State signifies that although the patriarchal structures of the household are still active and important and have a bearing on public patriarchy, it is these latter structures which have become the primary source of women's oppression in contemporary society.

To illustrate her case, Walby argues that two factors have been especially important in instigating this shift. First has been 'the demand for cheaper labour by employers within the capitalist labour market'. As we have seen the relative 'cheapness' of women's labour (and thus the relatively lower status of women as employees) had been the major object of the strategy of exclusion during the nineteenth century. Second, within the State, 'feminist struggle has helped undermine patriarchal exclusionary strategies' (Walby 1990, p.59).

She cites a number of instances of these struggles including the entry of women into factory work during the nineteenth century, 'the recruitment of women to the munitions factories' during the two World Wars, and the entry of women into clerical work (ibid pp.41-2).

Through its engagement with the State, first-wave feminism also made important political gains including access to political citizenship through the right to vote, access to higher education and the professions, and legally sanctioned rights to property and divorce. For Walby, the winning of citizenship rights, and the entry of women into paid employment constitute respectively the first and second 'moments' of the change from private to public patriarchy: 'It is only with women's access both to waged labour and state welfare payments in the post-war period that the possibility of full economic as well as political citizenship is realized... the increasing entry of women into waged labour... could not have occurred without first-wave feminism' (Walby 1990, p.191). This change in the form of patriarchy is therefore accompanied by a change in the degree or intensity of patriarchy within its various structures.

The State has clearly played an important role in these changes. Firstly, once women had gained citizenship rights and were beginning to have a stronger public and political role, it could no longer support exclusionary strategies within the labour market and so actively sponsored corrective legislation culminating in the Equal Pay Act in 1970 (implemented in 1975) and the Sex Discrimination Act in 1975. Second, the expansion of the State and particularly of the Welfare State in the post-war period opened up many employment opportunities for women who wanted to work. The fact that the service-oriented nature of many of these jobs continues to accommodate the domestic stereotype of women as 'carers' remains problematic, as is the fact that since men still hold the best jobs within these institution there is a clear possibility that 'previously privatized domestic work is carried out under more public forms of patriarchal organization' (Walby 1990, p.168). Nonetheless these developments can be seen as a step in the right direction, and as far as Walby is concerned, certainly signify that important changes are taking place in both the structure of patriarchal relations located within the State and within paid work.

Social Reproduction

Although perspectives which use the concept of patriarchy as the chief explanatory device for understanding the gendered nature of relationships

133

between women and men are very influential, other feminist theorists have struck a different balance between the various causes of women's relative disadvantage within the home and at work. Whilst all agree that it is men who generally get a better deal in both family and working life, they argue that this situation cannot be explained in terms of the operation of various structures and practices of patriarchy since these structures and practices *are themselves* a product of the prevailing social and economic milieux in which they are situated.

It is not simply a matter of describing how one form of patriarchy has superseded another, but of looking much more closely at how the social and economic systems of capitalism affect all aspects of social relationships within society. Some of these effects may have specific implications for gender relationships, but they also have implications for the relationship between the economy of the household and the formal economy of paid employment, between women and men in different social and economic classes, and between the economy and the form of the State. As Charles puts it:

> Changes in women's economic activity have been linked to varying demands for female labour, the economic strategy of the household unit to which they belong, industrial and economic development and gender ideologies.... (Charles 1993, p.61)

To take one example, whilst the State has certainly moved towards giving positive support for equal opportunities for employment, its motivation for doing so, and the precise manner in which it has done this, has a great deal to do with developments within the capitalist division of labour. In this sense, the suggestion that first-wave feminism played an important role in this process during the earlier part of the century is certainly true, but it is not the whole explanation. One might ask why it is that the State has not gone further by, for example, providing nursery facilities for all or by actively enforcing equal opportunities legislation at work. To put it bluntly, what we are dealing with here is not just 'a state' or 'an industrial division of labour' understood as abstract analytical categories of institutions and practices, but a concrete and historically specific form of the *capitalist* State, and the *capitalist* division of labour (Barrett 1980). One might say that this form of economic organization sets the limits within which gender relationships are formed and reformed.

What unites both these perspectives though, is the recognition that access to economic opportunities, and thus the relationship between the household and the realm of paid employment, are key to understanding the gendered nature of 'working' relationships between men and women both at home and at work. In trying to understand what role women will play in the future of work we therefore need to look more closely at the interconnections between these two domains and the distribution of the 'working' activities involved. Two of the most important explanatory concepts which link the economic interests of the household with those of the world of paid work are those of 'social reproduction' and 'gender ideology'.

The first of these is particularly important to those approaches which draw upon a Marxist-type class-based model of social structure, and describe the social and economic position of women in terms of the struggle for resources. There are two aspects to the concept of social reproduction. First is that whatever else it requires, the capitalist division of labour needs a continuously renewed supply of workers to meet its demand for labour power. Labour power (meaning the ability and preparedness of people to exchange their efforts and skills for wages) is a renewable resource both in the sense that people who are already working need to be 'renewed' on a daily basis during their time away from work, and in the sense that 'new' recruits replace those who have reached the end of their public working lives.

Second, the household itself needs to be reproduced, since clearly it cannot exist unless its members remain healthy and increase in number. It is important to emphasize here, that the concept and practice of social reproduction involve more than the physical or biological 'reproduction' of household members since clearly entrants to the workforce have to be suitably educated and healthy, and have to have assimilated appropriate expectations about what 'going to work' is all about. Further, although biological reproduction and the specifically female type of child-bearing 'labour' which it involves overwhelmingly takes place within the household, many of the resources of social reproduction are produced publicly rather than privately:

> It is often forgotten that much besides women's domestic labour enters into the reproduction of labour power and, in advanced capitalist societies, many of these processes, such as the production of food, may take place in the capitalist sector, may involve men and may be defined as 'productive' rather than 'reproductive' activity. (Charles 1993, p.91)[2]

These observations are important in rebutting 'universalist' or 'naturalist' explanations of women's reproductive role within the division of labour, since beyond the immediacies of pregnancy and child-birth there is no 'biological' reason why women should take sole responsibility for younger members of the household (for further discussion of these points and in addition to Charles 1993, see: Harris and Young 1981, Humphries 1977a and 1977b, Brenner and Ramas 1984).

Up to a point then, the economic motivations and interests of employees within private households and employers within the public economy coincide; household members need to generate resources in the form of income, and employers need to attract resources in the form of their employees' labour. In other respects however, these two sets of interests do not coincide since the employment opportunities and choices which are available to household members are not chosen by them but are imposed in various degrees by employers. This lack of correspondence inevitably gives rise to conflict within the capitalist division of labour, and equally inevitably, these conflicts have a highly significant bearing on the conflicts which may arise between men and women both at work and within the household. Within the former for example, conflicts between men and women within the labour movement (conflicts which may take the form of exclusion and occupational segregation of the kind described by Walby and others) are part of the fall-out of the struggle that all employees face in trying to gain a living wage. To the extent that these internal conflicts may undermine a more concerted effort to challenge the basic advantages that employers have over their employees, it is clearly in the interests of employers, and arguably of the State, to allow them to continue.

Within the household, the pressure of maintaining the well-being of family members, gives rise to conflicts over who should be responsible for which tasks. To the extent that men earn higher wages, it makes economic sense for women to take responsibility for domestic tasks. The working activities of men and women thus circulate within both a public division of labour in paid employment *and* within a private or 'domestic' division of labour in unpaid work. Although therefore women's 'labour' is typically confined within the private domestic realm, and is thus less visible than the public paid-labour of men, it nonetheless creates essential use-values within society:

> The crux of all these arguments is that domestic labour within the home, far from being unproductive in the marxist sense, actually contributes to the creation of surplus-value by lowering the value of labour power and thus keeping wage levels down. It does this by producing use-values within the home - food, clothes and so on - which would otherwise have to be bought on the open market with the wage and the wage would therefore have to be higher. (Charles 1993, p.87)

Whilst then, the creation of the use-values of social reproduction is necessary for both employers and employees, it is again very much to the employers advantage that responsibility for them is located within the household. If conflict arises between members of households over the distribution of reproductive tasks, then, conveniently, this remains a 'private' matter. Analytically then, rather than attributing such conflicts and tensions to the presence of various 'structures of patriarchy', this perspective uncovers the fact that they are an integral part of the much more readily identifiable struggle for economic survival and well-being which *all* members of society are involved in; a struggle which is overwhelmingly determined by the unequal way in which employers and employees have control over, and access to, paid employment in the labour market. It turns out then, that the concept of patriarchy may be useful as one way of *describing* in retrospect various aspects of the relationships between women and men, but it cannot *explain* them since the concept itself has no real explanatory power (for a more detailed exploration of these issues see Fine 1992 and Pollert 1996).

There is a considerable body of historical evidence which supports the fact that the economy of the household, and thus the relationships between its members, is heavily circumscribed by the particular form taken by the public division of labour with which it has to engage. Clearly both the public and private economic relationships between men and women living within modern industrialized societies are not the same as those which existed during the pre-industrial period.[3] Most interestingly, since the capitalist division of labour developed out of the divisions which preceded it, a dual process of change was involved in which some practices 'became rigidified' whilst others were 'transformed' (Charles 1993, p.95).

The way in which these two sets of relationships have developed therefore provides us with a number of important explanatory clues as to *why* contemporary working relationships between women and men are gendered in the way they are. Following a detailed review of the evidence, Charles has usefully summarized a number of these. Firstly, as part of the process of introducing new ways of organizing various kinds of production, employers made use of the 'authority relations' which already existed in the way that fathers and elder brothers tended to supervise the work of women and younger family members: 'This authority, deriving from pre-industrial family relations, was retained through men's adoption of supervisory roles within industrial production; capitalist production was organised in a way which reflected family authority relations' (Charles 1993, p.97).

Secondly, and again building on a situation which was already widespread, industrialists sought to employ larger numbers of women on the grounds that they worked for lower wages. This tendency to substitute 'cheap' women for 'expensive' men gathered pace in step with increasing mechanization during the late-eighteenth and early-nineteenth centuries which resulted in falling demand for 'skilled' men and rising demand for 'unskilled' women employees. Thirdly, and in an attempt to defend their weakening position, skilled men drew support from their guilds. Since membership of the guilds was almost exclusively male, this gave a particularly gendered tone to conflicts between employees and employers over wage levels, hours of work and working conditions.

Whilst accepting that the upshot of these conflicts can be described in terms of a general attempt by men to exclude women from the public workforce, their motivation for doing so was simply to keep the best jobs for themselves, but was actually part of a much more complex process of struggle aimed at maintaining the economy of the household for *all* its members. Men's insistence, which became central to the labour movement's campaigns into the twentieth century, on the need for jobs which paid a 'family wage', was at least as much to do with the urgent need to maintain the welfare of all members of the household as it was to do with the selfish desire to exclude women from the public realm.

Changes in the material organization of production which accompanied the industrialization of the public economy also contributed to the rigidification of a particularly gendered division of responsibilities over biological reproduction within the household. Whilst, as Charles notes 'there was no hint that women should not work to earn a wage; on the contrary, their contribution was necessary to the survival of the family unit' (Charles 1993, p.97), the new dynamics of the household economy meant that differences in the life-cycle between men and women became more problematic for the household economy. Whereas women had once been able to accommodate pregnancy within the shared productive activities of the household, the shift towards an almost total dependence on earned income gave rise to a much more structured separation of child-bearing and child-rearing from paid employment:

> Constant pregnancies and nursing are seen as incompatible with the demands of capitalist production. These material conditions produce the specific gender division of labour associated with capitalism.... Thus the gender division of labour is related both to the organisation of production and to the material reality of biological reproduction. (Charles 1993, p.93)

To the extent that fertility rates and decisions about the optimum size of the family are also determined by economic circumstances - how much food is available to feed a family, how much income can younger family members contribute towards their own upkeep, what standard of living does the household wish to maintain and so on - biological reproduction, and the

138

divisions of labour which emerge to accommodate it, are themselves significantly determined by production outside the household.

Gender Ideologies of Work

Common to both the feminist perspectives discussed so far is the recognition that both the public and private divisions of labour draw upon and are legitimated by a powerful set of assumptions and expectations about which kinds of activities and responsibilities 'should' or 'ought' to be done by men and women both inside and outside the household. Because these assumptions and expectations are not random or isolated from each other, but form a definite and identifiable system of ideas, they amount to what has been called a 'gender ideology of work'.

In the public realm, this ideology takes the form at the common-sense level of a set of stereotypes about what work is and about who should be doing it. In the private realm, it takes the form of assumptions about what constitutes 'the household' and the distribution of 'roles' and responsibilities within it. The penetration of this ideology is such that both men and women recognize it, and, whether implicitly or explicitly, tend to construct their own sense of work around it. To the extent that these ideologies and stereotypes penetrate into people's core understanding of who and what they are, we can begin to see that at a deeper level there is a complex relationship between these ideologies and fundamental ideas about femininity and masculinity. We will look more specifically at these connections in the following chapter. From a feminist perspective, the gender ideology of work and its stereotypes constitute a second part of the mechanism through which men attempt to justify and legitimate the attribution of greater social status and higher economic value to 'their' activities, and lower status and value to the activities of women.

Beechey has summarized 'a number of assumptions' which constitute what can be labelled the 'dominant ideology' of work which operates in the public sphere:

> That people work for a wage or salary, that work takes place outside the home, and that people either work full-time or are unemployed. It is generally assumed that people work in manufacturing jobs in manufacturing industries, and are working-class. It is also assumed (at least implicitly) that workers are men. Women... tend either to be ignored or treated as deviants from the masculine norm. (Beechey 1987, p.190)

On this basis, particular attitudes and expectations towards work have been ascribed to women by people in general, and also by male researchers. Dex has listed a number of those which were commonplace until quite recently:

> Women find it hard to reject the notion that their prime role is in the home 'servicing' male breadwinners. Women work only for pin money. Women do not mind and even prefer boring work. Women have an instrumental orientation to work: young women are only interested in work as a means to find a husband; older women work to finance home improvements. Women only work for money and are not involved in work personally. Women do not like to show initiative in their work and they are less interested in challenging jobs or promotion than men. (Dex 1985, p.37)

As we have already seen, this gender ideology can have far-reaching practical consequences:

> Gender can play a role in determining the forms of authority and supervision which are used in the workplace, it can affect the status, income and forms of contract of certain jobs, it can influence the skill categorisation of particular tasks, and finally it can play a role in dividing the workforce, both structurally and politically. (Beechey and Perkins 1987, p.140)

Although as we shall see, some aspects of these stereotypes now seem quite laughable, there is strong empirical evidence that these attitudes are extremely well established and consequently very difficult to shift. For example, in their survey of 'Women and Employment' in 1980, Martin and Roberts found that 25 per cent of the women they questioned agreed that 'a woman's place is in the home' and over 50 per cent agreed that 'a husband's job is to earn the money; a wife's job is to look after the family' (Martin and Roberts 1984, cited in Charles 1993 p.68). A more recent study of the extent to which employers use notions of 'sex-typing' (where jobs are seen as reflecting 'inherent characteristics of men and women') as part of their recruitment procedures is quite clear that across a wide range of industries such stereotypes are alive and well:

> A rigid sexual division of labour was sustained on the demand side by low turnover to established posts, and on the supply side by a widely recognized gender-labelling of vacancies.... In both plants, gender segregation was prominent and highly conventional.... There were few signs of any tendency to change the gender composition of jobs.... Gender segregation in these two organizations was deep-rooted historically and rationalized by gender stereotypes. (Lovering 1994, pp.327-48)

This ideology is closely related to, and is often seen as emerging out of, a deeper or underlying set of assumptions about the kinds of social roles and responsibilities which are taken by women and men within the private realm of the household. This has its roots in the now largely discredited but nonetheless still latent functionalist allocation of men and women to different social 'roles', and the attribution of the gender-specific and apparently 'universal' attributes such as 'expressiveness' and 'instrumentality' to women and men respectively. In Klein's words: 'women constitute not only an essential but also a distinctive part of our manpower resources... distinctive... because the structure and substance of the lives of most women are fundamentally determined by their function as wives, mothers and homemakers' (Klein 1965, p.83; quoted in Beechey and Perkins 1987, pp.120-1).

Articulating a highly biologistic attribution of 'natural' talents, this perspective also tends to suggest that the types of employment 'suitable' for women are those which reflect housewifely activities such as cleaning, childminding, cooking and other personal and social services. The domestic division of tasks within the household is thus also used to legitimate divisions of labour between the domestic and public realms as a whole:

> Child-bearing and child-rearing are assumed to be naturally linked, and therefore to fall to women, which makes married women imperfect substitutes for men in market work. Women's expectations of marriage and children are held to make them less willing to invest in education and job-training and more prone to labour market behaviour that is unstable from the employers' point of view. The gender division of paid and unpaid labour is thus perceived as 'naturally' complementary and as maximizing the gains of both partners. (Lewis 1992, p.83)

Thus emerges what Beechey and Perkins have called a 'ideology of domesticity' in which women are characterized as socially and economically subordinate and largely dependent on their partner's ability to earn that old chestnut of the labour movement, 'the family wage'. As we have already seen, the apparent accuracy and thus legitimacy of this situation is further reinforced by the State which has no compunction in assuming that women are financially dependent on men, particularly if the couple are legally married, and that women are 'naturally suited' or 'best placed' to take care of the business of bearing and raising children.

The way in which these 'naturalistic' and 'biologistic' perceptions of male and female attributes and predispositions are replicated in the actual segregation of jobs between men and women in the public realm of formal paid employment is clearly demonstrated in recent survey research in which respondents were asked why they thought some jobs were/should be done by women and some by men.[4] Summarizing these data, Scott concludes:

> As far as 'male' jobs are concerned, both the 'male' elements of these jobs and men's masculine qualities are given high priority. 44 per cent of the responses are to do with the fact that 'men's' jobs are heavy, dirty, dangerous, or involve outdoor work; heavy work is far and away the most important factor.... 'Masculine' qualities involve such things are aggressiveness, ambition, ability to exercise authority and cope with stress, a natural affinity with machines, and superior intelligence (!). These three factors, 'male' job characteristics, men's masculinity, and social pressure are 55 per cent of reasons given for the existence of 'male' jobs. (Scott 1994a, pp.16-17)

Parallel reasons were given for why other jobs are 'female': 'Feminine qualities and social pressures amount to nearly a third of the responses. Women's qualities include their caring abilities, the fact that they are "better with people", the job resembles their domestic work, it involves dexterity, or it is "not a masculine job"' (Scott 1994a, p.18).

The embeddedness of these perceptions is demonstrated by the fact that around a quarter of responses cited 'tradition' as one of the major *reasons* for these distinctions. When added to the number referring to the specificity of gender-roles, this figure rises to over 54 per cent: 'These data indicate that as far as employee perceptions and attitudes are concerned, gender segregation is strongly associated with social roles and traditional customs' (Scott 1994a, p.18). More abstractly, some of the ideas involved here can also be associated with the persistence of symbolic and cultural 'representations' of women and men which characterize the former as being 'closer to nature', and the latter as operating much more fully in the public 'cultural' realm (see Simone de Beauvoir 1972). This emphasis on what we can call the 'social construction' of gender attributes and thus of gender-type roles and types of work has been taken up by cultural theorists who, as Vogler puts it: 'focus on the socialization of men and women into different social and cultural values. The main argument is that people choose jobs which are in line with their beliefs about appropriate masculine or feminine behaviour, and which sustain their conceptions of their own masculine and feminine identities' (Vogler 1994, n.1. p.76).

However, it is one thing to describe a situation and quite another to explain *how and why* it came about. The first thing we need to do is reflect a little on what we mean when we call something 'ideological'. Without getting too technical, the label 'ideology' is used here to distinguish sets or collections of ideas which are 'false' in the sense that they misrepresent the reality of the situation which they claim to represent accurately. Although many if not all ideologies have this tendency, the use of the label in a pejorative way signifies that such misrepresentations are deliberately used by one group in society to maintain their own advantage over other groups (see Ransome 1992). In order to debunk the current gendered stereotype of work, and thus to declare the gender ideology upon which it is based as exploitative, we need to look at evidence which allows us to separate out 'false' ideas from 'true' ideas, to see whether or not the representation is accurate or inaccurate.

The Gender Ideology of Work within the Household

A first area of inaccuracy, is that the prevailing stereotype of who should be doing what and why they should be doing it tends to assume from the outset that *one form* of the 'the household' - namely the nuclear type made up of two adults and 2.4 children - is *the only* form in society. Within functionalist and liberal accounts, the argument runs that this form of the household emerged during the modern industrial period because it was this form which is most suited to that kind of social and economic organization. Apart from the fact that various manifestations of the so-called nuclear household existed before the industrial period and that increasing reliance on income earned outside the household tended to encourage an increase in the size particularly of working-class families during the nineteenth and early-twentieth centuries (Laslett 1977, Anderson 1971, Pahl 1984), it is evident, as Charles puts it, that: 'the majority of households have never conformed to this "perfect English family" and that the composition of households has varied enormously' (Charles 1993, citing Tilly and Scott 1987, Lewis 1984 and Gittins 1985).

If the ideal-typical family has never actually been the norm, then where did the idea of it come from? For liberal, Marxist and feminist theorists alike (Pahl 1984, Macpherson 1962, George 1973, Tilly and Scott 1987, Charles 1993, and Humphries 1977a and 1977b) an important shift came with the emergence of the new bourgeois middle-class household during the late-seventeenth and early eighteenth-centuries. Where previously women had played a full and public part in paid work, these emerging affluent households introduced the idea that it was not 'proper' for wives and female children to stray much beyond the household. Their social and economic dependence became part of their gentility.

More practically, and as we have already noted, this shift was also associated with further moves to consolidate private property and primogeniture within the law, and to create an aura of financial stability and thus creditworthyness which was so essential for success in business. This trend in the development of a distinctively bourgeois family ideal continued

143

throughout the eighteenth and into the nineteenth centuries and was further reinforced by the absorption of Protestant religious ideals concerning the moral integrity of women and their position as 'angels' of the household. From the late-nineteenth century onwards, the domestic household has emerged as a distinctive private realm which is quite separate from the public realm of working life. Within the private realm, femininity itself came to be seen as quite incompatible with productive employment. Public paid employment was simply something which respectable women did not do.

As an account of the emergence of middle-class households with a distinctive culture of familial respectability, and leaving aside the issue of the potential ideologicality of some of the values and beliefs on which it was based, these ideas about the nature of the household are accurate enough. They may however become ideological if it is assumed that *all* households follow this pattern, and thus that they can all be judged against the same criteria. The reality is that throughout this period, working-class households continued to depend on the earned income of wives and daughters. Whilst it is certainly true that patterns of employment shifted away from agricultural work in rural areas towards domestic service, factory and shop work in the rapidly expanding towns and cities, it remains the case that the new middle-class pattern has never been universally applicable. What has happened though, is that in their desire to emulate their more affluent suburban neighbours, working-class households have absorbed middle-class *ideas and ideals* about the kinds of activities which are appropriate for men and women to do:

> This solution came about through a process of class struggle in which the working class fought for improved living and working conditions, while adopting the gender ideology of the bourgeoisie which defined a woman's place as the home. This process of class struggle, combined with the reforming zeal of the philanthropists, meant that a specific gender division of labour became institutionalised within the working class as well as the bourgeoisie from whence it originated. This gender division of labour is seen as arising from a gender ideology which had its roots in bourgeois ideals of family life and it both shaped the aspirations of the working class and guided the moral sensibilities of the nineteenth-century reformers. (Charles 1993, pp.92-3)

Recent changes in the composition of households expose once and for all the mythical, inaccurate and thus ideological nature of this stereotype of the 'ideal family'/'family ideal'. Walby reports findings derived from official statistics which show for example that: 'The divorce rate in the UK has risen from 0.5 per cent per 1,000 in 1960, to 3.1 per cent in 1993.... The proportion of women aged 18-49 who are married has declined from 74 per cent in 1979

144

to 57 per cent in 1994... [while] the proportion of women aged 18-49 who are single rose from 18 per cent in 1979 to 29 per cent in 1994' (Walby 1997, pp.2-3/55). The collapse of the traditional household is likely to continue as the number of women without partners, and especially those with dependent children continues to grow. The 1993 *General Household Survey* notes for example that: 'The proportion of households containing a "traditional" family of a married or cohabiting couple with dependent children fell from 32 per cent in the early 1980s to 24 per cent in 1992 and 1993.... The proportion of families headed by a lone parent rose from 8 per cent in 1971 to 22 per cent in 1993, mainly due to the increase in lone mother families' (*General Household Survey* 1993, pp.7-8). A recent United Nations study reports that between 1970 and 1992, the percentage of births to unmarried women rose from 8 to 31 per cent in the UK. Increases of a similar magnitude were reported in the majority of the developed regions of the world. ('The World's Women in 1995', United Nations, 1995, chart 1.27a).

In terms of the experience of living within these apparently balanced and 'symmetrical' households, where partners may be thought to contribute in equal measure to keeping the household going, a large body of research has shown that quite apart from the power differentials which persist between men and women (Pahl, J. 1985, 1989), the functionalist/bourgeois-liberal model is found wanting. A first point which needs clarifying, is that rather than being peripheral, the income generated by women is essential to the economic well-being of the household. For example, Burchell and Rubery report findings which show that amongst the 600 male and female respondents they questioned, over two-thirds cited 'the need for money for basics such as food, rent, and mortgage' as one of the main reasons for working (Burchell and Rubery 1994, table 3.5, p.102).

Although the desire 'to earn money to buy extras' was the second most common reason given by female respondents - a view which might support the stereotype that women only work in order to earn 'pin money' - this reason was equally important amongst the whole sample and amongst male respondents. These priorities are confirmed by other survey data which show that if households 'have difficulty making ends meet' over 40 per cent said that they would have to 'cut back on *necessities*' (Main 1994, p.140, emphasis added). Lewis suggests: 'It remains the case that women in low paid, low status work are more likely to be working out of economic necessity than for reasons of personal fulfilment' (Lewis 1992, p.3). These women are unlikely to be impressed by the suggestion that they 'do not value economic rewards highly'.

In addition, and closely related to changes in the composition of the household, recent increases in the economic activity of married women with dependent children (up from 52 per cent in 1977-79 to 63 per cent in 1991-93) shows the falsity of the dependent mother/male breadwinner stereotype. Although the percentage of lone mothers with dependent children who are working has fallen over the same period (down from 47 per cent to 41 per cent), it is clear that for those 41 per cent, the economic well-being of their households is heavily dependent on income from their own rather than from any 'breadwinning' partner's earnings.

The weight of the burden of raising children which falls to both married and lone mothers within the household is reflected in the fact that they are much less likely to be formally employed if they have younger children (73 per cent of married women with children over five years compared with 49 per cent with under-fives), and that full-time employment is more common amongst married than amongst single mothers (22 per cent as against 17 per cent in 1991-93; for more details see *General Household Survey* 1993, p.54). We should also note that the ageing of the population is creating a new burden on households as more and more of them are now providing care for elderly and infirm relatives. Walby reports for example, that among adults aged 45-64, around 20 per cent of women and 14 per cent of men are engaged in care outside the home and a further 6 and 5 per cent respectively are co-resident carers (Walby 1997, p.54 referring to *Employment Gazette*, March 1995, p.103).

These changes in the structure and composition of the household uncover the falsity of the assumption that all women, and particularly married women, are entirely dependent on there being a male breadwinner within the household, and that the household can be maintained with a single income. Charles suggests for example, that 'if women didn't work, 40% of households would fall below the poverty line' (Charles 1993, p.63). This change is particularly marked in households with women working full-time, since the proportion in which men earn the majority of the income has fallen from 83 per cent in 1973 to 55 per cent in 1993. There have also been steady increases in the proportion of households in which both partners earn similar incomes (up from 14 to 30 per cent) and in those where the women earns more (up from 3 to 15 per cent) (Walby 1997, p.52, drawing on Irwin 1995).

Survey data show that this situation is closely related to attitudes about who should or ought to be doing what. Table 4.1 shows the percentage of respondents agreeing with two statements about the main responsibilities of partners within the household. Looking at these data we can see that taking all classes together, over two-thirds of both men and women thought that women should be ultimately responsible for housework (65 and 61 per cent respectively). Clear differences emerge between women working full- and part-time however, with only 44 per cent of the former holding this view. These expressed beliefs tend to be more firmly held as one moves from the service class to the working class i.e. from higher clerical and other non-manual occupations to skilled- and unskilled manual occupations. The fact that only 56 and 44 per cent of men and women respectively thought that men should be ultimately responsible for breadwinning, shows the falsity of the idea that women have, and/or think they have, no role in providing earned income for the household. As one would expect, acceptance of dual responsibility in generating income is particularly strong amongst women working full-time with 71 per cent rejecting the male breadwinner idea.

Table 4.1: Attitudes towards male/female responsibilities by class and gender
percentages agreeing with the two statements - (1) 'The female partner should be ultimately responsible for housework', (2) 'The male partner should ultimately be responsible for breadwinning'

	all men	all women	full-time women	part-time women
Statement 1:				
All classes	65	61	44	80
Service class	58	49	44	77
Intermediate class	75	61	39	94
Working class	66	69	59	74
Statement 2:				
All classes	56	44	29	60
Service class	50	29	25	41
Intermediate class	66	48	27	77
Working class	57	51	40	55

Source: Adapted from SCELI data (Household and Community Survey), reported in Vogler 1994, table 2.12, p.55. *Note*: Data based on responses from 544 respondents. 'Class' categories are taken from a collapsed version of Goldthorpe's (1980) class schema.

Clearly these attitudes have an important bearing on the division of responsibility for tasks within the household. Whilst, as Vogler observes: 'it may be thought that when women are in full-time employment, they should do a smaller proportion of the total [housework] than when they are in part-time work' the reality is that 'there is very little difference' (Vogler 1994, p.60).

Similarly, Gershuny *et al.* report that: 'Studies of domestic work-time allocation show that the reduction in the wife's proportion of the household's domestic work following her entry into the workforce is insufficient to compensate for her increase in paid work' (Gershuny *et al.* 1994, p.152; see also Morris 1990, and Schwartz Cowan 1989). Confirmation of the weight of the burden which falls to women is found in a recent review of the amount of time spent by adults in doing domestic-related tasks.

Table 4.2: Average minutes spent per day by women and men on domestic tasks

	Women	*Men*
cooking	68	28
looking after children	86	55
washing	25	3
shopping	46	26
cleaning	70	46
Total unpaid housework	**295**	**158**
paid work	**127**	**212**
sport/exercise	20	38
self-education	22	33
DIY	6	22
Totals	470	463

Note: Of the remaining time in the day, approximately 8 hours is occupied with resting and sleeping, and 8 hours with eating and leisure activities.

Source: Office for National Statistics, reported in *Guardian* newspaper, 7 Oct 1997, p.1.

As Table 4.2 shows, on average, women spend nearly 4 hours per day on unpaid domestic tasks, compared with only 2.5 hours for men. This report also applies a monetary value to non-paid domestic activities and concludes that if these were valued 'at the same average rate as paid employment' they would be worth 22 per cent *more than* the total value of the formal economy (*Guardian*, 7 Oct 1997, p.1).

In light of this information, we can already see that important elements of the gender stereotype of 'work' and of women's role within it outlined at the start of this section are quite ideological. First, there is a considerable gap between the ideal of the happy, balanced and symmetrical family, and the true reality. Given that the choices made by women about their employment opportunities are bound to be circumscribed by these real circumstances, we can agree with Vogler that: 'It cannot therefore be assumed, as human capital and cultural theorists do, that households are egalitarian consensual units within which both partners are equally free to realize their 'choices' on the labour market' (Vogler 1994, p.63).

Second, given that the economic integrity of so many households depends on the income of both male and female spouses/partners and/or on the earned income of women alone, it is quite ridiculous to suggest that women are motivated to take paid work for different reasons than men. It may well be that fewer women would work if their families could get by without, but so too would men. Third, rather than there being an equitable distribution of domestic and paid activities between men and women within and household, women are still expected to bear a considerable extra weight of responsibility for domestic tasks. As suggested by our earlier discussion of social reproduction, these tasks are just as necessary for the integrity of the household as is the earning of income outside it. Although then, the myth of the ideal and balanced family would have us believe that women's earned income is 'secondary', and that they are thus 'subordinate' in social and economic terms, the actual number of households for which this is the case (perhaps 10 to 15 per cent) is already extremely small and is likely to shrink even further over the next ten years.

The Gender Ideology of Work at Work

Turning from the gendered stereotype of the division of activities within the household to the public and equally gendered stereotype of the division of labour in paid activities, five further assumptions can be shown to be inaccurate and ideological. First, and as is now well known, the considerable shift away from employment in manufacturing industries to employment in services means that it is no longer the case that 'proper work' has something to do with working in stereotypically heavy, dirty and physical manufacturing industries. In the UK for example, and expressed as a percentage of those in employment, the proportion employed in manufacturing fell from 36.4 per cent in 1971 to 20 per cent in 1994, while the proportion employed in services rose from 52.5 per cent to 74 per cent (a movement of some 4 million jobs from one sector to the other) (see *Social Trends* no.21, 1991, table 4.11; and *Annual Abstract of Statistics*, no.127, 1991; and no.131, 1996, table 6.1). Similar changes in the aggregate distribution of employment between agriculture, industry and services have taken place in each of the larger EC countries between 1978 and 1989 (see *Eurostat Annual Review 1976-1985*

149

(EEC Brussels 1986), tables 3.4.13-18; Eurostat: *Basic Statistics of the Community* (EEC Brussels 1988, 1989 and 1991), tables 3.17 and 3.18). A more recent survey for the United Nations records that between 1991 and 1994 in Western Europe, the annual change in employment in industry declined by an average of 3.0 per cent per year, while employment in services increased by an average of 0.5 per cent. In North America, while employment in industry suffered a similar decline, employment in services grew more strongly by an annual average of 1.5 per cent (United Nations, 'Economic Survey of Europe in 1994-1995', table 2.3.3).

Second, historical data show that women always have played a very important part in the formal workforce, and thus that it is quite false to suggest that 'work' is something only done by men. Walby reports for example that in Britain and apart from a decline in the proportion of adult women (i.e. those aged twenty years and over) who were 'economically active' to around 32 per cent at the turn of the century, throughout the nineteenth century and from the mid-twentieth century onwards, between 40 and 50 per cent of women were actively employed. This proportion rises to over 70 per cent in 1995 amongst women of working age (i.e. aged 16 to 59 years). Recent significant increases in the number of working women, and in the proportion of the workforce accounted for by women should more properly be seen as an extension of the historical norm rather than as a complete break with the past (Pahl 1984).[5]

Table 4.3: Employees in employment, GB 1959-1995

	1959	1966	1971	1981	1991	1995
Total	20983	22787	21648	21386	21719	21355
All male	13824	14551	13424	12278	11253	10777
All female	7159	236	8224	9108	10467	10584
% female	34.1	36.1	38.0	42.6	48.2	49.6

Source: Walby 1997, table 2.1, p.27.

As Table 4.3 shows, by 1995 women constituted almost half of the total workforce in employment, a rise of over 15 per cent since the 1950s. As Walby notes, the most marked increase has been amongst married women 'whose economic activity rate has risen from 26 per cent in 1951 to 71 per cent in 1991' (Walby 1997, p.27).

150

Whilst the proportion of the workforce accounted for by men has obviously fallen by the same percentage as the proportion of women has increased, the economic activity of men of working age (16 to 64 years) has fallen consistently from almost 80 per cent in 1975 to 64 per cent in 1994 (Walby 1997, table 2.3, p.30). Similar shifts in patterns of economic activity amongst men and women have been recorded throughout the leading industrialized economies. Between 1970 and 1990 in Western Europe for example, economic activity rates amongst men declined from 78 to 72 per cent, whilst rates amongst women increased from 37 to 51 per cent. In the other developed economies outside Europe, activity amongst men declined from 81 to 75 per cent and increased for women from 40 to 54 per cent. In South-eastern Asia, economic activity amongst women has increased less dramatically from 49 to 54 per cent ('The World's Women in 1995', United Nations, 1995, chart 5.4b).

Third, the fact that almost all of the increase in employment amongst women has been in part-time rather than full-time work, clearly shows that work is no longer a predominantly full-time activity. Between 1971 and 1995 in the UK for example, of the overall increase of around 2.2 million jobs, 90 per cent were part-time. Since women account for a much higher proportion of part-time employees than men, 'women are now almost as likely to be working part-time as full-time, that is, 47 per cent' (Walby 1997, pp.31-2). Writing in 1995, UK Government researchers have summarized these trends:

> Part-time working has become much more common in the last decade for both men and women. Over [the period 1984 to 1994] the number of men working full-time has fallen by 3 per cent, while the number of women who work full-time has risen by 13 per cent. Over twice as many men as women work full-time, while more than five times as many women as men work part-time. In 1994 there were one and a half million more women working, either full or part time, than there were ten years earlier. (*Social Trends* no.25, 1995, p.69)[6]

While increases in part-time working have had an impact across all industries, this has been particularly so in the service sector, where just under half of the total increase of 2.25 million jobs between 1981 and 1989 was accounted for by increases in part-time jobs. For men, full- and part-time employment in this sector increased by 403,000 and 227,000 respectively, while the number of women employed full- and part-time increased very substantially by 790,000 and 800,000 (See *Census of Employment* 1981, 1984, 1987, 1989. Final results published in *Employment Gazette*: December 1983; September 1987; October 1989, and April 1991, table 5). International comparisons show that although part-time working has grown particularly quickly in the UK over the last two decades, it is now a very well established feature of many of the leading economies.[7]

A fourth inaccuracy is the tendency, particularly amongst employers, to assume that 'women' form an entirely homogenous group of employees and potential employees. Whilst differences between men may also tend to be overlooked, the false impression that all women approach employment from the same social and economic position is more critical, since, as we have seen, the choices they make about employment are much more heavily circumscribed by household factors. Having taken the trouble to look more closely at the balance of costs and benefits which women are forced to make in deciding whether to enter paid employment, feminist analyses have therefore uncovered the fact that it is quite inadequate to lump all women together into a single group since very significant differences exist *between* different groups of women. Following Walby, amongst the most important differences we should note here are in educational achievement, in the ages of women looking for work, that increases in rates of economic activity are higher amongst women in higher socio-economic groups, that participation rates vary according to locality and region, and that each of these differences are overlaid by differences generated by class and ethnic background (Walby 1997, p.26):

> Ethnic diversity and class inequality mediate the impact of employment on gender relations, so that while employment may be a viable route for emancipation for more privileged women, this may not apply to Black and working-class women for whom employment is frequently poorly paid and tedious as compared with the alternative of motherhood. (Walby 1997, p.24)

These differences between women at the point of access to employment are also found within employment itself: '[It cannot] be presumed that women simply fill the jobs created at the bottom of the pile for, as the distinction between horizontal and vertical segregation illustrates, women will themselves be incorporated into a hierarchy of employment, relative to one another as well as to men' (Fine 1992, pp.87-8). Whilst we can certainly agree with Lewis that: 'the experiences of both groups of women are fundamentally subject to a gender order which establishes a hierarchical relationship between men and women, and according to which definitions of femininity and masculinity are constructed', it is also true that:

> One of the most significant differences in income and expectations in late twentieth-century society must be that between the teenage unmarried mother, unable to escape from dependence on state benefits, and the professional woman in her late thirties, married to another professional, having her first

152

child and able to pay for a nanny. Whenever attention is drawn to this particular dimension of inequality, the cry goes up about women exploiting other women. (Lewis 1992, p.10)

A fifth and final inaccuracy relates to the fact that although ideally it might be thought that women and men have equal employment opportunities this is patently not the case. The true reality is that women are heavily segregated into particular occupations both within and outside the service sector, into particular types of work tasks, into jobs where they are likely only to work with other women, and into part-time rather than full-time jobs (for detailed accounts of segregation in various occupations see: Hakim 1979, Stamp and Robarts 1986, Pollert 1981, Glucksmann 1986, Witz 1988). Amongst other things, segregated jobs tend to provide lower levels of pay and other economic rewards, much poorer opportunities for training and career advancement, and generally much lower levels of social status. It will be useful to look briefly at these negative consequences of segregation.

Segregation and the Occupational Sex-typing of Jobs

Picking up on a number of issues already considered, segregation is closely associated with what has been labelled 'occupational sex-typing' or 'job-gendering'. As Lovering puts it, this 'involves a dual process whereby the characteristics of employees are defined in terms of their gender (rather than individual abilities or qualifications) and jobs become known as 'men's work' or 'women's work' (Lovering 1994, p.329). Lovering lists the following factors which are associated with the sex-matching of jobs with employees: the physical nature of the task; perceptions of the 'psychological and social characteristics' attributed to men and women; social relations (meaning employers' preferences for keeping single-sex teams intact); women's preference for shorter hours of work; and their apparent acceptance of jobs offering lower pay, status and career prospects (Lovering 1994, p.352). Referring to the overall sample survey of around 6000 respondents in the Social Change and Economic Life Initiative (SCELI) carried out in the UK in 1986, Scott reports clear evidence of 'a high degree of polarization of the sexes between 'male' and 'female' jobs':

Men [were] much more highly concentrated in 'male' jobs than women in 'female' ones, particularly at the extreme ends of the spectrum: 83 per cent of men are in 'male' jobs and almost half of these are in 'almost exclusively male jobs'; in comparison, only about a fifth of women are in 'exclusively female'

153

jobs and a higher proportion are in 'mainly female' or 'mixed' jobs. (Scott 1994a, p.8)

As might be expected, levels of gendered job-segregation between men and women vary across occupations and industries with the highest levels in 'traditional' male enclaves in private manufacturing and lower levels in public and private services. Although 'women are less segregated than men in all industries, most of them being in moderately segregated jobs', the only industrial sector made up largely of jobs which are not categorized in this way is in distribution, hotels and catering (Scott 1994a, p.12).

Segregation and the Disadvantages of Part-time Working

Part-time working is perhaps the clearest manifestation of the likely negative effects of segregation. First, part-time working *as a whole* is highly feminized and is separated away from full-time working: '44 per cent of women work part time compared with only 1 per cent of men. Both full-time and part-time women are concentrated in moderately segregated jobs (42 and 49 per cent respectively), but part-time women are much more likely to be in highly segregated jobs than full-time women (29 per cent compared with 17 per cent)' (Scott 1994a, p.15). Second, *within* part-time working, further and highly disadvantageous segregation is evident. In terms of the types of skills (and thus of likely job satisfaction) Rubery *et al.* note for example, that amongst their sample of 600 respondents:

> 36 per cent of female part-time jobs were found in the partly and unskilled social classes compared with only 13 per cent of female full-time jobs and 19 per cent of male full-time jobs.... [While] 38 per cent of female part-time jobs were in the routine non-manual worker category, a similar percentage as for female full-time jobs... a much smaller percentage were in the top classes and much larger ones in the lower classes.... (Rubery *et al.* 1994, p.209)

Apart from the researchers's own conclusion that 'almost all these data support the view that part-time jobs differ significantly from full-time jobs and in practice constitute a less skilled stratum of the job market... no less than 69 per cent of part-time jobs fall into the lowest skill band', the generally poor quality of part-time jobs is also evident in the opinions of those who actually do them: 'Only 43 per cent saw their jobs as 'skilled'.... Only 29 per cent of part-timers considered their job offered promotion prospects (Rubery *et al.* 1994, p.214):

> Part-timers were less likely than both male and female full-timers to have access to employer pension schemes, paid time off, meal subsidies,

accommodation, life insurance, private health schemes, subsidized transport, finance or loans, recreation facilities, and maternity pay. (Rubery *et al.* 1994, pp.210/213-14/218)

Because women are much more likely to be working part-time, and because the number of women entering this kind of work is increasing, these researchers reach the somewhat pessimistic conclusion that 'trends towards increasing part-time work thus seem likely to depress the share of women's jobs found in higher categories and the increase in lower categories, while maintaining the over-representation in middle level clerical and similar work' (Rubery *et al.* 1994, p.209).

Segregation and Pay and Career Prospects

Patterns of gendered occupational segregation are closely associated with lower levels of pay and career prospects for female employees. Although, as Walby points out, there has been a narrowing of the gap between men's and women's earnings during the last 25 years (rising from only 63 per cent of men's full-time earnings in 1970 to 80 per cent in 1995, Walby 1997, table 2.4, p.31),

Table 4.4: Hourly earnings by sex and whether full- or part-time

	1974	1977	1981	1986	1991	1995
Full-time women as % of Full-time men	66	74	73	74	78	80
Part-time women as % of Full-time men	54	60	58	57	58	60
Part-time women as % of Full-time women	82	81	79	76	75	75

Source: Walby 1997, table 2.6, p.32.

Table 4.4 shows that a considerable gap still remains, particularly for those women working part-time whose earnings are still as much as 60 per cent below the equivalent full-time earnings amongst men. Given that increasing numbers of women are working part-time, it is particularly alarming that compared with their full-time contemporaries, the hourly wages of part-timers are actually *decreasing*. The closeness of the relationship between earnings and the type of work being done (i.e whether it is perceived to be 'male' or 'female' work), is confirmed by Scott: 'Men earn more than women within each social class but their earnings tend to be even higher in more 'male' jobs. Similarly, women earn less than men within each class, but their earnings are lowered further by being located in more 'female' jobs' (Scott 1994a, pp.14-15).

Looking at career prospects, whilst it is obviously the case that these tend to be quite poor for women working part-time, there is evidence that the position of other groups of women employees may be improving. Walby reports for example, that both in terms of absolute numbers and as a proportion of employees in 'higher order occupations' (i.e. senior, high-grade, non-manual professional jobs as distinct from skilled and unskilled manual jobs), women are closing the gap with men. Between 1981 and 1991 for example, and using the 1980 occupational classification, the average proportionate increase accounted for by women in the top five occupational categories was over 70 per cent compared with just 12 per cent amongst men (calculated from Walby 1997, table 2.9, p.37). These changes have to be treated with some caution however, since apart from the fact that this trend is partly a consequence of the overall increase in the proportion of the total workforce engaged in these kinds of work, there is much evidence that women still face considerable difficulties in passing through the 'glass ceiling'. For example, following her survey of 324 senior managers in five multinational companies (all of which were members of the 'Opportunity 2000' project supporting increased equal opportunities), Wajcman reports that although there were no significant differences between male and female managers in terms of hours of work, individual characteristics and motivation, they express quite different opinions about their career prospects:

> Whereas 70 per cent of men think that men and women have equal chances of promotion in their company, fewer than 40 per cent of the women think so. In fact, 71 per cent of women believe that a "glass ceiling" exists limiting women's ability to move up the ladder, and almost a third of men agree with them. (Wajcman 1996, p.271)

The barriers to advancement most frequently mentioned by women were: 'that senior management is perceived to be a "club" (54 per cent giving this as a reason), the prejudice of colleagues (23 per cent), the lack of career guidance (50 per cent), and family commitments (43 per cent)'. Sexual discrimination/harassment was mentioned by a further 17 per cent of female respondents (Wajcman 1996, p.271-2. For further accounts of the circumstances which affect women's success in reaching high-level employment see: Corti and Dex 1995, and Evetts (ed.) 1994). If these difficulties are still being strongly felt by women high-achievers in so-called 'enlightened' companies, one is bound to wonder what are the prospects for women at lower levels?

Explaining Gender Segregation

Having reviewed recent evidence of the difficult circumstances which women face in making choices about employment, and of the restricted opportunities they encounter once they have entered formal paid employment, we are now in a position to assess what contributions the various feminist accounts discussed here have made to understanding *why* this situation has come about, and what they tell us about women and the future of work.

The first point to make, is that the various debates which make up the feminist discourse on work have moved on from the earlier dichotomy between those who emphasized the role of 'supply-side' factors (principally that the burden of domestic responsibilities limits women's ability to take paid work), and those who emphasized 'demand-side' factors (principally the fact that employers seek to exploit women through the operation of various structures and prejudices which discriminate against them).[8] As we have seen, the debate is now much more concerned with practices and processes which tend to cut across these rather crude distinctions. As the detailed empirical evidence makes clear, we obviously need to look at both supply-side and demand-side factors and the various ways that they are combined. It is quite spurious to 'factor out' the domestic division of labour in looking at participation rates, levels of education, training, skills, experience and so on, and equally spurious to disregard levels of pay and other inequalities when looking at women's and men's household decisions about taking paid employment.

Amongst the most important insights which have been uncovered in this process of argument and analysis are the following. First, that 'segregation' is something which applies to the experience of women both within and outside the household. Second, that gender ideologies cut across the domestic/formal paid employment divide, since quite obviously the gendering of domestic tasks and the gendering of tasks at work are, both analytically and in terms of their practical effects, two aspects of the same whole. Third, that since domestic activities are just as important to the well-being or social reproduction of the household as are activities which generate financial income, the assumption that it is only the latter which constitute 'work' proper is highly problematic. Fourth, and drawing on each of these insights, feminist discourses lay bare the way in which the different manifestations of gender discrimination tend to be

157

self-legitimating. If women actually do spend more time doing domestic work, or if they are apparently better at some kinds of activity that at others, then it appears to be quite legitimate that they should continue to do them.

This division of practical activities is absorbed at the ideational level as a justification for people's perceptions of what they are doing and of why they are doing it; the practical and ideational aspects of gender divisions are justified by recourse to each other. The tautological nature of this process of self-legitimation renders it extremely durable since there is strong evidence of the fact that relationships between men and women, and expectations and ideas about their respective roles, are saturated by long-standing and deeply-rooted beliefs about who should be doing which kinds of work. As we have seen tradition, expressed beliefs that 'things have always been done this way', and that such divisions are natural, are all part of the dead weight of inertia which women have to face in making their choices about work. Not only then, do 'sexist attitudes play a crucial role in stabilizing and legitimizing segregation in the labour market', they may also 'lag behind demand-led changes and prevent the potential for desegregation being realized' (Vogler 1994, p.73):

> There is much evidence that naturalistic beliefs about gender... play a fundamental role in the sex-typing of jobs. These beliefs seem to be much more enduring than economic and family structures. Finally, there is substantial inertia in the labour market; traditional employment practices persist despite pressures for change. Patterns of gender segregation are sustained by 'tradition' as much as by the rational strategies of individual employers and employees. (Scott 1994a, p.35)

By uncovering these processes of ideological contamination, feminist accounts have also usefully exposed the myth that women make free choices about their working lives in the context of an allegedly perfect or balanced labour market. Although it might be comforting to believe that all women start off from the same position and make fully rational choices, or develop rational strategies about how they can best contribute to the economy of their households, these choices are much more restricted.

Within the household, they have to find practical ways of redistributing the domestic activities for which they are likely to have become responsible. They then have to balance the costs of going to work against the benefits of entering paid employment in the context of segregationist structural constraints which tend to undermine their ability to make the most of their human capital as employees. These constraints tend to be self-supporting since domestic responsibilities may severely limit their ability to raise the

158

market value of their human capital (for example by gaining further qualifications or training), whilst time spent at work may undermine their value as providers of activities within the household. This situation becomes even more complicated if the household also has to take account of welfare benefits paid by the State (see Morris 1990, Glendenning and Millar (eds.) 1987). Since the distribution of activities between men and women within the household is not properly balanced, and since the market for labour is very far from perfect, the choices made are more likely to be a best guess than a fully rational judgement:

> Women make choices, but not under conditions of their own making. Women choose the best option that they can see, rationally, though usually with imperfect knowledge, but only within the range of options open to them. The decision as to whether to spend more time on the home or more time on paid work is a rational choice. But those choices cannot be understood outside of an understanding of the development of the institutions and structures which construct those options. (Walby 1997, p.25)

Women and the Future of Work

Each of these insights has made a very significant contribution to our understanding of the problems women face before and after their entry into formal paid employment. Realistically however, and despite the considerable effort that has been expended on this problem, we must also recognize that none of the analytical positions discussed in this chapter have provided a full explanation of *why* this iniquitous situation persists. Put bluntly, and as a number of recent researchers have declared, the feminist discourse on work is much better at *describing* the situation than it is at *explaining* it. In the case of trying to *explain* familial ideology for example, many accounts regress to the *descriptive* position that things are the way they are, because that's the way they are. The point is of course, that this actually explains nothing at all:

> It is surely women's responsibility for reproductive activities and the associated undervaluing of their work which is in need of explanation, and it cannot be explained simply by observing that it is a common feature of developing and developed societies and must therefore be the cause of women's subordination. (Charles 1993, p.258)

We can even go so far as to suggest that it is a recognition of this failure of explanation which has led some researchers to abandon the attempt altogether and to turn instead to producing ever more detailed descriptive accounts, perhaps in the hope that some 'final' explanation will reveal itself in the mass of empirical detail. In trying to understand the position of women in the future of work, it will be useful to note briefly a number of weaknesses of the various contributions.

Looking first at the explanatory potential of patriarchy theory, the initial attractiveness of this approach is that in cutting across the domestic/private and practical/ideological divides, it appears to provide a 'unifying' theory of gender discrimination. On this understanding, and accepting for the moment that formal paid employment *is* the most important source of social and economic prestige, women's main priority for the future is to continue increasing their activities as members of the formal workforce. Unfortunately however, at least in Walby's narrative, the *mechanism* by which this transition occurs, and the obstacles which women face, are represented as being largely political and ideological, rather than economic and practical. In her latest account for example, Walby explains recent success in women's entry to formal paid employment almost entirely in terms of the political successes of the women's movement:

> These changes in employment relations are part of a general change in the form of gender regime. In the long run they are the ultimate consequence of the working through of the shift in gender regime brought about by the success of first-wave feminism in winning political citizenship and the increase in demand for labour with economic development. In the recent period these changes have been further accelerated by changes in state [and trade union] policy towards equal opportunities... changes in family practices; and the massive increase in women in education at all levels. (Walby 1997, pp.37-8)

Whilst her detailed evidence of changes in Sate policy, trade union activity and so on is well-documented and persuasive, we are told almost nothing about the 'increase in demand for labour', or about the 'economic development' to which this is attributed. Similarly, although there have been changes in what she calls 'family practices', her account says very little about these or why they have come about. It is difficult to accept that practical changes in the demand for labour, patterns of working and work-organization, changes in the composition of the household, only some of which have been helpful to women, *can all be attributed* to the success of first-wave feminism. In reality of course, these have also been brought about by structural and material changes both within the world of work (technological development, the impact of the increasingly global economy), and within the household (changes in household membership and new patterns of child-bearing and child-rearing) many of which are only connected with the women's movement in a very tangential way.

The limited explanatory power of this approach is demonstrated by the fact that political advances in equal opportunities have not in themselves produced entirely satisfactory practical changes for all women. For example, although Walby quotes much evidence of the intention by various agencies to move towards equal opportunities, and of the increasing educational achievements of younger women - the 'gender revolution in education', the results of these policies have been very slow to take effect. The greater is the desire for change, and the better educated is the female workforce, the more disappointing it is that such changes have had little effect on the majority of women. As she says:

> The significance of [the gender revolution in education] depends on the significance of educational qualifications for access to social and economic opportunities. *If* employment chances are primarily structured by qualifications, then these changes in education will have dramatic consequences for gender relations in employment. If, however, employment chances are determined by other factors than this type of merit, then the consequences will be less important. Other intervening variables include: structures of sex segregation; work commitment; discrimination. (Walby 1997, p.49, emphasis added)

The point is, that this is a very big 'if' indeed. As the empirical data we have been looking at show, it is precisely the 'intervening variables' of sex segregation and discrimination at work which *do* inhibit employment opportunities for women. Walby's account tends to assume a highly liberal reading of what we know to be the mythical ideal of a meritocratic society characterized by a perfectly balanced labour market. The labour market is not in balance, women do not enter it on the same terms as men, and once in work, they do not have equal opportunities for advancement. If better education allows them to see this more clearly, then perhaps things will change more quickly. It may also mean however, that they find the world of work even more alienating and frustrating than older and apparently less well educated women do. Indeed in their survey of a local labour market, Rubery *et al.* conclude that many women (and indeed many men) are *already* over-qualified for the kinds of work they do: '*relative to the jobs they do*, female part-timers are overqualified, compared with male and female full-timers' (the percentage of over-qualified respondents were 27 and 28 per cent amongst male and female full-timers, and 40 per cent among female part-timers; Rubery *et al.* 1994, pp.225/6, original emphasis). And referring to women who have suffered what they call 'a drop in the social-class rating of their job', these authors go on the suggest that: 'This segment may be indicative of future labour market trends as women, particularly those with more qualifications, become more dissatisfied with their confinement to low-paid and low-status jobs' (Burchell and Rubery, 1994, p.115).

To the extent that the majority of women are confined to jobs which are poorly-paid, insecure and unstimulating, it would seem that the political successes of first-wave feminism are only really being felt by a fortunate minority of women. As Walby willingly concedes, there must be something other than shifts in political perspective going on here to explain why it is that at one and the same time, some women make progress while others do not: 'It is in the areas of education and employment that we find *both* the leading edge of the shift from the domestic to the public gender regime [meaning the private and public forms of patriarchy], *and* increased inequality between women' (Walby 1997, p.23 emphasis added).

The patriarchy approach inevitably finds itself leaning on the idea that a particular form of gender ideology - patriarchal ideology - is the key explanatory device in understanding the origins of structured gender inequality. Whilst, as we have seen, discrimination against women is certainly deeply embedded in, and legitimated by reference to, gender ideologies, it is difficult to accept either that these ideologies are principally or wholly an expression of an underlying patriarchy, or that ideological attitudes alone can explain these paradoxes. A major problem with the 'ideological inertia' or 'dead weight of tradition' hypothesis is that if tradition and inertia are so all-powerful, then how is it that things change at all? What we must be careful not to do, is to confuse detailed accounts of the actual and continuing inequalities faced by women with explanations of *why* such discrimination still exists. To resort to the position that things are like this because they always have been.

Ultimately, this view may regress into the highly naturalistsic and biologistic explanation which feminist accounts have tried so hard to overcome. Up to a point, it can be suggested that researchers themselves have been so struck by the apparently non-economic/non-material factors affecting the choices which women make about their domestic and working lives, that they attribute scientific validity to the common-sensical and highly ideological perceptions of gender roles reported by their respondents. It remains the case that it is the origins of these gender ideologies, and the practices through which they are sustained which need explaining, not the fact that such gender ideologies are commonplace within society. It is this lack of explanatory bite which undoubtedly lies behind the summarizing comments of a recent editor of one of the most detailed empirical investigations of gender segregation yet carried out: 'Most of the employer- or industry-focused chapters stress the importance of occupational sex-typing in the way jobs are defined and labour recruited into them... At this stage it is not possible to say *why* this occurs' (Scott 1994a, p.20). And further:

> Despite the recent growth of interest in the relationship between work, gender, and sexuality, we still lack an adequate explanatory theory for job-gendering.... [W]e still do not know how job-gendering interacts with other economic processes, why it should take one form rather than another, why it should be more resistant to change in one case rather than another, or even why it should matter. Why should personal identities affect or be affected by the supposed masculinity or femininity of a job? (Scott 1994b, p.238)

Given the extreme efforts which have gone into this project it is remarkably disappointing to find its contributors reaching the somewhat unsurprising conclusions that: 'gender ideology strongly permeates the labour market as well as the family' (Scott 1994a, p.20), or that 'sexist attitudes play a crucial role in stabilizing and legitimizing segregation in the labour market and may also inhibit possibilities for change arising on the demand side' (Vogler 1994, p.73).

Once again then, we are provided with descriptions and not explanations. It is the ideologicality of the ideas which needs explaining; why is it that women are associated with some attributes and aptitudes and men with others? At least some part of this explanation must come from the economic circumstances in which households find themselves. Unless we want to suggest that the gender-typing of roles and activities is historically invariable, and that the current version would be as familiar to those living within pre-industrial households as it is to us living in late-industrial period, we are compelled to seek out causes and explanations which are not purely to do with notions of social and cultural normativeness. Indeed, one of the prerequisites of the idea of socialization, is that there is some kind of advantage to be gained from behaving in one way rather than in another. What we need to find out, is *what kind* of advantage and *for whom*?

This brings us back to the idea of social reproduction as a key device for explaining gender inequality. Whilst accepting that part of this advantage is ideational in the sense that we tend to prefer falling-in with other people's ideas and beliefs (including incidentally, ideas and beliefs about what work is), it is also material in the sense that we need access to necessary resources. As employees, the advantage of complying with the status quo is simply that in the absence of any realistic alternative, the current mechanisms of employment are the only means through which people can generate the financial and other resources they need to sustain their households. As employers, the advantage is that much is to be gained from the preservation of particular, and historically specific, employment and organizational practices: economically they generate profit; socially and politically they consolidate the stability of the overall system within which this is seen to be a legitimate undertaking. Even to the extent that these practices do derive from a particular construction of gender attributes and suitabilities, the need for income is likely to be prioritized above the desire to uncover and change the various gender ideologies which lie behind them. This lack of motivation may appear to be, and can be labelled in terms of 'inertia' and 'tradition', but this mistakes the fact that employers have a vested interest in maintaining the status quo; lack of enthusiasm for change derives less from apparent apathy than from a *positive* motivation to leave things as they are.

To the extent that the economic integrity of the household *also* depends on stability within the mechanisms and practices of employment, it is not surprising that both male and female employees might also prefer things to remain unchanged. When someone says 'things have always been done this way', they could legitimately be interpreted as saying 'I would prefer not run the risk of change since I can at least get by with things as they are'. The clear advantage of the social reproduction approach is that it grasps these essential facts and continues to keep them at the centre of its analysis. It might go against current academic trends to say again that technological and organizational change of the kind discussed in previous chapters has altered the balance of demand for employees between manufacturing and services, and between full- and part-time working, or that both functional and numerical flexibility have brought about new patterns of working and new concentrations of skills, or that women may still be seen by many employers as constituting a 'reserve army' which can be drawn into, and then pushed out of, the workforce as and when required, but it is surely counter-factual to leave these basic economic-structural circumstances out of account. Women would not be in low-pay and low-skill jobs *if* these kinds of jobs were not available. These kinds of jobs would not be available *unless* employers have sound economic reasons for employing people on this basis. These reasons might be quite *different* if work were organized in order to do something other than generate profit. Judgements about who is 'the best person for the job' are bound to be influenced by the fact that as potential employees women constitute a factor of production which has, and more importantly *is seen by employers to have*, particular properties of employability.

What does this analysis tell us about women and the future of work? At the analytical level of feminist accounts themselves, it is clear that the factors which contribute towards women's differential access to paid employment are quite varied and that they interact with one another in highly complex ways. To the extent that no single explanation has yet been able to accommodate all the facts, we can say that this failure tends to confirm the multiple, rather than single origin of gender inequality: no single causal explanation can be found because gender inequality simply does not have a single cause. The greater the amount of descriptive empirical detail, the more obvious this becomes.

In practical terms, current data suggest that although things are changing, it is highly unlikely that current trends and practices are suddenly going to disappear. For as long as households require earned income, and for as long as employers seek to employ people as cheaply as possible, the spaces which female employees fill within the employment matrix are likely to remain. As for possible changes in the rationale of why it is women rather than men who tend to fill these spaces, we know that there is not going to be any revolution in people's attitudes and orientations towards work. Such changes as there are, are most likely to develop at the level of what was referred to in the previous chapter as ideational flexibility. This refers to one of the identifying characteristics of the latest technological paradigm, namely that it is flexible at the level of ideas about what 'work' is and how it should or could be organized.

Accepting that we don't have a free hand here, since obviously potential changes will be limited by the prevailing social and economic environment, we can note a number of tentative possibilities. In the first place, if Freeman and others are correct in suggesting that the current transformation of work will require significant changes in public and political attitudes, and in the institutional framework, then this could create a suitable environment within which a movement towards greater state provision of child care and other facilities, for equality of training opportunities, and for legislation which more fully recognizes the equal worth and value of non-full-time patterns of working, could progress at a more accelerated rate.

Secondly, within the world of work, if HRM and other management strategies are successful in moving towards more diverse methods of planning and decision-making, and towards various forms of group- and team-working, this could accelerate the rate at which old prejudices about how work should be organized can be put to one side. Within such a process, women could have an extremely influential role especially in terms for example, of demonstrating that decisions can be made through co-operation and compromise rather than through typically male approaches of hierarchical authority and argument. In the search for greater efficiency and competitive advantage, how much longer can employers delay in asking themselves what are the qualities of approach and judgement which women can offer at work?

Thirdly, as consumer demand for services increases, and as the economy becomes increasingly dependent on this sector for growth and prosperity, both the people who work in these occupations, and the quality and necessity of the work that they do, could receive a considerable boost in terms of public recognition and status. How realistic is it for society to continue to degradate and denigrate service workers and service occupations when in reality we know that they are indispensable to our personal and economic well-being?

Fourth, and most ambitious, the kinds of changes we have been discussing in this chapter are likely to place increasing pressure on what we mean by 'work'. If it were more explicitly and forcefully acknowledged that in terms of their usefulness to the social reproduction of the household and of the economy, domestic activities are just as valuable as paid activities, that part-time work is not secondary, and that service-type activities are just as worthy as the now almost extinct activities associated with the traditional industries of the recent past, then we might allow ourselves the luxury of imagining that the old stereotype of work is at last being rendered redundant. To the extent that this stereotype has played a pivotal role in the disadvantages women face, then such a change can only be regarded as positive and beneficial.

Since work-roles provide an extremely important basis of familial and personal identity, we need to be aware that a successful decline in the current gender-typing of activities also has deep implications not only for current perceptions of what femininity and masculinity are, but also of the role that 'work' will continue to have in people's lives. These kinds of fundamental changes are made all the more complex and urgent because of other changes which are being set in motion by globalization. We will look at what these new perspectives have to say about the future of work in the following chapter.

5 Work, Identity and the Production/Consumption Debate

One of the most important contributions made by feminist perspectives on work, is that in the future, the idea and meaning of the activities we call work are likely to change. To the extent that work provides people with important opportunities to express their self-perceptions of who and what they are, changes in the concept of work are bound to have repercussions for people's sense of identity, and for perceptions of what their economic and social roles are. If we accept that particular types of jobs, ways of working, and work organization are likely to be matched or paired with particular perceptions of what work is and what it provides, then to the extent that the material organization of work and the composition of the workforce are changing in the ways discussed in previous chapters, we also have to consider the possibility that established distinctions between the roles of men and women, masculine and feminine identities, and between work and non-work activities are also entering a period of transition.

These changes may also prefigure a general reconsideration of the relative weight of importance of work when balanced against all the other types of activities in which people are involved. Although these issues always have lurked in the backs of people's minds, increases in the range of non-work activities in which people are now typically involved may suggest that people have greater choice over how to spend their time. To the extent that work has been 'emptied out' of people's daily activity, a much wider range of non-work, recreational and leisure activities is now available. Non-work time is thus highly valued as an important and expanding terrain upon which people can explore new perceptions of who and what they are. Similarly, the amount of time typically spent on or at work has decreased as a proportion of daily activity, as has the immediacy of that activity in terms of keeping the household going.

This is not to say that work is no longer necessary since, as we have already seen, at least within capitalist societies, households cannot survive without earned income. Rather, and at least amongst the more affluent households, loss of work does not signal immediate disaster in the way that it did for example, during the economic collapses of the 1930s. Up to a point, relative affluence (including property and savings) for some, and welfare payments (unemployment benefit and social security) for others, has allowed a noticeable relaxation of the urgency once associated with work. In these terms then, not only has work changed significantly within its own established public realm (changes in patterns of working, new skills and modes of organization and so on), but the whole concept of work has been thrown back into the melting pot along with all the other activity-ingredients out of which people make the stew of their daily lives. In looking at the future of work, we can identify three areas of current debate. First, if identity and work are closely linked, what might happen to people's sense of identity once or if this important crutch has been removed? Second, if people become less preoccupied with work, what will the new balance between work and non-work activities be in the future; are we witnessing a shifting of the boundaries between work and non-work activities? Third, and assuming there is going to be significant movement in these areas, to what extent will consumption replace production as the primary site of people's life activities?

In looking at each of these debates we need to bear in mind that although both men and women are being affected by the kinds of changes described below, some areas of impact are being more acutely felt by men since, historically, their sense of identity has been much more fully bound up with the world of work. For this reason, the discussion in the earlier part of this chapter will focus more on the experiences and circumstances of men than on those of women.

Identity Crisis

To begin with we need to clarify what we mean by 'identity' in the context of a discussion about work. Most straightforwardly, and as we have already touched upon in chapter one in our discussion of the narratives of work put forward by Marx, Weber and Durkheim, work provides a sense of social identity and social location. We draw upon recognisable and widely shared perceptions of the kind of work that we do, both in terms of the skills and activities involved, and in terms of social value associated with different industries or professions, as a means of registering or calibrating where we stand in relation to other people. To the extent that we have internalized these comparitors, we use them 'externally' as a means of understanding the social and economic gradations of society, and 'internally' as a way of measuring our personal progress against the ideas and aspirations we have set ourselves for our working lives.

168

From a Marxian perspective, the most important signifiers are grounded in our needs for social and economic well-being. Since we cannot survive without meeting these needs, we obviously identify ourselves with the working activities which provide this sense of ontological security. To the extent that we spend a good deal of our time working, the realm of work tends to prefigure other sources of selfhood. For Weber, the signifiers of work are described more in terms of 'market position', 'human capital', or 'life-chances', meaning that the sense we have of who we are as social beings is part-and-parcel of the terms on which we enter the employment relationship. The greater the level of our credentials, the higher is our market value to prospective employers, and thus the more robust is our social and economic position with respect to other people.

Unlike Marx however, Weber introduces the idea of 'status groups' to emphasize how the register of social position is not limited to the realm of work, but is fully active in the non-work realm as well. A doctor for example, has relatively high social and economic status not just because she or he earns a good income but also because of the type and level of lifestyle which this allows. Individuals therefore identify with, and are identifiable to others, in both the working and non-working aspects of their lives. In some instances, this partial dislocation of identity- or status-markers at work from identity- or status-markers at home, means that an individual can have or aspire to a style of life which may seem incompatible with their work-based identity. A dockworker for example, who for Marx would plainly be a member of the working class and would presumably lead a working-class lifestyle, could be a member of a conservative political party, join the local golf club and thus begin constructing their identity according to precepts more usually associated with the middle class.

In making this distinction between 'economic classes' and 'status groups' Weber suggests that individuals are just as, if not more likely, to engage in collective social and political action if they feel that their social status or 'estimation of social honour' is threatened, as they would be if their jobs are threatened. Because work-based and status-based senses of identity are not entirely coterminous, and can thus vary in respect to each other, Weber's account has opened the way for a considerable raising of the stakes in discussing the importance and relevance of non-work-based sources of self- and social identity.

For Durkheim, the sense of identity which derives from work goes beyond the particularities of income, status and lifestyle, and becomes an essential part of our sense of ourselves as participants in the wider social body. From the Durkheimian perspective that 'society' exists over and

169

above the individuals of which it is made, work anchors people's sense that they are securely located as social beings. A sense of social-beingness is a necessary precursor for people's sense of themselves as individuals: without the common identity of being a member of society, individuals would not be able to register their sense of individuality and difference (Durkheim 1933, 1964).

The importance of work, both in terms of particular activities and skills, and in terms of work-as-social-activity, is clearly demonstrated by empirical evidence of the negative consequences of unemployment. Loss of work signifies the removal of the individual from the milieux of working life, and thus seriously undermines the whole range of identity-markers we have just described. As Fineman, and Kalvin and Jarrett put it, there is 'a very powerful image presented of the job satisfying these fundamental needs in a way which no other existing social institution could' (Fineman 1983, p.153):

> [There is] consistent evidence that human beings need a sense of purpose and structure to their lives; that the vast majority derive this purpose and structure very largely from their work; and that to be unemployed is therefore for most people deeply disturbing, distressing, and debilitating. (Kalvin and Jarrett 1985, p.6)

Time and again research has uncovered the direct link between unemployment and economic and ontological distress:

> Redundancy signifies a crucial change in social identity for those who experience it, and one which exposes them to powerful pressures... it involves not simply a change from a secure position of regular employment, with relatively confident expectations about the future, to one of insecurity and uncertainty; but also an exit from an organization, where the daily routine is of collective shared experience with those working alongside, to a highly individualised place in the labour market where the general rule is competition with other unemployed individuals for scarce employment. (Westergaard et al. 1989, pp.81-2)

> Discussions of human consequences of unemployment are full of references to how it lowers self-esteem, saps self-confidence, undermines self-reliance, induces self-disgust, heightens self-consciousness, and so on - all of which cumulatively implies a profound change in the individual's self-concept. (Kalvin and Jarrett 1985, p.44)

Whilst emphasizing that economic insecurity is the primary and overwhelming concern experienced by the unemployed (Jahoda et al. 1971, Eisenberg and Lazarsfield 1938, Beales and Lambert (eds.) 1973, Daniel 1974, Dennehy and Sullivan 1977, Hill 1978, Hayes and Nutman 1981, Marsden 1982, Mann

1986, Gallie *et al.* (eds.) 1993, Ransome 1995), there is clear evidence of people's attachment to work in terms of the more intrinsic senses of identity it provides. To take just one example, respondents to the British Social Attitudes Survey during the 1980s (when unemployment and job insecurity were particularly high in Britain) were asked whether they would still choose to work if there were no financial need to do so (see Table 5.1).[1]

Table 5.1: Attitudes towards work and income
If without having to work, you had what you would regard as a reasonable living income, do you think you would still prefer to have a paid job, or wouldn't you bother?

(Percentages)	1984	1985	1986	1987
Employed respondents				
Still prefer paid job	69	71.9	72.1	-
Wouldn't bother	29	26.5	25.9	-
Other/Don't know	1	1.5	1.8	-
Unemployed				
Still prefer paid job	94	70.0	68.1	77.5
Wouldn't bother	6	21.0	28.8	19.7
Other/Don't know	0	-	2.3	1.4

Source: Jowell *et al.* (eds.) *British Social Attitudes Annual Reports*, 1984, 1985, 1986, 1987, questions 34,26,29; 45,50,54 and 44.

Clearly both employed and unemployed respondents expressed a strong desire to be economically active *over and above* their desire to satisfy basic material needs, with around 71 and 77 per cent respectively preferring a paid job. The strengthening of this preference amongst the unemployed towards the end of this period may indicate that having experienced unemployment themselves, and despite the possibility that they may have been able to develop new areas of activity in the absence of work, these respondents had developed an even stronger desire for paid employment.

Further evidence of people's commitment to the non-financial benefits of working emerges from the 1986 survey, in which a number of questions were asked regarding people's general attitudes towards employment (see Table 5.2).

Table 5.2: Attitudes towards benefits of working
On balance, is your present job...

(Percentages)	Employed	Unemployed	Self-employed
Just a means of earning a living	29.9	35.6	34.4
Means much more than that	70.1	63.7	63.8
of those answering 'much more'... would you feel the same about any job you had?	12.1	16.9	12.0

Source: Jowell *et al.* (eds.) *British Social Attitudes Annual Report*, 1986, questions 8a,28b,57a,57b,45a and 45b.

It is clear that although a degree of instrumentality is evident in all groups, two-thirds of respondents clearly feel that work provides, or at least should provide, more than income alone. The generalized nature of this expectation is born out by the fact that a sizeable minority, particularly amongst unemployed respondents, say that they would feel the same about *any* job (similar findings have also been reported by Field 1977, Brown *et al.* 1983, Westergaard *et al.* 1989, and more recently by Gallie *et al.* (eds.) 1993).

Given that identifying with the work one does and with the people one works with is a crucial forum within which such identifications are articulated and 'made real', it would not be surprising to find that loss of self-concept through loss of social contact is keenly felt by the unemployed (Jahoda 1982, Gershuny 1993). After material insecurity and loss of a sense of purpose and meaning, loss of social contact is heavily emphasized. Such feelings of social deprivation are noted by Hayes and Nutman: the unemployed 'missed the feeling of being one of the team, of having people outside the family and neighbourhood to talk to, the politics and the intrigue of the workplace, and the gossip about people and events' (Hayes and Nutman 1981, p.49).

Illustrating the fact that over 60 per cent of their respondents' comments about the effects of unemployment 'related to a deterioration in social life, some demonstrating extreme loneliness and feeling of losing touch with society', Martin and Wallace quote an unemployed engineering assembler: '"You can become in a little world of your own, nobody to say hello to. You get very lonely. I've been for a walk around just to see another person"' (Martin and Wallace 1984, p.256). These authors also found that this loss of social contact was often associated with a loss of 'self respect'. In addition to the 92 per cent who said that unemployment caused 'boredom', and the 69 per cent who said it made them 'feel useless', over 80 per cent 'considered work to be important for self respect'; 'This suggests that almost half the women looking for work found their work role necessary for the social contact and interesting activity it provided and also for their self-respect' (Martin and Wallace 1984, p.267).

The corrosive effect which these losses can have on the integrity or 'identity' of the household are quite clear: 'It seems wholly likely that family life is shaken by unemployment - often to the point of disintegration - and we have evidence that points towards possible increases in divorce, domestic violence, abortions and unwanted pregnancies, parental and infant mortality, and morbidity in wives and children, as well as evidence of failure of growth in children' (Smith, R. 1987, p.137. Similar findings have been reported by Lampard 1993). Writing about the implications of unemployment for social work practice Keefe concludes that: 'Several studies of people anticipating and experiencing unemployment have found that these people suffer loss of self-esteem, loss of personal identity, worry and uncertainty about the future, loss of a sense of purpose, and depression' (Keefe 1984, p.265). For some, and apart from well-documented increases in stress leading to deep physical and psychological illness (Beales and Lambert 1973, Kasl and Cobb 1979, Nicholas 1986, Gallie and Vogler 1993), a total collapse of a sense of identity can lead to the ultimate abandonment of 'self' itself through suicide (Dennehy and Sullivan 1977, Hayes and Nutman 1981.[2]

Although the relationship between work- and self-concept is known to be one of the underlying identifiers of working-class communities,[3] there is clear evidence that the consequences of loss of identity, social status and self-respect through unemployment are also keenly felt by professionals whose sense of being 'bound in' with the collective work-identity of a particular group might be thought to be less strong. In his account of the effects of job insecurity on lecturers in Further Education for example, Portwood found that:

> Many of these [FE] lecturers suffered severe mental anguish even to the point of temporary loss of identity and purpose. Their career commitment became a major handicap... many considered that monetary compensation could not make up for loss of style of life associated with their careers. Indeed, this career style, especially its physical location, was the basis of self-identity for several of them. Once it was removed, they felt they had lost not only status but meaningful existence. (Portwood 1985, pp.457/461)

This much seems clear enough. Pushing the relationship between work and identity a little further however, and picking up on themes raised within feminist discourses on work discussed in the previous chapter, it becomes clear that work is not simply associated with a *general* perception of self-identity, but with *particular versions* of what the self is and of what kinds of attitudes, expectations and behaviours go with particular identities. This takes us into a more complex set of debates surrounding the important distinction which needs to be made between 'self' and 'identity'.

The issue here is that a person's sense of self - their fundamental inner identification of themselves as a unique being in the world - tends to be prefigured or overshadowed by their perception of what it means to be either a man or a woman. Being a man or a woman means adopting a distinctly *masculine* or *feminine* kind of identity. As the experiences of gay men and lesbians clearly demonstrate, one of the major sources of prejudice they face is precisely that they may adopt identities which seem to others to be quite incongruous with the 'normal' or 'expected' pairings of self with gender identity. Thus, gay men are often ridiculed as being effeminate, and lesbians as being 'butch'. People may be being less critical of femininity or masculinity as such, or even of the 'self' of the person concerned, than of the mis-matching of this identity with the physically gendered body to which it is being attached. Much of the tension which this disengagement of self from identity causes stems from the fact that it may oblige non-gay people to reassess the basis upon which their own assumptions of selfhood and identity are based (for discussions see: Plummer (ed.) 1981, Devor 1989, Wolff 1979, Butler 1990, Garber 1992, Dunne 1997).

At a more personal level, Seidler suggests that for men in particular, the pressure to conform to a 'correct' matching of the male self with masculine behaviour, may actually result in men adopting a highly restricted sense of self:

> We can still experience a strong tension between the ways we experience ourselves and the images we are supposed to live up to.... This denial can mean that we no longer have a sense of self which exists separately from our sense of male identity. We are so anxious as boys to prove that we are *not* girls... that we come to identify our sense of self directly with our sense of male identity. (Seidler 1989, p.18)[4]

In the context of a discussion about the future of work, these observations are important, since one of the central ways of expressing a male self, of being a man, of acting in a masculine way, is through having a job. Put simply, one of the reasons why work is so important to men as a means of understanding what they are and how they should behave, is because work is seen as being an indispensable ingredient of masculinity. As the literature on unemployment shows, for men, loss of employment has serious consequences for their sense of masculinity. To be without work means losing the battle of demonstrating how manly one is. If one's sense of self is constructed entirely in terms of, or is at least heavily dependent upon this demonstration of manliness, then loss of work results in loss of sense of self. This notion of manly status is well described in Marsden's account of Mr Vicker's attitude towards his wife going out to work:

> "You see, I've never lost my, sort of, *manly status*, if you like. That's what he's done, isn't it, the bloke who sends his wife out to work. Fine, O.K. if it's the only way of providing a reasonable standard of living, and the option is for them to both sit at home on national assistance and both be even more miserable. But at the same time you would certainly feel - well, I would - I would certainly feel as though I'd lost a bit of my manly status". (Marsden 1982, p.126)

This account also shows that quite aside from constructions of masculinity around the fact that until recently at least, men were typically involved in jobs which were physically demanding - one had to be a 'real man' in order to cope with the muscular and stamina demands of most jobs - masculinity is fundamentally perceived in terms of being able to provide for wife and family. Mr Vicker feels his loss of manly status in terms of not fulfilling his part of the household bargain. Similarly strong views were expressed by two of Oakley's respondents when questioned about the idea of a reversal of marriage roles - 'the replies given by a factory hand's wife and a journalist's wife were typical':

> "Oh, that's ridiculous - it's up to the woman to look after the kids and do the housework. It wouldn't be my idea of a man. I think a man should go out to work and a woman should look after the house".

> "I don't agree with men doing housework - I don't think it's a man's job... I certainly wouldn't like to see my husband cleaning a room up. I don't think it's mannish for a man to stay at home. I like a man to be a man". (Oakley 1974, p.156)

The longevity and cross-cultural grip of such views is clearly illustrated in the following opinion given by one of Connells's young Australian working-class male respondents during the 1990s:

I believe that a female is more adept physically and psychologically to endure the trials and tribulations of bringing up a home, controlling a home and family. While, a male may not necessarily be physically stronger... but... in a sort of majority basis more, not ambitious, but greedy for the work; and feel that they need the responsibility to bring home the bread, for example'. (Paul Nikolaou, quoted in Connell 1995, p.167)

This common perception of the social and familial ordering of responsibilities highlights two issues which are particularly important in discussions about the future of work. First, perceptions of male and female identities tend to be *relational* in that the attributes associated with the one are to be contrasted with those of the other. Clearly this echoes the idea of the gendering of work both in terms of particular tasks (men do heavy work, women don't), and in terms of who goes out to work (men) and who doesn't (women). As more and more women take up paid employment, both of these sets of assumptions about the 'natural' linkages between working, identity and sense-of-self become less and less certain. Whilst there are many explicit examples of the disengagement of women and men from their traditional roles (women doing 'male' jobs in industry, men doing 'female' jobs in services; women who opt for a career rather than motherhood, and men who leave work to raise children) a more subtle process may be at work here involving the gradual emptying out of the categories of masculinity and femininity themselves. It is not just that women can do men's jobs (the fact that women and children used to haul coal wagons underground in the mines, or that women provided almost the entire workforce in the munitions factories in Britain during the Second World War are clear historical precedents of this despite being edited-out of the collective memory), but that if women are doing this kind of work, then where does this leave the sense of 'maleness' or 'masculinity' which such jobs supposedly entail? Correspondingly, within the household, if a (new) man chooses to become a 'househusband', then doesn't this entail some rewriting of the script about what constitutes femininity? These dilemmas highlight the second point that the sense of loss of self-respect expressed by Mr Vickers, shows that perceptions of maleness and masculinity are very closely linked with the idea and role of men as 'breadwinners'.

Looking at the origins of this key-stone of male identity, and leaving the material compulsion of providing for households to one side for the moment, Seidler has argued that the breadwinner role is deeply rooted in, and is a constituent part of, a distinctly masculinized version of what the world is, how we should understand it, and how we should act within it. Adopting ideas about the importance of 'self-sufficiency', 'self-reliance' and 'individuality' from the Protestant Reformation, and combining these with Enlightenment ideas about the superiority of 'reason' over 'emotion', and thus of the need to exercise 'self-control', men not only identified themselves with an endless responsibility for providing for themselves and their families, but insisted that this masculinized, instrumentalized and acquisitive orientation towards life and how to deal with it, was the *only* 'rational' and reasoned way to proceed (see also Winter and Robert 1980, Giddens 1991, Rojek 1995, and Connell 1995, pp.156ff).

Men's monopoly of elite positions not only in social and economic life, but particularly in the world of academic debate and scientific discovery, allowed them to consolidate this position with relative ease:

> The new sciences of the seventeenth century saw themselves as a new masculinist philosophy. So a rationalist philosophy saw itself as essentially masculine, and was an integral part of establishing a new pattern of sexual relationships of power. (Seidler 1989, p.46)

A similar narrative is developed by Connell. He suggests the following main ingredients: 'the cultural change that produced new understandings of sexuality and personhood in metropolitan Europe'; 'the new emphasis on the individuality of expression and on each person's unmediated relationship with God [leading towards] individualism and the concept of an autonomous self'; 'the creation of overseas empires [which] was a gendered enterprise from the start'; 'the growth of the cities that were the centres of commercial capitalism'; and 'the onset of large-scale European civil war' which gave rise to 'the strong centralized state' (Connell 1995, pp.186-9).

Having committed themselves to this agenda, it was inevitable that being a man, and being a *successful* man, could only really be demonstrated by cultivating a state of independence and self-sufficiency. Success in this effort, both inwardly as measured against one's conscience, and outwardly as measured against one's social and material status, became a signifier of other 'manly' qualities such as physical and psychological strength, skill and professionalism, and perseverance and endeavour (Seidler 1989, pp.50/143). Not being able to live up to this personally and socially imposed set of expectations is often experienced in terms of becoming a burden on society, a scrounger rather than a provider. For example, Westergaard *et al.* record the feelings of a 63-year-old stamper facing this predicament: "I never thought I'd have to do that, never... that was for those who weren't bothered to try... scroungers... that sort, not for me"' (Westergaard *et al.* 1989, p.98). Indeed, Dennehy and Sullivan found that this sense of loss of face actually inhibited one of their respondents from taking part in an interview at all: 'We were told by the wife of one man who had been out of work for two years and had several children that her husband did not wish to talk of his experiences of unemployment - [because] he had come increasingly to think of himself as a "scrounger"' (Dennehy and Sullivan 1977, p.62).

This testimony vividly shows the closeness of the linkages between outer material 'failure' as measured against the canons of competitive-acquisitive individualism, and the inner and deeply personal perceptions of the integrity of the self as measured against the ideal of self-sufficiency. The grip of the former over the latter within capitalist societies is such that it requires an enormous effort to maintain a sense of self unless one is successful in material terms. This suggests that the construction of a sense of self is subject at one and the same time to inner or self-imposed pressures (akin to the psychological pressures of the threat of spiritual damnation identified by Weber), and to the pull of external forces (akin to changes in the mode of production identified by Marx), and all of this in the context of possible shifts in perceptions of what the relationship between the individual and society has actually become (the basic tension identified by Durkheim).

To the extent that the integrity of the self depends on an at least minimal degree of correspondence between the goals set by these inner and external pressures, one would expect that as changes occur in the material circumstances in which people live, so also will people, and particularly men, have to reassess or re-negotiate with themselves what those goals are or have become. There would be little point for example, in a man investing large amounts of their sense of self in the identity-capital of belligerent chauvinism once these attitudes have become the subject of popular derision.

In recognizing the identity-pull of the exterior world on people's sense of self it is possible to see a way out of the dilemma noted in the previous chapter where the apparent fixity of particular perceptions of femininity and masculinity, of femaleness and maleness, and of the roles and behaviours which are seen as consonant with them, act as a dead weight to change. Whilst accepting that these gendered ideologies are deeply rooted in a sense of tradition, and that people are disinclined to abandon them, this does not mean that they can *never* be changed. The possibility of relinquishing these markers of identity becomes even more likely, if to the increasing pull of material changes in the world of work and the household division of labour, we add the increasing push of people trying and wanting to alter their sense of self from within. *Separately*, external pressure for change and internal desire for change may be insufficient to generate shifts in prevailing assumptions about identity; *together*, they may establish a new momentum for change. Whilst we should acknowledge that these shifts may have different kinds of impact on men and women - it cannot be assumed for example that women have ever been so fully intimidated by the pressures of acquisitive self-interest as men have - it is nonetheless the case that the possibilities open to women in terms of how to construct their sense of self have had to engage with these perceptions. Indeed, pressure from women to have equal access to the identity- and status-markers of employment, and to expose the fact that activities within the household play a crucial part in social reproduction, constitutes one of the most significant aspects of change itself.

This idea of the re-negotiation of the self, and thus of the kinds of identity markers which are appropriate to it, has become a dominant theme in discussions about what exactly constitutes masculinity and femininity, and more particularly, of what they might become. As Giddens has described it, the quest for selfhood has become a highly reflexive process:

> In the post-traditional order of modernity, and against the backdrop of new forms of mediated experience, self-identity becomes a reflexively organised endeavour. The reflexive project of the self, which consists in the sustaining of coherent, yet continuously revised, biographical narratives, takes place in the context of multiple choices as filtered through abstract systems.... Because of the 'openness' of social life today, the pluralisation of contexts of action and the diversity of 'authorities', lifestyle choice is increasingly important in the constitution of self-identity and daily activity. Reflexively organised life-planning... becomes a central feature of the structuring of self-identity. (Giddens 1991, p.5)

In terms of analytical and theoretical approach, the point of departure here is the idea that rather than being fixed and irreducible, gendered perceptions of masculinity and femininity, and thus of self, are much more fluid constructions which vary in relation to changes in historical and social circumstances. Following a detailed critique of 'sex-role theory' which, despite adopting the now largely discredited paradigm of sociobiology, had popularized the idea of fixed roles up until the 1970s, (see for example David and Brannon 1976, for a critique see Carrigan *et al* 1985, and Connell 1983, 1987), Connell suggests that rather than treating perceptions of appropriate roles and behaviours as 'pre-existing norms which are passively internalized and enacted, the new approach explores the making and remaking of conventions of social practice itself' (Connell 1995,p.35):

> Masculinities are configurations of practice structured by gender relations. They are inherently historical; and their making and remaking is a political process affecting the balance of interests in society and the direction of social change. (Connell 1995, p.44)

179

Engaging with the notion that the construction of the self is symbolic as well as material, and taking up ideas developed by Turner about the importance of the physical body (Turner 1984, 1992) and its embeddedness in processes of identity formation, Connell goes on to point out that notions of sociobiology have also been pushed aside by a greater emphasis on the semiotics of self construction. Whereas the earlier approach had tended to use signifiers borrowed from engineering as a means of describing the way people approached their bodies, semiotic variants of the social-constructionist approach represent the body and thus the self which lies within it, in much more fluid and non-mechanistic terms:

> Rather than social arrangements being the effects of the body-machine, the body is a field on which social determination runs riot. This approach too has its leading metaphors, which tend to be metaphors of art rather than engineering: the body as a canvas to be painted, a surface to be imprinted, a landscape to be marked out. (Connell 1995, p.50)

The active subject no longer works on their body as a receptacle of the self in the manner of Captain Picard on the bridge of the *USS Enterprise*, the chief engineer in the control room of the brain, but more in the manner of the conductor of the orchestra, the choreographer or artistic director.

From the point of view of working identities, we can suggest that at least a part of the perception of manliness associated with heavy industrial jobs was the sheer physicality of the activity; as we have already noted, physical strength and stamina were signifiers of manliness in these working contexts. To the extent that these kinds of tasks are becoming much less common, one could anticipate that this criterion of masculinity is becoming less important, or has at least shifted out of the working realm and into the realm of sport and leisure (Connell's description of the desired attributes of sporting activities in terms of their involving 'the combination of force and skill' could just as easily be applied to someone operating a piece of equipment in a factory).

Interestingly though, and as Connell points out, the association of masculinity with particular kinds of activity which fulfil these criteria of physicality are being gradually displaced by criteria of technical competence. It may not be very 'manly' in the now displaced traditional sense to work with computers in offices, these activities do not 'use up' or 'exhaust' the body in quite the same way, but the way is still open for at least some male employees to express their manliness through the intellectual rather than muscular 'mastery' of the technology:

> The combination of force and skill is thus open to change. Where work is altered by deskilling and casualization, working-class men are increasingly

defined as possessing force alone.... Middle-class men, conversely, are increasingly defined as the bearers of skill. This definition is supported by credentialism, linked to a higher education system that selects and promotes along class lines.... The new information technology requires much sedentary keyboard work, which was initially classified as women's work. The marketing of personal computers, however, has redefined some of this work as an arena of competition and power - masculine, technical, but not working-class. These revised meanings are promoted in the text and graphics of computer magazines, in manufacturers' advertising that emphasizes 'power'. (Connell 1996, pp.55-6, drawing on Donaldson 1991)[5]

This is quite a neat trick since it accommodates structural changes in patterns of working whilst retaining at the level of ideational legitimation the post-Enlightenment association of scientific expertise with manliness, an association which has been periodically recast first with the post-industrial theorists highlighting of the importance of 'technical knowledge' (Bell and Galbraith), and more recently still with the 'expert systems' described by Giddens (see chapter two above).

These kinds of shifts in the ways in which masculinity and femininity are signified and constructed shows that people have available to them more than one type of masculinity or femininity; masculinities and femininities are *plural* rather than *singular*. At one level this plurality refers to differences in the constitution of masculinity and femininity which are influenced by broad differences of class and ethnicity. For example, although middle-class men may share some of the same masculine traits as their working-class contemporaries, these two varieties of masculinity are not identical. Similarly, a black woman's sense of her femininity will not be quite the same as that of her non-black neighbours.

At a slightly deeper level, this variety opens the possibility that as the pace and scope of change in contemporary society increases, men and women respectively are not actually faced with a choice between having *a* masculinity or *a* femininity or of having none at all (akin to the experience of many unemployed men during the 1980s), but of shifting their self-perception and their sense of self from one variety of masculinity or femininity to another variety. As the proportion of the workforce which is involved in non-manual and largely non-physical kinds of work increases we can anticipate that new measures of manliness and womanliness will be on offer. Connotations of weakness, sensitivity and passivity once associated by men with non-manual and non-industrial work are bound to change as more and more men are employed in these kinds of work. These individuals will not cease to be 'men', they will not loose their male bodies, but will simply redraft their sense of masculinity to match the new circumstances.

For women, and recalling the discussion in the previous chapter about how more and more women are acquiring high-level credentials, we can also anticipate that since physical strength is of little importance when it comes to judging a person's aptitudes and suitability for an increasing number of jobs, one of the earlier barriers to women's employment opportunities is on the way out. Further still, as the criteria of employability are extended to include the kinds of skills and experiences where women hold the advantage - less argumentative approaches to decision-making, a greater willingness to overtly accept and accommodate the feelings and expectations of other people, and perhaps a more universalist approach to work-organization - new and enlivened debates might emerge about the true social status and actual economic importance of people who have those skills. Rather than relying wholly on male-oriented criteria as the base-line for making such evaluations, a new kind of balance might emerge between these and female-oriented criteria.

The Relationality of Gender Relations

Having recognized that notions of maleness and femaleness are socially constructed, and having noted that masculinity and femininity are plural rather than singular constructs, we also have to acknowledge that like the broad categories of masculinity and femininity, the different versions of identity to which they give rise are not self-contained and free-standing but are *relational*. As Connell puts it:

> To recognize diversity in masculinities is not enough. We must also recognize the *relations* between the different kinds of masculinity: relations of alliance, dominance and subordination. These relationships are constructed through practices that exclude and include, that intimidate, exploit, and so on. There is a gender politics within masculinity. (Connell 1995, p.37)

This sense of relationality between available identity markers underscores something which we noted in our earlier discussion of patriarchy, namely that according to this theory, it is not just men who seek to dominate women, but that it is older and/or more powerful men who attempt to dominate younger/weaker men (see Cockburn 1983). Similarly, those who operate with a highly heterosexual perception of masculinity are likely to try to dominate other men who do not. Borrowing ideas developed by Antonio Gramsci (see Ransome 1992), Connell has usefully characterized this process of contestation, of alliance, domination and subordination, in terms of what he calls the emergence of 'hegemonic masculinity'. Put simply, the point he wishes to get across is that at any one time, one particular variety or version of masculinity tends to hold sway; all manifestations and representations of masculinity or femininity are equal but some are more equal than others:

> There is an ordering of versions of femininity and masculinity at the level of the whole society... the forms of masculinity and femininity constituted at this level are stylized and impoverished. Their interrelation is centred on a single structural fact, the global dominance of men over women. This structural fact provides the main basis for relationships among men and women that define a hegemonic form of masculinity in the society as a whole. 'Hegemonic masculinity' is always constructed in relation to various subordinated masculinities as well as in relation to women. (Connell 1987, p.183)

Although '"hegemony" does not mean total cultural dominance, the obliteration of alternatives' (ibid., p.184), Connell goes on to paint a picture of how this dominant/dominating masculinity tends to represent other versions of masculinity and representations of femininity as somehow incomplete or immature. To the extent that masculinities have tended to dominate femininities, one important consequence of the strategy of cultural domination has therefore been to prevent the development of fully mature alternatives to the prevailing form, alternatives which might come to threaten its dominant position. As a result of this, and because ideas about femininity have tended to develop under the shadow of, and in relation to, the precepts and criteria of the prevailing masculinity, the development of a properly hegemonic femininity has been greatly hindered:

> There is no femininity that is hegemonic in the sense that the dominant form of masculinity is hegemonic among men.... At the level of mass social relations, however, forms of femininity are defined clearly enough.... One form is defined around compliance with [the subordination of women to men] and is oriented to accommodating the interests and desires of men. I will call this 'emphasized femininity'. (Connell 1987, p.183)

Whilst at the surface the currently prevailing version of masculinity may appear to be quite solid - Connell emphasizes how the culture industry has played an important role in creating and replicating a gloss of powerful images of the rugged, determined, predatory male, and has contrasted these with derogatory images of the effeminate male and the weak female - on closer inspection it is clear that its dominance is actually built on rather insecure foundations. He suggests for example, that in as much as the prevailing form is highly stylized very few men actually live up to the image they are supposed to have, and that many men are only 'dominant' because the framework of gender relations allows them to be so and not because of any inherent properties of superiority which inhere in them as men.

Perhaps most important is the recognition that hegemonic masculinity tends to impose within its own apparently consistent overall framework, quite different kinds of demands on the aspiring male: 'hegemonic masculinity can contain at the same time, quite consistently, openings towards domesticity and openings towards violence, towards misogyny and towards heterosexual attraction' (Connell 1987, p.186). Once we have recognized that hegemonic masculinity is a dynamic and inherently historically variable construction which exists in relation to competing alternatives, we can also see that through various 'strategies of resistance or forms of non-compliance', and by means of complex 'strategic combinations of compliance, resistance and co-operation' (ibid. 184), the prevailing form is always open to challenges from newly-emerging alternatives (in Gramscian terms, the emergence of a new 'historical bloc' of identity).

As one might expect, the extent to which such a challenge is likely to be successful depends on the arena in which the conflict takes place, and on how essential are the facets of hegemonic masculinity which are being challenged. Borrowing Habermas's idea of a 'legitimation crisis' (Habermas 1976), Connell suggests that during the 1980s and into the 1990s four of these key realms or dimensions of support have indeed weakened. First, changes in patterns of working, in the types of tasks being done, and in the composition of the workforce, have undermined important aspects of the work-based anchors of 'traditional' masculinity and thus of received perceptions of male identity. Second, a gradual erosion of both the reality and the perception of what constitutes a household and how it works have undermined stereotypical notions of the breadwinner role. Third, changes in the nature and register of sexual expression (both between and within genders) have undermined assumptions about the inevitability or 'naturalness' of heterosexuality. Fourth, and echoing elements of Walby's account of the role of the women's movement in instigating a transition from the private to the public form of patriarchy, the 'movement for the emancipation of women', and an increasingly universal rejection of the 'underlying contradiction between the inequality of women and men' has resulted in 'a historic collapse of the legitimacy of patriarchal power' (Connell 1995, pp.84/85).

Furthermore, since it is highly likely that the realms of work, the household, sexuality and social and political beliefs are going to continue to be of central importance as bases of identity formation, and since it is precisely in these realms that women are gaining ground, it will be extremely difficult to resist the legitimacy of what they have to say. An attempt for example, to suggest that it does not matter that women are taking a leading role in the workforce because the realm of work is not as important as it once was (meaning when men held the upper hand), would clearly be idiotic since these realms of experience *are* just as important as they ever were.

In summarizing these arguments, we can see that there are reasonably strong grounds for anticipating that both the range of different masculinities and femininities on offer, and the content of those choices are likely to continue to change. To the extent that the renegotiation of what gender means and of how the various relationships between different gender positions are organized is now being conducted *across* as well as *between* the main categories of maleness and femaleness, new possibilities would seem to be on offer in terms of the kinds of linkages which can be made between self and identity.

It is important to recogize however, that *greater* choice does not mean *complete and unrestricted* choice. Firstly, and as Connell concludes: 'despite the emphasis on multiple masculinities and on contradiction, few researchers have doubted that the social construction of masculinities is a systematic process' (Connell 1995, p.38). As we have seen, there are identifiable patterns of change at work in all of this, a goodly number of which are more or less directly related to structural changes in the world of work and in the household. Without denying the importance of changes in perceptions of gendered identities we have to accept that they are in many cases consequential rather than originating. Second, although it is tempting to imagine that earlier stereotypes and assumptions about what constitutes masculinity and femininity have been laid to rest, there is clear evidence that advocates of the old hegemony will not give up without a fight, and that new and reactionary counter movements will also emerge to fight this rear-guard action (Petchesky 1986, Bly 1992, Pfeil 1995, Abbott and Wallace 1992, Garner 1996).

Thirdly, having usefully identified that perceptions of identity have a symbolic dimension to them, it would be quite inaccurate to imply *that the whole of* the self and identity can be understood in these terms:

> The social semiotics of gender, with its emphasis on the endless play of signification, the multiplicity of discourses and the diversity of subject positions, has been important in escaping the rigidities of biological determinism. But it should not give the impression that gender is an autumn leaf, wafted about by the light breezes. Body-reflexive practices form - and are formed by - structures which have historical weight and solidity. (Connell 1995, p.65)

185

In the same way that the highly dichotomous characterization of gender-identity, of masculinity and femininity is gradually being set aside in favour of a much more open and dynamic approach, so also are perceptions of the divisions between the realms of work and non-work. In the following sections we will look at these debates first in terms of a possible shifting of the boundaries between work and non-work activities (both in terms of the activities themselves and in terms of the attribution of value and status to them), and second in terms of the extent to which consumption may replace production as the primary site of people's sense of identity and self.

The Work/Non-work Divide

Although it is certainly premature to suggest that the work/non-work divide is about to collapse, the more modest claim that there is a shifting of the boundaries between these two realms finds much support in established debates about the way in which the concept of 'work' is socially constructed. The basic point at issue here, is whether or not a highly dichotomous perception of work and non-work as quite distinct realms of activity each having specific characteristics not found in the other is actually very useful or realistic. Whilst there always has been a considerable blurring of the two realms, recent changes in the composition of the workforce and patterns of working (greater female participation, numerical and functional flexibility, shifts into part-time working and so on), together with changes in people's perceptions and expectations of work, may be leading towards a more forthright recognition of just how porous the work/non-work divide actually is. Even more significantly, they may also highlight the inherent *arbitrariness* of some of the criteria which are currently used in defining which activities count as 'work' and which do not.

To illustrate these possibilities, whilst we have already seen how specific notions such as skill and authority have been utilized by men as a means of excluding women from various jobs and careers, this process of social construction is also evident at the more general level of divisions between activities within and without the household. In her now classic study the *Sociology of Housework* for example, Oakley shows that with the single exception of being paid for doing it (and despite 'its isolation and the lack of social recognition accorded to the responsibilities carried by the housewife' Oakley 1974, p.75), on any reasonable measure of what constitutes 'work', the constituting activities of housework certainly fall well within this category.

Moreover, and specifically recognizing the experiential aspects of these

186

activities (degree of autonomy, levels of satisfaction, skills and routines involved and so on) in terms of what they mean for the sense of identity of those who do them, Oakley chastises researchers and others for 'tacitly subscribing to the myth of feminine passivity' by failing 'to represent the meaning of housework to the actors (actresses) themselves' (ibid p.27):

> The women in the sample experience and define housework as labour, akin to that demanded by any job situation. Their observations tie in closely with many findings of the sociology of work; the aspects of housework that are cited as satisfying or dissatisfying have their parallels in the factory or office world. This equivalence is emphasized further by the women's own tendency to compare their reactions to housework with their experience of working outside the home. (Oakley 1974, p.40)

Similar points have been made by liberal writers such as Pahl, who draws on historical accounts of pre- and early-industrial households to show how the economic well-being of the household is not achieved through a simple dichotomy between (public) working activities which are paid for and (private) working activities which are not, but involves its members in a much more complex 'strategy' of participations in what he labels 'by-employments' (meaning jobs done in addition to one's main occupation), 'occupational easements' (privileged access to resources associated with the place of work) and 'self-provisioning' (doing it yourself):

> Household work strategies are made up of the different kinds of work undertaken by members of a household and the use of other sources of labour on which they can draw.... Typically, in most accounts of work, much attention is given to the regular waged employment undertaken by men. [In this account however], more attention is given to the other work that men do - the easements of their occupations, their by-employments, whether waged or unwaged, and the work they do within and for their domestic groups. (Pahl 1984, p.30)

He goes on the suggest that despite the fact that most households have become entirely dependent upon wage labour: 'it is quite possible to describe households in the 1980s where the mix of work is broadly the same as it was in the thirteenth century' (Pahl 1984, pp.54/55). Pahl's contribution also added detail to the importance of the informal or 'black' economy as a kind of twilight realm of resource-getting, and to a wider understanding of the so-called 'informal work' associated with it, both of which further undermined dichotomous perceptions of the realms of work and non-work (Pahl 1984, see also Pahl and Wallace 1984, Gershuny and Pahl 1979, Gershuny 1979, Gershuny and Miles 1983).

Writing from a much more radical perspective, and despite the fact that his contribution has been lambasted for its utopian and idealist overtones (Pahl 1984, Sayers 1987, Frankel 1987; for a defence see Bowring 1996, and Lodziak and Tatman 1997), Gorz (1982, 1989) has persuasively argued that the productivistic ethic of capitalism has fallen foul of its own framing of 'work' in terms of very specific economistic criteria:

> *Work* has not always existed in the way in which it is currently understood. It came into being at the same time as capitalists and proletarians. It means an activity carried out: for someone else; in return for a wage; according to forms and time schedules laid down by the person paying the wage; and for a purpose not chosen by the worker. (Gorz 1982, p.1)

Having defined work primarily in terms of the payment criterion, serious problems arise when this kind of work is becoming more and more insecure, or is disappearing altogether. Writing at a time when this was happening throughout Western society Gorz concludes: 'Work and the work-based society are not in crisis because there is not enough to do, but because *work in a very precise sense* [i.e. work-for-a-wage] has become scarce, and the work that is to be done now falls less and less into that particular category' (Gorz 1989, p.153, original emphasis).

Trapped within their productivist logic, and preferring to salvage their own particular definition of work-as-paid-activity rather than allowing any wider reconsideration of alternative criteria and thus definitions of work, capitalist employers sought to create 'work' by allowing economic rationality to colonize spheres of activity which had not previously been included within the category of work-as-paid-work. He suggests for example, that this has happened most clearly in the 'commercialization' of 'private' tasks and services which were previously done by and for members of the household outside the 'public' labour market. Furthermore, the process of commercialization does not render the doing of these tasks more efficient and thus less time consuming, but actually results in an *increase* in the amount of time which society spends on them:

> The idea is that these tasks should occupy the greatest number of people and absorb as much working time as possible, but in the form, in this instance, of commercial services.... It is no longer labour that is scarce, but paid jobs. Now more hours of paid work are to be devoted to domestic tasks than they would actually take up if everyone did them for themselves. 'Making work', 'creating jobs': these are the goals of the new tertiary anti-economy. (Gorz 1989, p.155)

Ironically then, and quite *irrationality* from the point of view of furthering the development of a society in which the amount of time spent on socially necessary work could be reduced and the amount of non-work activity increased, the evident labour-saving benefits of technological advance (first in manufacturing and more recently in services), and the subsequent commercialization of previously non-commercial activities, cause a crisis of work rather than a liberation from it.

Following this theme of the origins and continuing appropriateness of the criteria which are used to distinguish between work and non-work, and as I have argued extensively elsewhere (Ransome 1996), one of the most significant future possibilities of recent material and attitudinal changes in the world of work is that they might lead to a shedding of such inflexible and formalized divisions between the two realms of activity, and to a loosening of the perceptions of value and status attached to them. Whilst at an extrinsic level it is appropriate to use the payment criterion as a way of distinguishing between the doing of identical activities (a woman who cares for her child at home is 'mothering', while the *same* person doing the *same* activities within a hospital is 'working'), at the deeper level of the significance and meaning of those activities we might choose to place much more emphasis on the intrinsic criteria of 'work'. In Gorz's words:

> It is not therefore enough merely to define the criteria on which economic rationality is based. *We have to define the criteria by which we judge them to be applicable.* If we are to do this, we must examine our activities more closely and ask what meaning the relations they allow us to establish with other people contain and whether these relations are compatible with economic rationality. (Gorz 1989, p.137, emphasis added)

Although there would be as much resistance to this kind of approach as there is to the changing of gender ideologies, the present tendency to assess the worth and value of an activity almost exclusively in economistic terms does not preclude the possibility of alternatives. A first step is to recognize that unlike criteria of creativity, purposefulness and sociability, the criterion of productivistic/economistic utility is a feature of the systemic relationships within which work is currently organized rather than being a characteristic of activity as such. Whilst it is quite unrealistic to propose a concept of work which *does not* include criteria such as the expenditure of energy, or purposefulness, or creativity, *it is* possible to imagine one where work is not primarily defined in terms of the payment criterion. It is not wholly unrealistic to imagine that such alternatives may be given more of an airing as part of the process of reconsidering the work-non-work divide.

189

Returning to our opening discussion about the impact of work on identity, a more realistic perception of important similarities of experience which cut across the work/non-work divide may be accompanied by a shifting of people's sense of how they see themselves and of what they would like to get from work. We have already seen for example, that the prevailing dogmatism of competitive acquisitiveness gives rise to a highly unidimensional sense of what work means in terms of identity. One of the possibilities for the future is that a new and much more multidimensional sense of individualism or identity-as-an-individual might emerge in which people feel able to sustain their sense of ontological security across a span of activities including, but not exclusively associated with work proper. This process may draw its momentum from, and indeed feed into, a more general review of the attributes which are currently associated with work and non-work respectively. For example, rather than being seen and experienced as a burden, as a realm devoid of autonomy and enjoyment, a greater emphasis might emerge within the realm of work on the more creative and pleasurable attributes usually associated with the non-work realm.

Whilst it is false to suggest that 'work' will become fully transformed into a realm of 'play' - we do after all have to work in order to gain an income - or that this kind of transformation will emerge equally within all kinds of work - many jobs are inherently non-creative and burdensome - there may still be a general shift in what we can call the *ambience* of work. Similarly, and to the extent that work casts a paler and shorter shadow over the non-work realm, a less mechanical or automatic distinction might emerge between the two, such that expectations of what work *should* offer might be more explicitly formed in terms of the rewards and satisfactions we expect to get from our leisure activities. This is another example of the ideational flexibility noted in previous chapters; given that it is often and increasingly technically possible to exercise greater choice over *how* work should be organized, then why not incorporate into this planning process ideas and expectations from outside work?

If it is the case that greater choice of non-work activities is resulting in an expansion of people's desires and expectations about the activities they do - even perhaps to the extent that 'choice' is now seen as a basic entitlement or 'right' - then surely it is only a matter of time before these demands are felt at work. Seeking to restrain demands for more convivial working arrangements, for more creative types of work, and for a greater accommodation of household responsibilities, can only lead to a new and enhanced state of dissatisfaction and alienation.

The Production/Consumption Divide

Continuing with the theme of identity, and picking up on the idea that individuals' own desire to change their sense of self acts as a push against earlier preconceptions of selfhood and individuality, debates have arisen over *where* such alternative markers of identity might be found. The point at issue here, is not just that the boundaries of work and non-work are shifting in the ways just described, but that the non-work realm of leisure and other forms of consumption may actually be *replacing* the world of work as the primary source of identity. In Mort's words: 'Carrying the significance which once had been ascribed to work, it was argued that consumption had now come to occupy the 'cognitive focus of life'.... Self-reflexivity - the cultivation of the self, physically as well as psychologically - was understood to be enshrined in the current orchestration of consumption' (Mort 1996, p.6). There are a number of steps to this argument.

It is widely accepted that since the affluent days of the 1960s and despite the recessions of the 1980s, a significant proportion of the population has been able to divert increasing amounts of its income and to spend larger proportions of its time in consuming rather than producing goods and services.[6] The major sites of increasing consumption are not (as they were during the 1950s and early-1960s) devoted to buying more and more of the basic necessities on which physical well-being depends, but on purchasing new kinds of goods whose 'necessity' relates to the satisfaction of more elaborate kinds of needs, many of which are directly related to identity-formation:

> Consumption has ceased to be purely material or narrowly functional - the satisfaction of basic bodily needs. Today consumption is both symbolic and material. It expresses, in a real sense, a person's place in the world, his or her core identity. (Stewart 1992, p.204 quoting Gardner and Sheppard 1989, p.3)

This transition from consuming things associated with traditional necessities towards consuming things which satisfy new or acquired necessities links to part of the Fordism/post-Fordism debate which we looked at in chapter two, about how the mass consumption of the 1950s and 1960s has been superseded by the much more bespoke or personalized demand for goods which emerged during the 1980s and 1990s. It is no longer sufficient to be able to purchase the same goods and services as everyone else; it is the *differences* in the choices we make and the things we buy which makes *us* different. Mass consumer goods are now only 'mass' in terms of how they are produced but not in terms of how they are consumed:

Rising overall affluence and changing production methods have provided both the desire and the means to move away from mass-produced products and hence mass consumption. In this environment less status accrues from the simple ability to buy goods and services, but more from what specifically is bought and how that is different from what others buy. This has resulted in the increasingly fragmentary nature of consumption. (Stewart 1990, p.217)

Although in its exterior manifestations, consumption remains a 'communal' activity in the sense that we are all part of 'consumer society' (a trip to the local shopping centre or mall will confirm this point), its interior manifestation is very much to do with self-perceptions of individuality. This introduces the possibility that in the same way that a particular construction of individuality tends to be associated with person-as-worker, a new kind of individuality might be associated with person-as-consumer. The really interesting point here, is not just that these twin senses of individuality exist alongside one another (people always have made an at least minimal distinction within themselves between their work and non-work identities), but that the limits or restrictions imposed by traditional perceptions of what individuality is are much less fixed in the non-work realm of consumption than they are in the world of work. It is not just a question of moving out of one field of identity formation and into another, but of considering the new possibilities which are now on offer; possibilities which might come to affect *both* realms. As Stewart puts it:

> Once an individual acquired certain real features, in terms of age, sex, and so on, then the expectation was that they would acquire a fairly narrow set of values which 'limited' their behaviour. Increasingly, as society has become more affluent and the old social mores, relating to age, class, and gender have broken down, it seems evident that we are free to 'appropriate' meanings into our lives from just about wherever we choose. (Stewart 1992, p.220)

A very similar diagnosis of the possible breaking down of these traditional markers of social position and identity, and of the 'authority structure' which goes with them was famously put forward by the Henley Centre for Forecasting as early as 1986. Suggesting that 'deference to traditional authorities in Britain has now hit an all-time low', they proposed that the new source of 'authority' comes from *within* people rather than being *imposed* upon them by society:

> After years of the ideology of individualism... 'production side values' have fallen into low esteem.... Nowadays, we no longer know our place.... But does this imply the absence of any authorities at all? The answer is no. Whilst the authority of class, of the production side of life, has declined, that of the

consumption side has risen... we talk of a more discriminating form of materialism in which, in essence, the motive has changed from one of seeking to keep up with the Joneses to one where we are seeking to keep away from them (so to speak). The authority we tend to use for this is from within rather than external. (The Henley Centre for Forecasting, 1986, p.117, quoted in Mort 1996, p.103)

The chief referent for both judging and constructing this new approach to the world is thus a revised or modernized type of individuality centred on the self: 'The demise of the ethos of production, together with a corresponding rise of a reformulated code of individualism, was generating a more internalised hierarchy of authority. It was the self, Henley claimed, which now functioned as the highest court of appeal' (Mort 1996, pp.103-4).

At a slightly more abstract and generalized level of analysis, and joining the throng who have followed the diagnosis of late-modern capitalism as 'disorganized' (Offe 1985, Lash and Urry 1987, 1994), Rojek suggests that there are significant differences between the practice of leisure and consumption in the earlier and later stages of modernity. In the period of 'Modernity 1' (say from around 1780 to 1980), which is characterized as being orderly and controlled, individuals were faced with relatively limited choices; choices which only offered a semblance of true individuality and freedom:

Our consumption and leisure experience is composed of mass-produced items and standardized accessories which can be found anywhere. On this reading, leisure in mass culture is not about a search for authenticity or fulfilment; instead it consists of distraction activity. What one is distracting oneself from is the realization that originality, uniqueness and spontaneity are dead. (Rojek 1995, p.85)

With the coming of 'Modernity 2' (from the 1980s onwards), which is characterized as being disorganized, fragmentary and thus tendentially out of control, people's experiences, both within and outside work have become much more transitory and diverse. With diversity of experience comes diversity of self.

The highlighting of the self in this way is seen as being a highly significant development in late-industrial consumer society since both perceptions of identity and selfhood, and more importantly *the desire* to achieve them are not limited in the same ways as basic material needs are. Whereas there are limits to the volume of food one can eat or to the number of clothes one can wear at one time, there are, so it is claimed, no such limits in matters of identity. The seeming limitlessness of this new adventure was seized upon by innovators and producers in the commercial world as they set about trying to satisfy the new demand for the ingredients of do-it-yourselfhood. The availability of these new ingredients further boosted consumers' appetites for individualizing goods and so the cycle continued. Summarizing the thrust of prophecies made during the late-1980s, Mort suggests that this amounted to a new stage, or a 'new and improved' variant of the 'consumer revolution':

> Commercial explanations of the significance of the 1980s drew on a familiar motif. This was the idea of the 'consumer revolution'. Such a model understood contemporary shifts as epochal and totalising, breaking with what had gone before. It was a modernising logic which dominated. With its constant search for innovation, it was claimed that the commercial sector would transfigure not only the realm of economics, but would have far-reaching effects in social and cultural life as well. (Mort 1996, p.4)

Having taken matters of identity under their wing, producers were thus able to represent the consumer's search for new and exciting variations of identity as part-and-parcel of the search for individuality itself. Being an individual was no longer simply a matter of accepting and living out the pre-fabricated ascriptions of social location (including those deriving both from employment and from the traditional attributes and attributions of social status), but became instead a more complex and dynamic process of salvaging from the traditional, and of excavating fresh sites on which to build new constructions of identity.

It is important to note here, that whilst it might be supposed that this general undermining and partial discarding of traditional identity markers would result in a kind of anomie of the self, or in a new kind of self-alienation, the business of seeing one's self as an object of consumption is actually a continuation rather than a complete abandonment of the logic of acquisitive/possessive individualism. Only this time, it is the self which becomes the object (or subject to be worked on) of consumption rather than being the (active) subject which does the consuming (Seidler 1989, pp.25-6).

The New Individualism

Having identified the self as the new subject/object of late modernity, and having mapped the new terrain of identity formation, commercial commentators and academics alike turned their attention to trying to describe what the characteristics of the new individuality and the new individual might

194

be. In looking at these debates three points should be born in mind. Firstly, and in contrast to the tendentially self-effacing and guilt-ridden psychology of the protestantesque perception of individualism, the new individualism absorbed the idea that it is all right to feel good about one's sense of self; it is not necessary to feel embarrassed about exploring new ideas about identity, nor to feel that consumption is somehow self-indulgent as compared with the honest and more earthly business of earning a living. Indeed, being positive in these efforts is an essential part of the new game plan.

Secondly, and as an extension of the idea that identity-markers have been set free from earlier constraints, the search for the paraphernalia of identity-formation has been represented as being as much a symbolic process as it is a material one. Thirdly, and picking up on themes developed earlier by Weber (1976), Simmel (1978), and Veblen (1925), both these new emphases have shifted the centre of gravity of academic debate away from the productivist stance of 'industrial sociology', and towards the wider cultural arena within which work takes place.

Within the academic discourse of cultural theory itself, these changes were reflected in a move away from 'the concept of cultural manipulation' as represented in the critical theory of the Frankfurt School during the 1940s and 1950s (e.g. Horkheimer and Adorno 1972) and of 'rational choice theories of consumer sovereignty' (Mort 1996, p.6), both of which had tended to represent the consumer as the passive plaything of market forces, towards a much more reflective and active conception of the consumer. The explicitly culturally-oriented contributions of writers such as Featherstone, Baudrillard and particularly Bauman and Bourdieu, have since suggested that differential social position, and thus the identity markers which go with them, need to be assessed in terms of the consumption-oriented 'habitus' as constituted by the 'signs' and expectations of 'taste' and 'lifestyle', rather than in terms of the grit and toil of productivism.[7]

The abandonment of the strict work/non-work dichotomy discussed above is thus accompanied by a similar abandonment of attempts to theorize 'culture' as being dichotomously separate from 'work'. As one of the leading advocates of 'the turn to culture' has put it:

Culture was too often regarded as readily circumscribed, something derivative which was there to be explained. It was rarely conceived of as opening up a set of problems which, once tackled, could question and overturn such hierarchically constituted oppositions and separations [including economy/culture, production/consumption, work/leisure.] A set of problems which, when constituted in its most radical form, could challenge the viability of our existing modes of conceptualization. (Featherstone, (ed.), 1992, p.vii)

By pairing the notion of 'post-modernism' with 'post-industrialism', and by making culture a primary locus of the former, culture itself becomes not only the main locus/focus of study, but the main generator of social change: 'postmodernism [reflects] important changes, not so much in the structure of industrial capitalism, but in the place and nature of culture' (Turner in Rojek and Turner (eds.) 1993, pp.73/4). Whether one chooses to follow Baudrillard's characterization of 'mass society' being dominated by 'sign-values' and 'simulation', (Baudrillard 1983, 1986), or Jameson's characterization of postmodernism as the cultural superstructure of late/multinational capitalism (Jameson 1991), or Eco's notion of 'hyperreality' (Eco 1986), or Bourdieu's concept of 'habitus' (Bourdieu 1984), or Berman's diagnosis of 'paradoxical unity' (Berman 1982), or Bauman's idea of 'the contingency of the self' (Bauman 1992), there is no question, it would appear, that culture has become the key signifier of modern experience.

Following this line of argument, such major shifts in perceptions of the stage-settings, scenery and venues of contemporary experience necessarily required the emergence of new actors to live out the late- or post-modern drama. Betraying their origins in not-so-post-modern society, and very much in line with the debates around identity, selfhood and masculinity just discussed, it was the male persona which was given the leading role. Without further ado, 'the creative innovators and the style *cognoscenti*', 'the entrepreneurs and the intellectuals of the consumer industries - retailers, advertisers, marketers and the rest', produced 'an extended interrogation of masculinity, which scrutinised the character of young men' (Mort 1996, pp.3/144).[8]

Responding to the need 'to assemble a type of synthetic male personality out of the flotsam and jetsam of contemporary commodities' (ibid., p.18), the agents of social-cultural engineering defined and described various species of 'the new man', rising phoenix-like from the carcass of traditional manhood with his new sense of liberated individualism, a new pride in his autonomy, and a flatteringly high level of regard for other members of the cast. Conveniently, and in direct contrast with the apparently static and unimaginative origins, the fixed menu of choices from which 'the old man' had to make his choices, the resources now available for identity reconstruction, for the make-over of identity and selfhood are multiple, dynamic and cafeteria-like:

These speculations were produced through multiple concepts, which varied according to the goods in question and their position in the marketplace. There was no one model of consumption which dominated, despite the evangelical claims of the creative innovators and the style *cognoscenti*. The dynamics of transformation were plural and diverse. (Mort 1996, p.144)

Whilst accepting that these developments have emerged as a necessary counterbalance to the heavily productivist stance of established sociological and social theoretical discourses on work, there are clear limits to its usefulness in these debates. Firstly, and most simply, there has always been a certain tension in the argument that consumption is replacing production as the primary site of people's activities because a fully developed 'consumer-ethic' assumes that affluence will be sustained, and that almost everyone in society will have the wherewithal to participate in it. Under present circumstances of increasing job insecurity and persistently high levels of income inequality and poverty however, it would seem that consumption only dominates the lives of the fortunate minority. Indeed, to the extent that those who are marginalized have to stand by and watch the affluent playing with their new toys, one can suggest that any switch to consumption may replicate and recharge social tension rather liberating us from it.

Second, at the level of individual motivation, we can note that a consumer-ethic has to be based on a work-ethic of some kind, since people still have to earn enough money to support their consumer lifestyle. Indeed, some would argue that maintaining such high levels of disposable income actually reinforces the work-ethic, and may motivate people to work more rather than less energetically. As Gorz might put it, consumption does not provide 'liberation from work' so much as a renewed commitment to it.

Thirdly, whilst accepting that people are becoming increasingly skilled in the interpretation of signs and meanings, and that there has been a massive increase in the availability of these raw materials of identity, it also needs to be recognized that such resources still have to be paid for in some way; even MTV is not free at the point of reception. A multiplication of signs and their potential meanings and significances is not necessarily accompanied by any increase in the *practical means* of taking advantage of them. Whilst Baudrillard might be right in suggesting that some people now need to free themselves from the 'tyranny of signs', many more people are still preoccupied with freeing themselves from the 'tyranny of want'.

Fourthly, whilst it is certainly important and necessary to acknowledge the cultural dimensions within debates about the future of work, and while there is some justification in the suggestion that sociology in general and the sociology of work in particular have not been very good at theorizing 'culture', we also have to recognize that this shift of emphasis may be reaching a point where the importance of working activities as a constituent part of people's sense of who they are, of how they orient themselves in respect of other people, and of how working life provides a key realm of social interaction, is in danger of being lost from view altogether. It is perhaps disappointing that in tending to empty out the category of experience we call 'work', in representing it as a kind of sinking ship of identity, the shift towards abstract cultural analysis in postmodernist academic discourses actually means that they may not offer us very much in our present investigation into the future of work. As Mort puts it:

> Despite their sophistication, there is a general difficulty which shadows almost all of [these] perspectives. This is the recurrent tendency to over-abstraction. Consumption is evoked as a meta-concept, used to explain the most disparate phenomena. At once part of a debate on industrial and commercial restructuring, over the language and meaning of contemporary politics and about the reordering of identity, space and place, consumption is glossed as a composite and synthetic term. (Mort 1996, p.7)

To take just two examples, MacCannell and MacCannell have suggested the following:

> In the postmodern world, commodity *production* is no longer necessarily the site of exploitation. The reproduction of *simulacra* (...) can be organized in such a way as to be... either labour free, or providing a reasonable return to labour. Statistically, the individual's relation to production is no longer a place on the assembly line, or in the mine, but a 'niche' in a transnational or global bureaucracy, a pastel little office or cubicle with a potted plant and a computer terminal. 'Work' and 'labour' in these niches increasingly resemble little dramas of work, or work masquerades, everyone costumed for their part, their looking 'professional' or 'seriously engaged', or even 'presidential', as important as any other aspect of their job 'performance'. The manufacture of *simulacra* becomes a prettified *simulacrum* of manufacture. (MacCannel and MacCannel in Rojek and Turner (eds.) 1993, p.136)

Whilst accepting that the interactive experiences and identity markers of working in offices are (at least in form and context if not fundamentally) different to those of working in coal mines, it seems somewhat optimistic to suggest that this shift has transformed production into an entirely exploitation-free activity - what exactly is 'labour free' production, and how is a 'reasonable return for labour' being assessed here? More seriously, what grounds are there for suggesting that office workers (including those engaged in software programming or data analysis) experience their work as a 'drama' or a 'masquerade'? Can we seriously accept that a trainee nurse emptying bed pans, or a fast-food cook packing burgers are merely engaged in 'a prettified *simulacrum*' of some other more substantive or 'real' kind of production? Is it not more plausible to suggest that this kind of characterization of working activity (and by implication of the meaning it has for these people's sense of identity), actually originates from an ultimately futile attempt on the part of academic observers to re-apply abstract notions of simulacrum to the 'real' world? Mort seems to be moving towards a similar kind of critique when he notes that having identified the 'symbolic significance of consumer forms', 'cultural studies was also distinguished by a desire not merely to map commercial systems of provision, but also to intervene in them by legitimising the activities of the consumer' (Mort 1996, pp.5-6). One might add that to a greater or lesser extent, these researchers are also 'legitimizing the activities' of the theorists of consumption.

In a similar vein, and perhaps adopting a slightly more circumspect attitude, Featherstone applies the cultural studies schemata in describing what he calls 'the change from an industrial manufacturing order to post-industrial and informational order':

> In this shift from 'industrial society' to 'informational world' even the concrete labour process involves the abstraction of informationalized products and means of production that would seem further to de-situate, to hollow out meaning from forms of life. A number of authors in this book... contend that the seemingly empty and universalist signs circulating in the world informational system can be recast into different configurations of meaning. That these transformed social semantics can - in the context of traditional and self-reflexive social practices - instead inform the (re)constitution and/or creation of individual and communal identities. (Featherstone *et al.* (eds.) 1995, pp.2-3, 'introduction')

As reference to any number of empirical investigations of the labour process would show, people who make use of electronically-generated and electronically-transmitted information in their work would probably not be remotely interested in, and see no connection whatsoever between, these 'products' and questions of 'meaning'. One might just as well suggest that the driver of a Victorian train was concerned about the ephemeral properties of steam. What sense would it make for example, for a person processing data on customers' bank accounts to look for 'different configurations of meaning'. The point is that these data are just that: data. In the same way that we might be justified in suggesting that MacCannel and MacCannel have allowed themselves to get rather carried away with ideas about the universal importance of cultural analyses, the authors to whom Featherstone refers might also be confusing the 'transformed social semantics' of academic debate with something which may or may not be happening in the world beyond the academy. It may well be, as Featherstone puts it in an earlier volume, that 'postmodernism as a style of analysis can be seen as an attempt to provide an analysis of culture in late capitalism (Turner in Rojek and Turner (eds.) 1993, pp.73/74), but, as far as can be judged from current contributions, it adds very little to our understanding of the nature and organization of the labour process upon which 'capitalism' - late or otherwise - is based. If we really do want to understand what work will be like in the future, it is clearly necessary not to lose sight of the sheer physicality, the actual material substance of this (and for that matter any other kind of) activity.

6 Economic Globalization and the Future of Work

Globalization - meaning at its simplest the intensification of activity at a global level - has become a ubiquitous concept in current debates about contemporary society. Almost every aspect of our lives it would seem, is now overshadowed by processes and structures which operate at a global level largely beyond our reach and perhaps beyond our comprehension. Metaphorically speaking, 'globalization' is represented as having the same kind of all-pervasive and irresistible force over social bodies as gravity has over physical bodies. Although we are not preoccupied by gravity, we do not conceive of ourselves as being constantly drawn against the surface of the planet, we know nonetheless that this is the case. Similarly with globalization, although we may not constantly assess ourselves in terms of the global context, we do have an at least shadowy perception of ourselves as sharing the same planet as all the other people in the world.

Although this characterization conveys a sense of certainty and inevitability about globalization at the most abstract level, the specifics of its operation at ground level are much less clear. One of the areas where this ambiguity is most apparent is in the realm of economic processes and relationships. Beginning with a brief exploration of some of the ambiguities the concept contains, the purpose of this chapter is to look specifically at what *economic* globalization might entail. First, and accepting that whatever else they might involve, processes of economic globalization are closely related to developments in capitalism as a global system of economic production and exchange, we will look at whether late-industrialism is in fact taking on a more global character. Of particular focus here are the large multinational corporations, which, if we are to believe the globalist narrative, must surely be at the forefront of the global adventure.

Second, and taking Manuel Castells predictions of the emergence of 'network society' as a test case we will review the possible impact of globalization on aspects of the future of work already discussed including divisions between core and peripheral workers, new kinds of management, and changes in the form of organizations which operate at the international level.

The Antinomies of the Concept Globalization

It is not unusual to suggest that an important social-theoretical concept is ambiguous. Indeed the longevity of many such concepts depends on their ambiguity since it is differences in interpretation and application which gives them currency (and incidentally keeps academics in work). It will however be useful to explore briefly why globalization is an ambiguous concept specifically with regard to discussions about the future of work. A first point to grasp is that much depends on how strong a thesis of globalization one wishes to adopt. Whilst it is clearly ridiculous to suggest that all kinds of work in every place are being wrenched clear of their local moorings, it is equally unrealistic to ignore the impact of changes at a global level upon the organization of work at the local level. What we need to do is understand where the balance lies between the strong thesis that everything is changing and the antithesis that nothing is changing.

A second point is that one has to be clear what exactly the subjects and objects of globalization are. If one is referring to concrete material objects problems arise because although all material things are inherently global in the sense that they are all attached to the same planet, their physical presence, and the experience we have of them, is necessarily specific and local. It may be that I can buy an Indian ready-meal and eat it whilst watching a documentary about Antarctica, sitting on a chair based on a Swedish design, but the meal, the television images and the chair are all real things which I experience within the real place I call my home. The origins of these objects might be global but my experience of them is not. What *is* global about these objects however, are the economic mechanisms through which they become available to me. Strictly speaking then, economic globalization is much more useful as a means of referring to possible changes in the nature of relationships between objects and actors, the ways in which they affect one another, than it is of claiming that the objects themselves have been transformed.

Taking this a stage further, and having discarded the strong thesis that all things and all experiences are fundamentally altered by the global diversity of their origins, we can say that economic globalization most usefully refers to possible changes in the *processes* through which goods and services are produced and distributed. What is global about my new car is not the car itself but the internationalized labour process within which it has been made.

Thirdly, it is important to keep an eye on the extent to which these various relationships and processes are or are not combining to produce a fundamental shift in the overall nature and trajectory of the late-industrial labour process. This takes us back into the realm of narratives about historical transition discussed in the opening chapter. One of the major weaknesses of the strong version of the globalization thesis, is, as Hirst and Thompson (1996) have forcefully argued, that it assumes that just because important changes can be detected in one kind of relationship or process, *all* relationships and processes are not only also moving, but in *the same* direction: 'we should be cautious in a wider sense of ascribing structural significance to what may be conjunctural and temporary changes, dramatic though some of them have been' (Hirst and Thompson 1996, p.15). A recent example of this approach is found in the work of Manual Castells (1996), who argues that, taken together, the various fragments of globalization add up to a thoroughgoing transition towards what he calls the 'network society'. Whilst there is nothing inherently wrong with this kind of universalizing-speculative approach, it runs the risk of trying to fit apparently inconsistent if not entirely contradictory features of recent changes into the overall model; like Weber's bureaucrats for whom the maintenance of the organization becomes more important than the purposes for which the organization was designed, the grand plan, the big picture becomes more important than its constituent parts (we will return to this debate shortly).

Finally, and stemming from this, we also have to be specific about the time scale and scope of the phenomena we are talking about. It is one thing to predict that such-and-such a process or relationship *might* become more globally oriented in the future, or that one Indian meal signifies a *complete* transformation of one's diet, but quite another to establish that they actually *are* going to do so. Although it may disappoint the enthusiastic globalist to have to talk about trends, tendencies and possibilities rather than confidently describing real and actual changes, the picture that is drawn will be much more useful and realistic.

In order to put some flesh on these bones and to see how issues of relationality, process, time, scale and scope are being framed within the globalization debate, it will be useful to consider briefly four influential definitions of globalization which are currently being used. They will also serve to reinforce the point that although many accounts focus on the extent of globalization across and between the cultural rather than economic dimensions of social relationships and processes, almost all accept the fundamental and continuing importance of economic relationships and processes in the debate. Although this is partly a consequence of the fact that some contributions to the globalization debate have grown out of earlier attempts to understand and analyse global economic processes in terms of whether all societies will 'converge' towards the Western model (Levy 1966,

Kerr *et al.* 1973), whether capitalism has or will become an economic 'world-system' (Wallerstein 1974, 1979 and 1980, Frank 1971, Amin 1980), or of whether 'international relations' have displaced nation-states as the main locus of modernization (Rosenau 1980, Gilpin 1987), it also reflects the more substantive point that if it is to become in any true sense a 'real' phenomenon, globalization will be most keenly felt and most closely observed in the economic realm.

For Robertson, in trying to theorize the 'global field' or 'the global-human condition': 'globalization as a concept refers both to the compression of the world and the intensification of consciousness of the world as a whole.... In so far as [the discussion of globalization] is closely linked to the contours and nature of modernity, globalization refers quite clearly to recent developments' (Robertson 1992, p.8). For Giddens, globalization is inherently connected with disembedding in time and space, meaning 'the "lifting out" of social relations from local contexts of interaction and their restructuring across indefinite spans of time-space' (Giddens 1990 p.21), and with the increasing reflexivity of modernity, meaning the ways in which 'social practices are constantly examined and reformed in the light of incoming information about those very practices, thus constitutively altering their character' (ibid., p.38):

> In the modern era, the level of time-space distanciation is much higher than in any previous period, and the relations between local and distant social forms and events become correspondingly "stretched". Globalisation refers essentially to that stretching process, in so far as the modes of connection between different social contexts or regions become networked across the earth's surface as a whole. Globalisation can thus be defined as the intensification of worldwide social relations which link distant localities in such a way that local happening are shaped by events occurring many miles away and vice versa. (Giddens 1990, p.64)

Giddens characterizes modernity as 'multidimensional on the level of institutions' and identifies capitalism and industrialism as two of its four institutional dimensions. These correspond with the world capitalist economy and the international division of labour as key dimensions of globalization (the other dimensions are surveillance and military power which correspond respectively with the nation-state system and the world military order, Giddens 1990, pp.55-78).

Defining globalization as: 'A social process in which the constraints of geography on social and cultural arrangements recede and in which people become increasingly aware that they are receding' (Waters 1995, p.3), Waters concurs in this identification of globalization with the increasing interaction of the local with the global. For Waters, globalization refers to the extent to which social organization is related to 'territoriality' i.e. to particular physical and identifiable locations. The less related it becomes, the greater is the extent of globalization. The three 'arenas' of social relationships he identifies are the economy, the polity and 'culture', and these are associated respectively with material exchanges, political exchanges and symbolic exchanges. Waters argues that material exchanges 'tend to tie social relationships' to particular fixed localities, that political exchanges tend to tie relationships to 'extended localities', and, most importantly, that symbolic exchanges 'liberate relationships from spatial referents':

> The theorem that guides the argument of this book is that: material exchanges localize; political exchanges internationalize; and symbolic exchanges globalize. It follows that the globalization of human society is contingent on the extent to which cultural arrangements are effective relative to economic and political arrangements. We can expect the economy and the polity to be globalized to the extent that they are culturalized, that is, to the extent that the exchanges that take place within them are accomplished symbolically. (Waters 1995, p.9)

Historically, he suggests that in the political and cultural arenas globalization 'is the direct consequence of the expansion of European culture across the planet via settlement, colonization and cultural mimesis'. Within the economic arena, globalization is 'bound up intrinsically with the pattern of capitalist development as it has ramified through political and cultural arenas' (Waters 1995, p.3).

Adopting a more specifically geographical approach, the importance of economic relationships as an underlying basis of global processes is taken up by Amin and Thrift. In describing the 'reorganization of the world economy', they identify seven aspects as being most important 'in terms of both geography and pervasiveness of influence':

> The first is the increasing centrality of the financial structure through which credit money is created, allocated, and put to use, and the resulting increase in the power of finance over production.... The second aspect is the increasing importance of the 'knowledge structure' or 'expert systems'.... A third... is the transnationalization of technology coupled with an enormous increase in the rapidity of redundancy of given technologies.... Fourth is the rise of global oligopolies.... Fifth... is the rise of transnational economic diplomacy and the globalization of state power.... Sixth... is the rise of global flows and 'deterritorialized' signs, meanings, and identities.... Finally... is the rise of new global geographies... in which the processes of globalization are seen to

have produced borderless geographies with quite different breaks and boundaries from what went before. (Amin and Thrift 1994, p.5)

Taking these propositions as a point of departure, it is possible to see how easily one might slip into the kind of generalized hypothesis noted above. As a first approximation, these analyses would suggests that in the future, economic relationships are likely to be subjected to increasing pressures of compression and intensification in the sense that manufacturing and business organizations within particular domestic economies will have to respond more and more fully and quickly to organizational developments in competitor economies. This can be characterized as a natural extension of the process of adopting principles and techniques of flexible working which have proved to be highly successful elsewhere. The assimilation of Japanese working practice in motor manufacture by US and European companies during the 1980s and 1990s could be cited as a clear example of how competitive pressure intensifies the rate at which 'best practice' becomes generalized across and between different economies.

Secondly, and in line with the switch from mass production aimed at an undifferentiated mass-consumer market towards the 'mass customization' of goods aimed at a diffused 'prosmer' market (see chapter two above), processes of intensification and compression will also become increasingly important in the battle for consumer response and loyalty. Now that consumers have come to *expect* greater variety and choice in goods and services (I would be disappointed if I could *not* eat an Italian meal whilst sitting on my English sofa in front of my Japanese television watching an American documentary about African culture), both the rate at which new products are developed and their complexity and sophistication will have to accelerate to meet rising levels of 'wish fulfilment' within corporate and consumer markets. 'Standing still' in product development - even in the production of increasingly popular retro goods seeking to capture the craft-based artisanship of years gone by - is no longer a realistic option.

Thirdly, the observation that globalization will involve 'the intensification of worldwide social relations' and 'the networking of social relationships across the globe', reflects practices which are already developing at an accelerated rate in the fields of commercial and business relationships. We would also note that these developments have been greatly facilitated by the almost universal availability of relatively cheap and reliable technologies of communication. Technologies which endow the capacity to implement business strategy as easily at the global level as at the national and local levels. Indeed, as Castells puts it, these developments are likely to become constituent features of new types of global businesses and services: 'It is the historical linkage between the knowledge-information base of the economy, its global reach, and the Information Technology Revolution that gives birth to a new, distinctive economic system' (Castells 1996, p.66).

Finally, each of these processes would confirm our suspicions that the linkages between economic activity and particular geographical locations are becoming less and less fixed. Whilst this can partly be accounted for in terms of the 'working out' of various natural resources in particular regions, it also embraces the much wider realization that many practical operations within the contemporary manufacturing process can be shifted relatively easily from one location to another. This flexibility of location may also be accompanied by an increasing dispersal of operations across a number of regions, and, correspondingly, by significant leaps forward in the flexibility and geographical mobility of labour. Whilst conceding that it is relatively easy to provide an exaggerated model in order to knock it down, the point remains that many accounts of the globalized future of work do tend to get carried away with their own enthusiasm, and thus represent the future in a highly stylized manner. Clearly the way to avoid this is to shorten our future gaze a little, to resist the temptation of generalizing from one or two examples, and to limit the scope of the analysis by looking at concrete evidence of what actually is happening in a number of key areas.

The Future Narrative of World Capitalism

Although it might seem rather old fashioned to persevere with the idea that what is called the world economic system is a capitalist system, this is of course what it is. Even the most forthright evangelists of globalism accept that this economy will continue to be characterized by the production of goods and services for profit. More importantly, political economists were the first not only to recognize that such an entity had emerged (for example, Adam Smith's *Inquiry into the Nature and Causes of the Wealth of Nations* (1976), David Ricardo's *On the Principles of Political Economy and Taxation* (1817)), but to begin to provide a coherent account of its constitution. This is significant for our current discussion for two reasons. First, it lays to rest the highly misleading idea that the international if not fully global circulation of economic activity is something which has only happened during the twentieth century; that economic globalization is an inherently modern phenomenon. If we allow a degree of latitude in defining what economic globalization is, it is clear that cross-border proto-typical international trade has been going on at least since the time of the Ancient civilizations of Egypt and the Orient. As Hirst and Thompson put it:

> The present highly internationalized economy is not unprecedented: it is one of a number of distinct conjunctures or states of the international economy that have existed since an economy based on modern industrial technology began to be generalized from the 1860s. (Hirst and Thompson 1996, p.2)

Second, and noting how this kind of economic activity was reaching a high level of intensity during the nineteenth century, these early analyses took the first steps in showing how global capitalism could be described in terms of identifiable features of development and historical trajectory. Writing the *Communist Manifesto* during 1848 for example, Marx and Engels were already well aware that: 'The need of a constantly expanding market for its products chases the bourgeoisie over the whole surface of the globe. It must nestle everywhere, settle everywhere, establish connexions everywhere' (Marx and Engels 1952, p.46). Writing during 1916, and drawing on J.A.Hobson's *Imperialism* (1902) and Rudolf Hilferding's *Finance Capital* (1912), Lenin describes how the concentration of capital leads to international expansion:

> Monopolist capitalist combines, cartels, syndicates and trusts divide among themselves, first of all, the home market, seize more or less complete possession of the industry of a country. But under capitalism the home market is inevitably bound up with the foreign market. Capitalism long ago created a world market. As the export of capital increased, and as the foreign colonial connections and "spheres of influence" of the big monopolist combines expanded in all ways, things "naturally" gravitated towards an international agreement among these countries, and towards the formation of international cartels. (Lenin, *Imperialism, The Highest Stage of Capitalism*, 1970, p.79.

To the extent that these underlying features and tendencies are still characteristic of late-industrial capitalism, and that it has not deviated entirely from its earlier trajectory, this critical analysis provides us with a useful point of departure for understanding what path the global economy might follow in the future. A recent attempt, and one which usefully engages with issues around the current transitional phase towards post-Fordism discussed in previous chapters, has been put forward by Arrighi. He argues that the current transformation of international or global capitalism can be understood as the latest in a line of recurrent transformations which have marked the development of capitalism throughout its history. Following Marx, he suggests that:

> The central aspect of this pattern is the alternation of epochs of material expansion... with phases of financial rebirth and expansion.... In phases of

material expansion money capital "sets in motion" an increasing mass of commodities... and in phases of financial expansion an increasing mass of money capital "sets itself free" from its commodity form, and accumulation proceeds through financial deals.... Together the two epochs or phases constitute a full *systemic cycle of accumulation*.... (Arrighi 1994, p.6)[1]

This systemic cycle or 'regime of accumulation on a world scale' (Arrighi 1994, p.9), is very similar to what writers in the 'regulationist school' refer to as the 'regime of accumulation' i.e. the way in which capitalist enterprises achieve their aim of making money (see chapter two above).

For Arrighi, the argument runs that as the rate of return from invested capital begins to mature and then decline ('the tendency for the rate of profit to fall'), capitalists will withdraw from 'static' investment in production and commerce and switch into financial-capitalist activity. Money can therefore be made directly out of money without having to go through the intermediate stage of concrete investment and eventual return through profit. Periods of material expansion, such as the industrial revolution in Britain during the nineteenth century, and the emergence of American mass-productive capacity during the mid-twentieth century, are therefore interspaced with periods of financial expansion. The maturing of the 'American cycle' during the late-1970s thus gives way to a massive expansion of financial-capitalist activity during the 1980s and 1990s. This identification of massive increases in, and concentrations of, *financial* capitalist activity during the 1980s and 1990s is common to all accounts of recent global economic activity (e.g. Amin and Thrift 1994, Harvey 1989, Castells 1996).

Although Arrighi is at pains to point out that these *systemic cycles* should not be confused with the *secular cycles* identified in long-wave theory by Kondratieff and more recently by Freeman *et al.*,[2] it can be seen that the underlying logic of the two is quite similar. It will be recalled for example, that as Freeman *et al* have pointed out, the rate of emergence of a new technological paradigm is dependent on high levels of investment in research and development and innovation. Those regions which have the necessary capital available and are prepared to invest it in this way are likely to play a leading role in the next phase of material expansion, while those which are not will be left behind.

Essentially, and again reminding us that global capitalism is not an exclusively modern phenomenon, both systemic and secular cycles strongly suggest that the current transformation in the locus and nature of world capitalism should be understood not as a one-off event, but as part of a much larger pattern of historical development. Most importantly, Arrighi's model is useful in that it not only suggests that capitalism passes through a cycle of recurrent phases, but also provides a rationale for *why* there are significant differences *between* the phases in terms of direction and discontinuity. In essence, phases of material expansion are characterized by continuous change along a single developmental path or trajectory (for example the emergence of Fordist industrialism), while phases of financial expansion are characterized by *discontinuous* change, initially along the same path, but eventually onto a *different* path (for example the emergence of post-Fordist or late-industrialism). In trying to understand the future of work this is helpful, since even if we can not be certain as to when the new path will emerge, or what direction it will take, we can legitimately predict that the transition from one to another will certainly be marked by discontinuity and economic trauma. Conversely, periods of trauma (for example in the world economy during the 1970s and 1980s) are indicative of changes in the prevailing form of capitalist activity - in the current period from fixed to liquid capital.

In addition to discontinuity, and in line with the prevailing view that modernity is characterized by a particularly acute tension between order and disorder (Lash and Urry 1987, Offe 1985), this model also includes continuity in the sense that if the global economic system is to remain capitalist there will have to be a regime of accumulation in one form or another. The extent to which capitalism as a world system will continue into the future therefore depends on the degree to which it is or is not able to preserve or adapt its regime of accumulation to the new path. Turbulence in the financial markets of Japan and Southeast Asia during late 1997, provide yet another example of the crisis tendencies of global capital when the regime of accumulation is seen to be insecure. This model also has continuity in the sense that the factors which determine the continuation of capitalism at the global level - investment and innovation leading to the successful introduction of a new wave or paradigm of productive capacity - are of the same order as those which determine the survival of national economies and individual firms. On this understanding, it is quite wrong to characterize the global economy as something which circulates above and beyond national economies, or over the heads of individual businesses, because the same kinds of pressures are experienced at all levels.

Arrighi's analysis shares a number of features with that put forward some years earlier by Mandel. Although Mandel tends to place greater emphasis on the decline in the rate of profit than upon increasing financial-capitalist activity as a precursor to increased investment and economic growth, he too suggests that the capitalist system constantly passes through 'industrial cycles' or phases of upswing and depression, and that these short industrial cycles (seven to ten years) periodically combine into more dramatic phases or 'long waves' over fifty-year periods. The character of the long waves is governed by the shorter cycles in that 'in a phase of expansion the cyclical periods of boom will be longer and more intensive' while 'in those phases of the long wave where a tendency to stagnation is prevalent the periods of boom will prove less feverish and more transitory, while the periods of cyclical crisis of over-production will, by contrast be longer and profounder' (Mandel 1975, p.122).

Following Mandel's analysis, the global economy of the 1990s is coming towards the end of the downward phase of the fourth wave which began during the Second World War and peaked during the late-1970s in the then leading world economies of the US and Europe - economies in which the 'crisis of over-production' resulted in an extended period of stagnation and recession throughout the 1980s. The source of the next wave of global-capitalist expansion will be those economies and regions which have at their disposal a sufficient fund of liquid capital in search of profitable investment, and are making the strongest efforts to improve the profitability of their business and productive enterprises by developing cheap sources of labour, by technological innovation, and by developing new ways of organizing the labour process.

This neatly explains the emergence of Japan and the other 'tiger' or 'dragon' economies of the Pacific Rim (South Korea, Taiwan, Singapore and Hong Kong), and increasingly the 'tiger cubs' of Thailand, Malaysia and Indonesia, because it is in these regions that the above factors are found in their most concentrated form. Following Arrighi's analysis we can briefly note the beneficial consequences of these factors for Japan and the surrounding region (see also Francks 1992, Dixon 1991). Firstly, Japan has achieved a very considerable penetration of the world financial markets. Arrighi reports that between 1970 and 1990 Japan's share of *Fortunes*'s top 50 banks had risen from 11 to 22. Over the same period, their share of the *total assets* of these top fifty banks had risen from 18 per cent to 48 per cent (Arrighi 1994, p.335). These trends are confirmed in a recent OECD study which shows that Japanese external assets increased from 79 billion US dollars in 1977 to 2423 billion in 1994 (an increase of nearly 3000 per cent). This compares with increases in the US from 473 to 2378 billion (402 per cent), in Germany from 176 to 1433 billion (714 per cent), and in the UK from 273 to 2191 billion (702 per cent) (see OECD *Economic Outlook*, no.58, 1995, table 14).

Secondly, Japan has developed a highly innovative system of organizing its production and business enterprises around a complex set of contractual and sub-contractual arrangements both between larger and smaller firms, and between one firm and another. Historically, these 'family arrangements' emerged out of the internal commercial rivalries between the four giant 'industrial groups' or *keiretsu* (previously known as *zaibatsu*) which dominated heavy industry before and after 1945. To these can be added the equally giant 'general trading companies' or *sogo shosha*, which, as Francks puts it, played a key role in:

> Bridging the gap between the outside world and both large-scale *zaibatsu* companies and the smaller-scale businesses which produced much of what was exported as industrialization proceeded. General trading companies thus represented that link in the interlocking industrial structure which served to integrate Japanese businesses, both large-scale and small, into the world economy. (Francks 1992, p.239)[3]

Within organizations themselves, Arrighi suggests that the 'Japanese multilayered subcontracting system of business enterprise' has a number of advantages over the ostensibly similar, but organizationally inferior multinational conglomerates of the West:

> First, the Japanese system... is highly stratified into multiple layers [of primary, secondary and tertiary subcontractors]... until the chain reaches the bottom layer which is formed by a large mass of households that subcontract simple operations.... Second, Japanese subcontracting networks are far more stable and effective instruments of vertical and horizontal inter-enterprise cooperation than subcontracting networks in the United States and Western Europe.... Third [the Japanese system] has endowed Japanese big business with superior capabilities to take advantage of and reproduce wage and other differentials in rewards for effort between different segments and strata of the labor force. (Arrighi 1994, pp.344-5)

Thirdly, and as a combined result of these advantages and particularly the ongoing quest for sources of cheap labour, Japanese enterprises have been highly successful in expanding their system across a number of neighbouring countries instigating a 'spill-over' or 'cascade' effect of mutual economic regional benefit: 'The spillover contributed decisively to the take-off of the *regional* economic miracle [and contributed decisively] not just to overcome the overaccumulation crisis, but to strengthen its competitiveness in the world-economy at large through the incorporation of the labor and entrepreneurial resources of the surrounding region within its networks' (Arrighi 1994, pp.344-5). The increasing availability of capital for investment, and the continuing search for new sources of cheap labour has added great momentum to this first wave of regional development (from Japan to the four tigers) resulting in a second wave (from Japan and the four tigers towards Indonesia, Malaysia and Thailand) and now a third wave from these countries into Vietnam and China.

Rather then, than being confronted by limited opportunities for investment (the crisis of overaccumulation), by rising labour costs and technological and organizational stasis, Japan and its neighbours have taken advantage of a perhaps unique geographical opportunity to reinvest their capital gains in neighbouring regions which are very willing to trade cheap labour for inward investment in pursuit of their own desire for economic advance. Rising levels of disposable income among the workforce, initially in Japan but progressively throughout the region, have provided a very extensive new market for the goods and services being produced, thus maintaining the profitability of these enterprises.

During the late-1980s and into the 1990s then, the balance of power within the world economy has tilted in favour of the emerging economies of the Pacific Rim, who have taken the lead in implementing the new technological paradigm. The rapid economic expansion in this region has also been enabled by the fortunate presence of all the prerequisites of capitalist activity, namely access to a large pool of cheap labour, the capacity to reduce production costs through flexible forms of business organization and co-operative structures between firms, and expanding markets. Although it may be premature to predict the terminal decline of the West compared with the Asian East, the *accelerated relative advance* of the latter compared to the former is certainly both setting the pace and dictating the form which the world capitalist system will take in the future. It is not unreasonable to suggest that in the same way that the US displaced Britain's economic supremacy at the end of the nineteenth century, the emerging Southeast Asian economies are displacing the US at the end of the current century. Tentatively then, when applied to capitalist activity at the global level, theories of industrial cycles, systemic cycles or long-waves not only enable us *to describe* what is happening but to understand *why* it is happening.

Globalization and the Future of Late-Industrialism

Up to this point we have been looking at the possible impact of globalization on the future of work in terms of the likely trajectory of capitalism as a system operating at the global level. What we now need to do is to see how these kinds of pressures are likely to affect the industrial labour process at a more day-to-day level. Taking up the idea that globalization has to be understood in terms of how it affects economic relationships and processes, we obviously need to pay close attention to possible changes in the *modus operandi* of the those business organizations - namely the multinational corporations (MNCs) - which are already operating at a global level. If it turns out to be the case that these organizations are *not* significantly altering their ways of working, then the strong thesis of economic globalization looses much of its purchase.

A particularly useful account of the changing nature of MNCs and the kind of international economic system in which they operate has been put forward by Hirst and Thompson. Highly sceptical of the strong globalization thesis, their approach is to test it by contrasting two ideal-types of these enterprises and the kinds of economic relationships through which they operate. The first, labelled as 'an open international economy', describes the kind of international trading and commercial environment in which enterprises have been operating for some time. The key characteristic of these essentially national enterprises is that they retain strong links to particular national locations. The international economy then, 'is still fundamentally characterized by exchange between relatively distinct national economies and in which many outcomes... are substantially determined by processes occurring at the national level'. In this scenario, MNCs 'retain a clear national home base; they are subject to the national regulation of the mother country, and by and large they are effectively policed by that home country' (Hirst and Thompson 1996, pp.7/9).

The second ideal-type is the 'fully globalized economy' in which enterprises are no longer linked with, and identified in terms of, a particular national location: 'In such a global system distinct national economies are subsumed and rearticulated into the system by international processes and transactions'. Being free of the restraints of national-based systems of regulation and governance 'the international economic system becomes autonomized and socially disembedded, as markets and production become truly global' (Hirst and Thompson 1996, p.10). In this scenario, the MNCs would become, or would be displaced by truly *trans*-national corporations (TNCs), to emphasize the way in which they operate across and between different national economies without being located in any one in particular:

> The TNC would be genuine footloose capital, without specific national identification and with an internationalized management, and at least potentially willing to locate and relocate anywhere in the globe to obtain either the most secure or the highest returns. In the financial sector this could be achieved at the touch of a button and in a truly globalized economy would be wholly dictated by market forces.... In the case of primary manufacturing

companies the TNC would source, produce and market at the global level as strategy and opportunities dictated. (Hirst and Thompson 1996, p.11)

At its simplest then, and whilst conceding that since these two types are not necessarily mutually exclusive some form of hybrid might emerge, these authors argue that if TNCs are not replacing MNCs, and if the international economy is not moving towards the fully global type, then full-blow economic globalization is not happening either.[4]

Having identified the main players in the global drama, the next thing we have to do is decide which features of their activity are most heavily implicated in possible shifts towards a more fully global economy. We can phrase these, and organize our examination of the evidence, in terms of three questions: first, is it the case that patterns of international trade are shifting towards a more global model of activity; second, to what extent are the large enterprises changing their patterns of foreign direct investments (FDI); third, what evidence is there that the international division of labour is becoming more extensive. Although it is conceivable that an enterprise could become more globally-oriented in its relationships and mode of organization without significant changes in each of these three areas of investment, trade and employment, it is difficult to see how the strong thesis can be supported unless they do.

Before considering the evidence it will be useful to get a grip on the number and economic significance of MNCs. This is important because even if we adopt a weaker version of the thesis of economic globalization, one would expect to find some evidence of their growing importance. Besides, if there were only a few such enterprises, then it might not matter very much even if they were becoming more global or not. Sklair notes that according to the World Bank in 1986, while '64 out of 120 *countries* had a GDP (gross domestic product) of *less than* $10 billion':

> United Nations data for 1985-6 show that 68 [MNCs] in mining and manufacture had annual sales *in excess* of ten billion dollars, while all the top 50 banks, the top 20 securities firms, and all but one of the top 30 insurance companies had net assets *in excess* of ten billion. (Sklair 1991, pp.48-9, emphasis added)

The size and concentration of these enterprises is truly staggering. A recent study for the United Nations records that at the beginning of the 1990s, there were 37,000 parent MNCs controlling 170,000 foreign affiliates, and that 'over 90 per cent of [MNCs] originate in developed countries.... The five major home countries - France, Germany, Japan, UK and US - are home to over half the developed-country total': 'Roughly 1 per cent of parent [MNCs] own about half the stock of FDI in their home countries.... The largest 100 [MNCs] (excluding those in banking and finance), ranked by the size of their foreign assets, had about $3.2 trillion in global assets in 1990, of which an estimated $1.2 trillion was outside their home countries'.

In terms of *industrial concentration*, the report continues that '12 petroleum companies control over $250 billion in foreign assets, 21 per cent of the total of the top 100.... The petroleum, automotive, chemical and pharmaceutical industries together account for over half of the foreign assets of the largest 100 [MNCs]' (United Nations *World Investment Report 1993*, pp.19/25).

Using different data, and referring to Dunning 1993 and Emmott 1993, Waters notes that the 20,000 MNCs in 1988 accounted for: '25-30 per cent of combined GDP in all market economies; 75 per cent of international commodity trade; and 80 per cent of international exchanges of technology and managerial skills. The largest 300 MNEs account for 70 per cent of total FDI and 25 per cent of the world's capital' (Waters 1995, p.76). Spybey reports that according to *Fortune International* in 1993, of the world's 500 largest corporations 159 were located in the US, 135 in Japan, 41 in the UK, 32 in Germany and 26 in France. Added together, this accounts for over 78 per cent of the world's largest 500 corporations (Spybey 1996, table 6, p.89; *Fortune International*, 26 July 1993).

Patterns of International Trade

Trends in international trade are important in discussions about economic globalization because the strong thesis implies that such activity is becoming more and more intense at the global level. Specifically, we need to know not only about changes in the volume of such trade, but also about how that trade is *concentrated* between countries and regions.

Taking these issues in turn, there is no question that world trade is continuing to increase. The 1995 United Nations 'World Economic and Social Survey' records for example, that the total value of world exports increased from 2 trillion (thousand billion) US dollars in 1980 to nearly 3.7 trillion US dollars in 1992. Expressed as an average annual percentage change in the value of exports and imports, world trade increased by 8.9 per cent *each year* between 1985 and 1995. (United Nations *World Economic and Social Survey*, 1995, tables A15 and A19.0). On their own however, increases in world trade do not signify a shift towards the globalized economy, but merely an extension of the international trading system which is already in place.

Looking at total world trade in terms of country or origin, Tables 6.1 and

6.2 show the world league table of countries in terms of their share of total world exports in manufacturing (1978 and 1989) and in services (1970 and 1989).

Table 6.1: World league table in manufacturing: exports, 1978/1989

	Rank: 1978	Rank: 1989	Exports: Value ($Billion)	World Share (%)
US	1	1	364	11.8
West Germany	2	2	341	11.0
Japan	3	3	274	8.9
France	4	4	179	5.8
UK	5	5	152	4.9
Italy	6	6	141	4.6
Canada	9	7	120	3.9
USSR	7	8	109	3.5
Netherlands	8	9	108	3.5
Belgium/ Luxembourg	10	10	100	3.2
Total top ten:	-	-	1888	61.1
Next 15 countries	-	-	672	21.6
Rest of World	-	-	535	17.3
World total 1989	-	-	3,095	100

Source: Calculated from Gatt (1990), *International Trade 1989-1990*, table 1; Full table reproduced in Dicken 1992, table 2.5, p.30.

Immediately we can see that both in monetary value and as a proportion of total world exports, the top ten countries are in an extremely dominant position. In manufacturing, they accounted for over 60 per cent of world exports ($1.88 trillion), and in commercial services over 65 per cent ($4.3 trillion) in 1989.

Secondly, in the decades covered by these tables it is clear that apart from one or two changes in order, and with the exception of Austria (which moved up from fifteenth to tenth place in commercial services) there has been virtually *no change* in the countries which make up the top ten in either manufacturing or commercial services. Thirdly, and with the exception of Canada and the former USSR, it is clear that those countries which dominate manufacturing exports *also* dominate commercial services. Further still, and looking at the world economy as a whole, countries occupying *the next* fifteen positions account for a further and 21.6 and 21.9 per cent of exports in manufacturing and commercial services respectively. The remaining countries of the world account for relatively small proportions of 17.3 and 12.6 per cent of world exports.

Table 6.2: World league table in commercial services trade: exports, 1970/1989

	Rank: 1970	Rank: 1989	Exports: Value ($Billion)	World Share (%)
US	1	1	102.5	15.7
France	3	2	67.1	10.3
UK	2	3	47.3	7.2
West Germany	4	4	45.4	7.0
Japan	6	5	39.4	6.0
Italy	5	6	37.3	5.7
Spain	8	7	25.1	3.8
Netherlands	6	8	24.4	3.7
Belgium/ Luxembourg	10	9	23.1	3.5
Austria	15	10	17.2	2.6
Total top ten:	-	-	428.8	65.5
Next 15 countries	-	-	142.3	21.9
Rest of World	-	-	81.9	12.6
World total 1989	-	-	653.0	100

Source: Calculated from Gatt (1990), *International Trade 1989-1990*, table 12; Full table reproduced in Dicken 1992, table 2.13, p.42.

Whilst accepting that these are highly aggregated data which might disguise more subtle trends, on the face of it, it does appear that in terms of export activity, world trade has not become more globally dispersed. A slightly different picture does emerge however, if we look at things from the point of view of trends in the regional distribution of the world's manufacturing production.

As Table 6.3 shows, although there is still a high level of concentration in the regions dominated by the top ten countries (notably in Europe, the US and Japan), it is predicted that by the year 2000 the newly emerging industrial regions will increase their share. To this extent, the production of manufactured goods is becoming a more global affair.

It does not follow of course that the potential benefits of such shifts will result in greater parity in economic opportunity. As Dicken puts it: 'The fact remains that the actual extent of global shifts in economic activity is extremely uneven. Only a small number of developing countries have experienced substantial industrial growth; a good many are in deep financial difficulty whilst others are at, or even beyond, the margins of survival' (Dicken 1992, p.45).

Table 6.3: Share by region of the world's manufacturing production: 1988/2000 (percentage of world total)

	1988	2000
Western Europe	27.3	24.6
North.America	23.4	18.0
Developed Asia	22.1	15.2
Eastern Europe	17.6	15.2
Other Asian and Oceanic countries	4.9	8.0
Latin America	3.0	4.6
Africa and Middle East	1.7	2.7

Source: CEPII (Centre d'Etudes Prospectives et d'Information Internationales) calculations from Industries 2000 model and the CHELM and PIM data bases; reproduced in Castells 1996, figure 2.4, p.110.

More crucial from the point of view of the strong thesis of economic globalization however, is the fact that patterns of trade are still heavily concentrated *between* the three major economic regions which make up the 'Triad' of North America, Canada and Mexico (members of the North Atlantic Free Trade Agreement or NAFTA), Europe (members if the European Union or EU), and the Southeast Asian economic region centred on Japan (including the four 'tigers' of South Korea, Indonesia, Taiwan and Singapore, and 'tiger cubs' of Thailand, Malaysia and Indonesia (see Ohmae 1985)). The consensus here is that although the volumes and types of trade between these regions may be altering slightly, there is no evidence either that other regions of similar strength are emerging or that trading between the Triad and other countries outside it is increasing. As Dicken puts it:

> The 'triad'... sits astride the global economy like a modern Colossus.... The three regions dominate global production and trade. Seventy-seven per cent of

world exports are generated by them; 62 per cent of world manufacturing output is produced within them. They are also the dominant generators and recipients of international investment. (Dicken 1992, p.45)

Referring back to Tables 6.1 and 6.2 for example, if we had included data on imports, it would be found that each of the top ten countries are *also* the top ten importers of manufactures and commercial services. Similarly, and although the volume of manufactured exports from developing economies has increased, the proportion of these which are consumed within other developing economies is *falling*; in other words that the developed economies of Europe, the US and Japan are also dominant in their capacity to purchase manufactured goods. Although then, as Stallings suggests, trade within the Triad is increasing - a fact which might support a weaker thesis of economic globalization - these developments should not be taken to imply that economic relations either within the Triad, or between the Triad and other regions, are becoming more secure and settled:

> Present data show that trade and investment are increasing *both* within the so-called triad area... *and* within the three blocs. Other areas are being marginalized in the process.... The different types of capitalism that exist in the three regions have given rise to differential economic performance. The result is conflict *and* cooperation, divergence *and* convergence. (Stallings 1993, p.21; cited in Castells 1996, p.100, original emphasis)

Taking a somewhat different approach, Hirst and Thompson report findings based on an analysis of company-based data, which investigate the importance of MNCs within their own national economies. The issue here it that although, by definition, these large enterprises have an influence beyond their home base, they are still closely linked to these home economies because this is where much of their business activity takes place; the fact that they act internationally does not mean that they are no longer effective at the national level. They conclude:

> The main conclusion to be drawn from this analysis is an obvious one. The home-oriented nature of MNC activity along all the dimensions looked at seems overwhelming. Thus MNCs still rely upon their 'home base' as the centre for their economic activities, despite all the speculation about globalization. From these results we are confident that, in the aggregate, international companies are still predominantly MNCs and not TNCs. (Hirst and Thompson 1996, p.95)

Even though clear evidence for full-blown economic globalization in terms of volumes and regional distribution of production and trade is difficult to come by, we still have to consider the possibility that MNCs are adopting a more global strategy at the level of the kinds of investments they are making. Indeed following Hirst and Thompson's ideal-type of the truly globalized economy, the emergence of fully-fledged *trans*-national (rather than just *inter*-national companies) depends on their willingness to redirect their patterns of investment in order to relocate any or all aspects of their operations as the global situation demands.

Table 6.4: Foreign direct investment in the world economy: the changing relative importance of leading source nations, 1960-1985

Country of origin	Percentage of world total of outward direct investment		
	1960	*1975*	*1985*
US	47.1	44.0	35.1
UK	18.3	13.1	14.7
Japan	0.7	5.7	11.7
West Germany	1.2	6.5	8.4
Switzerland	3.4	8.0	6.4
Netherlands	10.3	7.1	6.1
Canada	3.7	3.7	5.1
France	6.1	3.8	3.0
Italy	1.6	1.2	1.7
Sweden	0.6	1.7	1.3
Total: Top ten sources	93.0	94.8	93.5
Developed Market economies	99.0	97.7	97.2
Developing market economies	1.0	2.3	2.7
World total	100.0	100.0	100.0

Source: Calculated from Dicken 1992, table 3.2, p.53.

The most often used measure of this kind of corporate investment activity is foreign direct investment (FDI). FDI includes: investments which an enterprise chooses to make in order to take a controlling share in a business in another country (for example, buying a company which supplies its raw materials); investments made to set up a new part of its own organization in a country which is different from the one where its operations are already based (a Japanese motor manufacture setting up a plant in France), and so-called 'portfolio investments' where an enterprise purchases shares in another company as a financial investment but without gaining control over it. The main difference here between MNCs and TNCs is that the latter would not regard *any* of the locations in which they make their various investments as their 'home' country.

Accepting that both the extent and variety of means of financial investment have increased dramatically during the past few decades (see Dicken 1992, figure 3.3, p.53, Castells 1996, table 2.7, p.94, Hirst and Thompson 1996, table 2.9, p.40), Table 6.4 shows (above) changes in the distribution of FDI in the world economy between 1960 and 1985. Once again we can note that the sources of world-wide FDI are almost exclusively concentrated in just ten countries of origin (providing around 94 per cent of the world total). Although they are increasing their share, the developing market economies provided less that 3 per cent of the total in 1985. In terms of trends over time, it is clear that the US, the UK, France and Sweden have fallen back, whilst the other European countries listed have increased their share. The most dramatic change is, not unexpectedly, the position of Japan which increased its share dramatically from less than 1 per cent in 1960 to nearly 12 per cent in 1985.

Table 6.5: Intra-Triad foreign direct investment in 1990 ($Billion)

From	To	Value ($Billion)
North America	European Economic Area	225.5
European Economic Area	North America	280.0
North America	Japan	21.7
Japan	North America	85.4
European Economic Area	Japan	7.0
Japan	European Economic Area	19.3

Source: Adapted from Hirst and Thompson 1996, figure 3.4, p.63.

Looking at the destination of this investment, the consensus is that direct investment activity follows much the same pattern as trade activity and is highly concentrated within and between members of the Triad. Table 6.5 shows the pattern and value of intra-Triad foreign direct investment in 1990. Using different data, and looking at the situation in 1989-91, Castells (1996, figure 2.3, p.101) has calculated FDI in terms of the proportion of total FDI in each member of the Triad which goes to other members of the Triad, and to some regions outside it.

These data show that for the US, 50 per cent of its total FDI is concentrated within the Triad (44 per cent to the EC, 5 to Canada and 1 to Japan), with a further 16 per cent going to Latin America. For the EC, 82 per cent stays inside (60 to *other* EC, 21 to the US, 1 to Japan), with 1 per cent going to Africa. For Japan, 69 per cent stays inside (46 to the US, 23 to the EC), with 13 per cent going to other countries in Asia (see also Dicken 1992, table 3.5, p.56). Apart from confirming the concentration of FDI within the Triad, these data also indicate the trend that where members *are* investing outside the Triad, this also tends to be concentrated in specific and largely neighbouring regions:

> Relatively isolated clusters of main actor and client states are emerging, which are geographically discrete and stabilizing.... Thus whilst *intra*-Triad investment relationships are particularly dense, a pattern of further discrete but robust *inter*-linkages between each of these and more marginalized country groupings is also evident. These country groupings tend to be regionally specific and 'adjacent' to one or other of the Triad members. (Hirst and Thompson 1996, pp.65-6)

These authors provide data which show that the EU tends to concentrate its direct investments primarily in Central and Eastern Europe and to a lesser extent in Latin America, Africa and West Africa and Asia and the Pacific, whilst the US favours Latin American, Asia and the Pacific and has a lower interest in Africa and West Africa. Japan is the dominant direct investor in Asia and the Pacific region.

The significance of this for the globalization thesis is that even though FDI is increasing, the locations where such investments are made have not so far become more global. In the same way that concentrated patterns of international trading within the Triad tend to isolate or marginalize countries and regions outside it, so also do patterns of international investment:

> Once again this goes against the idea of a 'neutral' or 'level playing field' in the global market place. Indeed it testifies to the relative lack of integration in FDI flows and stocks since the clusters indicate a geographical and regional

discreteness in the relationships between the countries. The direction of FDI relationships is between one or other of the Triad powers and its clustered 'client' states, rather than between these client states themselves. (Hirst and Thompson 1996, pp.65-6)

The same points are made by Castells, who, having noted that 'the structure of [the world economy] is characterized by the combination of an enduring architecture and a variable geometry', suggests that a pattern of 'asymmetrical interdependence' has emerged characterized by: 'an axis of opposition between productive, information-rich, affluent areas, and impoverished areas, economically devalued and socially excluded' (Castells 1996, p.145). This strongly suggests that whatever else it involves, economic globalization is devisive in its effects on economic relationships and processes: 'Between 57 and 72 per cent of the world population is in receipt of only 8.5 per cent of global FDI. In other words nearly two-thirds of the world is virtually written off the map as far as any benefits from this form of investment are concerned' (Hirst and Thompson 1996, p.68).

The International Division of Labour

The third type of evidence we need to consider is whether, or to what extent, patterns of employment are shifting onto a more global footing. This is a particularly complex issue since a distinction has to be made between movement of labour in the absolute sense of voluntary economic migration, and in the sense of changes in the distribution of tasks and functions within the division of labour between and across countries. Within the division of labour itself we also have to distinguish between changes in terms of possible shifts in patterns of responsibility and skill. In approaching these important questions we are moving towards a more detailed account of changes in the nature and organization of the late-industrial labour process under conditions of internationalization. Since these developments are discussed in more detail in the following section, we will confine ourselves here to the more general aspects of these issues. These can be dispatched with relative ease.

A first point to make is that there certainly is some *potential* for movement of labour. As Castells puts it, there are at least three sources of motivation for this:

Labour is a global resource at least in three ways: firms may choose to locate in a variety of places worldwide to find the labour supply they need, be it in terms of skills, costs, or social control; firms everywhere may also solicit highly skilled labor from everywhere, and they will obtain it provided they offer the right remuneration and working conditions; and labor will enter any market on its own initiative, coming from anywhere, when human beings are pushed from their homes by poverty and war or pulled towards a new life by hope for their children. Immigrant labor from all over the planet may flow to wherever jobs are.... (Castells 1996, p.93)

However, as Hirst and Thompson have pointed out, there is big difference between these kinds of potential and whether or not labour will *actually* move about in this apparently unrestricted way. In their critique of the strong thesis of economic globalization as it applies to movements of labour they begin by emphasizing that, in common with both international trade and investment, the fact that people may move from one country to another in order to find work is not new. Voluntary economic migration is not therefore an exclusively modern phenomenon which suddenly appeared in the late-twentieth century (Hirst and Thompson 1996, pp.22ff drawing on Castles and Miller 1993 and Livi-Bacci 1993). Indeed they go on to suggest that voluntary economic migration has become progressively *less easy* to achieve during the twentieth century than it was during the nineteenth century. Second, they point out that unlike capital, goods and services, labour is not a commodity which can be moved around with relative ease. This point is also made by Castells who, despite his inclination to see all things economic as potentially global, concludes that:

> While capital flows freely in the electronic circuits of global financial networks, labor is still highly constrained, and will be for the foreseeable future, by institutions, culture, borders, police, and xenophobia. Only about 1.5% of the global labour force (about 80 million workers) worked outside their country in 1993, and half of them were concentrated in Sub-Saharan Africa and the Middle-East. (Castells 1996, p.232)

The third criticism concerns the issue of what incentives enterprises have for shifting themselves around the globe in search of various kinds of labour. For Castells, this incentive is based on what he calls the four different 'positions' in the 'informational/global economy':

> The producers of high value, based on informational labour; the producers of high volume, based on low-cost labour; the producers of raw materials, based on natural endowments; and the redundant producers, reduced to devalued labour.... The critical matter is that these different positions do not coincide with countries. They are organized in networks and flows, using the technological infrastructure of the informational economy. (Castells 1996, p.147, emphasis removed)

The first difficulty here, is that whilst the other three positions could be seen as geographically detached, the 'natural endowments' of raw materials are certainly not; one can export raw materials but one cannot export the relationship between the material and the labour which recovers it.

Even more serious difficulties arise with the category of low-cost labour. Whilst it might seem like a good idea to travel the globe in search of easily exploited labour, the financial benefits of so doing depend on the savings that can be made in terms of the final cost of the product or service. In the current period however, this apparent advantage is declining for two clear reasons. First, increasing sophistication in products, and rising consumer expectations of quality (not to mention increasingly stringent safety legislation which tends to act against 'cheap imported goods') mean that employers require employees who have reasonably high levels of skill and reliability. Even though these kinds of employees can be found around the world, the advantage of employing them rather than people nearer to home might be quite minimal.

Second, and relatedly, the proportion of the final cost of many products accounted for by wages is decreasing. In order to make real savings enterprises would do better to look at reducing costs in other parts of the operations. As Hirst and Thompson put it:

> As labour costs typically represent no more than about 20 per cent of the cost of the final product in manufacturing in advanced countries, the benefits of cheap labour are unlikely to dominate all other strategies of firms for whom R&D costs or marketing costs are as significant or more so than labour costs, or those firms for whom quality of the final product (and, therefore, its close supervision) is a primary concern. Low wages alone are thus unlikely to be decisive in the location of production in all but the most labour-intensive products or phases of production.... (Hirst and Thompson 1996, p.117)

As with the other aspects of economic globalization we have been looking at, the search for 'cheap' labour is more likely to affect relationships and processes *within* the already established economies than it is to develop new kinds of labour relationships across the globe:

> The tendency to locate in or lose jobs to low-wage countries in certain industries must continue to put pressure on low-wage and low-skill employment in the advanced countries, but it does not mean that output in manufacturing will switch wholesale to less developed countries. (Hirst and Thompson 1996, pp.117-8)

The Global Future of Work in the 'Network Society'

This discussion about the impact of economic globalization on divisions of labour takes us neatly into specific questions about what impact internationalization might have on the late-industrial labour process of the future. As a means of organizing this discussion we will look critically at a recent and particularly ambitious attempt to pull all the threads of economic globalization together into a single grand design; following Hirst and Thompson's approach, we will use this as a test case for understanding the extent to which the future of work will be truly global.

Adopting a mode of writing and analysis reminiscent of Daniel Bell, and very much in line with the 'great transformation' narrative approaches with which we began our account, Castells suggests that global processes and relationships are converging to produce what he calls 'the network society'. Picking up on the importance of the new technological paradigm of microelectronics (or as he prefers to call it, 'the Information Technology Revolution'), and placing this within the now-familiar framework of long-wave theory, he argues that the leading trait of network society is that it is 'informational and global':

> It is *informational* because the productivity and competitiveness of units or agents in this economy (be it firms, regions, or nations) fundamentally depend upon their capacity to generate, process, and apply efficiently knowledge-based information. It is *global* because the core components (capital, labor, raw materials, management, information, technology, markets) are organized on a global scale, either directly or through a network of linkages between economic agents. (Castells 1996, p.66)

It is important to emphasize that the key words here are 'organization' and 'network'. Essentially, and adopting the perspective that economic globalization is all about changes in processes and relationships, the core of Castells model is that information technology offers new ways of connecting *information* together at a global level: 'New information technologies... act upon all domains of human activity, and make it possible to establish endless connections between different domains, as well as between elements and agents of such activities' (Castells 1996, p.67).

Perhaps contrary to first impressions then, what is 'global' about the process of internationalization is not primarily the *physical* relocation of 'capital, labor, raw materials, management, information, technology, markets' (although of course these do have some kind of physical location somewhere), but *the information-intensive network of connections* which link them

227

together. Looking at the international division of labour for example, although Castells gives the impression that labour can physically circulate around the globe in an unrestricted manner (which clearly it cannot), what he is really getting at is that people are *affected* 'globally' by the decision-making and other informational processes which are taking place at the international level. The increasing 'globalization' of the labour force is simply a manifestation of the fact that because information can be obtained more easily and in more detail, there appears to be greater interdependence of labour around the globe. He gives three examples of the types of mechanisms through which this might happen:

> Global employment in the multinational corporations and their associated cross-border networks; impacts of international trade on employment and labor conditions... and effects of global competition and of the new mode of flexible management on each country's labor force. (Castells 1996, pp.234-5)

Unfortunately, Castells is not always entirely explicit about this important distinction between the globality of the informational network, and the globality of its practical consequences. As we saw in our earlier discussion of the international division of labour, whilst at one level there is evidence that: 'interdependence is characterized by the hierarchical segmentation of labour not between countries but across borders', it is much more problematic to suggest that this interdependence is leading towards 'the simultaneous integration of work process and disintegration of the workforce' (ibid., 1996, p.239) if by this Castells means actual integration and disintegration of *practical* activities (rather than information about them). We have already seen for example, that industrial and other kinds of productive activities are heavily concentrated in particular countries and regions, and that investment activity tends to consolidate rather than undermine these already established patterns of activity.

We could also reiterate the point that at least since the expansion of international trade during the nineteenth century, employees always have been affected by the international context within which the enterprises that employ them have had to operate. Although it can be argued that employees, and particularly managers, may have become more aware of this during the course of the twentieth century, it remains an open question as to whether this awareness affects their expectations and experiences of work to any great extent. Knowing that the boxes one is stacking contain spare parts for a Japanese company operating in Europe, or that one's employer is sub-contracted to another company which is in turn a subsidiary of an American conglomerate is unlikely to make any real difference to one's experience of the labour process.

This tendency towards imprecision is a feature which recurs in Castells account of the network society. For our current purposes it will be to useful to review what he has to say about some of the fairly specific features of the late-industrial labour process which we have looked at in previous chapters. To start with, and continuing with the theme of how processes of internationalization might affect the division of labour in the future, we can agree with Castells that: 'labour markets are not truly global, except for a small but growing segment of professionals and scientists' (Castells 1996, p.93). Whist then, a proportion of this elite minority might constitute a genuinely global workforce in the sense that they literally do travel the world as a necessary part of their work, they are extremely untypical of the workforce as a whole. If we look at this mobility from the point of view of divisions between core and peripheral employees, it is likely that the vast majority of employees - not least because they do not have the kinds of high-level knowledge and skills which qualifies or requires them to be so - will continue to be overwhelmingly affected by local and at most national patterns in the distribution of skills and employment prospects. It may be that, on the basis of detailed information about the availability of skills and the cost of labour in different places, an international corporation might make strategic decisions about dividing its operations between plants and subsidiaries around the world, but these decisions are made retrospectively of patterns of work which are already in place: Japanese motor manufactures did not come to Europe in order to create a skilled workforce, but to take advantage of the one that was already there.

Looking more closely at the role of managers within the international division of labour, Castells sees their role as becoming an increasingly important one: 'the most important transformation underlying the emergence of a global economy concerns the management of production and distribution, and of the production process itself':

> For the firm to operate in such a variable geometry of production and distribution a very flexible form of management is required, a form that is dependent on the flexibility of the firm itself and on the access to communication and production technologies suited to such flexibility. (Castells 1996, p.96)

This perception is in line with the general trend towards more innovative forms of management that we looked at in chapter three. Beaumont notes for example, that 'if *strategic* human resource management was very much the phrase of the 1980s then it is a reasonably safe bet that *international* human resource management will be the term of the 1990s':

> [It] revolves around issues associated with the cross-national transfer and management of human resources... the cross-national interaction of human resources... and comparative HRM [practices].... Such issues will raise questions such as whether there is increasing divergence (convergence) across national systems, whether practices are culturally determined and to what extent practices in one system can usefully be adopted and modified in other systems. (Beaumont 1993, p.210)

Beaumont goes on to note however, that in the same way that clear evidence of any full implementation of HRM strategies in the domestic sphere is difficult to come by, moves towards a more international implementation of such a strategy are likely to be highly problematic. One important instance of this, noted by both authors, is that it is difficult to overcome evident differences in national-cultural approaches to management. Castells asks for example, whether the spread of the 'Asian model' of business organization will eventually be adopted around the globe. He answers no and goes on the explain that:

> Cultures and institutions continue to shape the organizational requirements of the new economy, in an interaction between the logic of production, the changing technological basis, and the institutional features of the social environment.... The architecture and composition of business networks being formed around the world are influenced by the national characteristics of societies where such networks are embedded. (Castells 1996, p.194)

Whilst managers of international firms might like the idea of developing a pan-national approach towards the organization of their workforces - that office workers in their New York subsidiary adopt the same ways of working as their European parent company - it is difficult to see how they will be able to overcome the national 'cultures and institutions', the 'national characteristics of societies' in which their different operations are located. Whilst accepting that some aspects of the international division of labour are likely to become more *coordinated* at the global level, this is not at all the same as saying, as Castells repeatedly does, that these rather piecemeal developments constitute *convergence* towards truly global patterns of planning and production.

A third important set of issues discussed by Castells relate to the kind of business organizations which might operate in the network society of the future. Once again we are on familiar ground here, with much discussion of how the global/informational enterprises will constitute the nodes of the global network of the new global economy. The need to combine 'flexibility and coordination activities, to ensure both innovation and continuity in a fast-changing environment' will give rise to a new kind of animal, the 'horizontal corporation', or 'network enterprise', which is 'a dynamic and strategically planned network of self-programmed, self-directed units based on decentralization, participation, and coordination':

> [The network enterprise is]: that specific form of enterprise whose system of means is constituted by the intersection of segments of autonomous systems of goals. Thus, the components of the network are both autonomous and dependent *viv-a-vis* the network, and may be a part of other networks, and therefore of other systems of means aimed at other goals. The performance of a given network will then depend in two fundamental attributes of the network: its *connectedness*, that is its structural ability to facilitate noise-free communication between its components; its *consistency*, that is the extent to which there is sharing of interests between the network's goals and the goals of its components. (Castells 1996, pp.166/171 emphasis removed)

Superficially, this definition seems to capture the increasingly dynamic information-intensive nature of relationships between business organizations quite well. On closer examination however, it is difficult to reconcile this image of the global enterprise of the future with something more tangible and substantive. The image here is very much one in which the network itself actually displaces, and becomes more important than, the concrete organizations it is supposed to serve. We thus reach the somewhat mystifying position that the 'needs' of the network are more important than the needs of the organizations which participate in it. Moreover, not only are organizations represented as being involved in more than one network, but the purposes of those networks might be quite different.

Now whilst one can appreciate that an international enterprise could be involved in a financial network, a producer network and perhaps a political network, there would seem to be a very high probability that with so many variables in play at the same time, the prospects of maintaining 'consistency' and 'connectedness' might be quite slim. If we are to imagine that the global economy of the future will be constituted by an increasingly large number of networks, then it becomes quite impossible to believe that there is any kind of direction to these changes at all. The developmental logic here is that once the networks have divested themselves of the inconvenience of having to trouble over the specific, concrete and particular needs of real business organizations, they will follow some new, and as yet unknown trajectory of their own choosing.

In order to consolidate his argument for the emergence of this new kind of organization, Castells suggests that the network enterprise will emerge in order to overcome the limitations of the international organizations which currently dominate the world scene. Reflecting a number of issues we looked at earlier, he begins with the uncontroversial suggestion that: 'We are not witnessing the demise of powerful large corporation, but we are indeed observing the crisis of the *traditional corporate model* of organization based on vertical integration, and hierarchical, functional management...' (ibid., p.156, emphasis added). Much more contentiously however, he proposes that although 'Multinational enterprises seem to be still highly dependent on their national basis':

> The networks formed by multinational corporations do transcend national boundaries, identities, and interests. My hypothesis is that, as the process of globalization progresses, organizational forms evolve from *multinational enterprises* to *international networks*, actually bypassing the so-called "transnationals" that belong more to the world of mythical representation... than to the institutionally bounded realities of the world economy. (Castells 1996, p.192)

A little later he says:

> The network enterprise is increasingly international (not transnational), and its conduct will result from managed interaction between the global strategy of the network and the nationally/regionally rooted interests of its components. Since most multinational firms participate in a variety of networks depending on products, processes and countries, the new economy cannot be characterized as being centred any longer on multinational corporations, even if they continue to exercise jointly oligopolistic control over most markets. This is because corporations have transformed themselves into a web of multiple networks embedded in a multiplicity of institutional environments. Power still exists, but it is randomly exercised. (Castells 1996, pp.194-5)

Again we are presented with a somewhat confusing and highly complex picture of how international organizations will develop in the future. This unclarity arises out of Castells's desire to acknowledge the continuing importance of the nationally-based MNCs (which 'continue to exercise jointly oligopolistic control over most markets'), whilst *also* wanting to argue that they are now transcending their links with particular national economies. This trick is performed by invoking the distinction between the organization and its information-based planning process; it is the networks that organizations form which have 'transcended national boundaries', while the organizations themselves remain 'highly dependent' on their national home bases. One is

232

bound to ask whether this is actually very convincing, since presumably the strategic decisions made by these enterprises must be based on knowledge of their already dominant position in particular national economies.

As we saw in dismissing the idea that MNCs and being displaced by truly global TNCs, it is simply not possible to ignore the fact that although MNCs have a presence in several countries, they are still fundamentally *national* organizations. Moreover and in order to sustain his argument, Castells is forced into suggesting not only that MNCs are no longer 'national', but also that they are no longer *organizations* in the sense that we currently use the term: 'corporations have *transformed themselves* into a web of multiple networks embedded in a multiplicity of institutional environments'. Thus the inconvenience of national linkages disappears along with the vanishing organizations themselves. With all this information-intensive planning going on, and with the magical networks becoming ever more autonomous and self-serving, perhaps it is not surprising that although 'power still exists', 'it is randomly exercised'.

A fourth issue relates to the impact that these network enterprises have at the level of production and trade. There is a clear implication in Castells' argument that both these basic features of economic activity will be transformed in network society; that the production and sale of goods in the future will become increasingly fluid and unrestricted at the global level. We begin again on familiar ground:

> The dominant segments of most economic sectors... are organized worldwide in their actual operating procedures, forming what Robert Reich has labelled "the global web". The production process incorporates components produced in many different locations by different firms, and assembled for specific purposes and specific markets in a new form of production and commercialization: high-volume, flexible, customized production. (Castells 1996, p.96; Reich 1991)

Immediately however, we encounter an important qualification of this apparently open and spectacularly well-organized activity. It turns out that it is not production and trade *in general* which are operating in this way, but that it is '*the strategic aim* of firms, large and small, to sell whatever they can throughout the world, either directly or via their linkage with networks that operate in the world market' (ibid., p.95, emphasis added).

Similarly (and quite apart from the fact that very many firms would probably not identify with, nor be in a position to operate this kind of strategy), it is not all economies, nor all firms within particular national economies, nor yet all parts of the operations of a particular enterprise which act in this way, but only '*the dominant segments and firms*', 'the *strategic cores* of all economies' which are 'deeply connected to the world market', and whose fate 'is a function of their performance in such a market' (ibid., p.95, emphasis added). Without denying the importance and perhaps 'leading-edge' nature of these specific core activities, the pan-global picture of production and trade we were offered in the earlier quotation has been whittled down to something which is much more discrete and specific. It is only some very specific aspects of production and trade which are moving towards a more global pattern, and certainly not the whole of the global economy; there may be some logic in the idea that 'all economic and social processes do relate to the structurally dominant logic of such an economy', but the current reality is, as Castells willingly admits that: 'while the informational economy shapes the entire planet, and in this sense it is indeed global, most people in the planet *do not* work for or buy from the informational/global economy (ibid., p.103, emphasis added).

What emerges from these limited examples of Castells' analysis, is that to the extent that his model of network society represents the thesis of economic globalization in its strongest and most all-inclusive form, there remain very serious impediments, both analytical and practical, in accepting that this is what the global future of work will be like. We will conclude by making two general criticisms.

First, the idea of the network itself is extremely elusive. In Castells' scenario 'network' ceases to be a description of the variously linked relationships through which enterprises interact with one another, and becomes instead an autonomous entity which not only has a life of its own, but actually reconstructs the very form of those relationships. However, there is a very large step indeed between *describing* changes in the mode of exchanging information necessary for conducting economic relationships such as those associated for example, with innovations in communications and data-processing technologies, and taking this as evidence of some fundamental change in what the production process *actually is*. When Castells says that 'the network enterprise makes material the culture of the informational/global economy: it transforms signals into commodities by processing knowledge' (ibid., p.172), the logic of his argument seems to be that actual production of tangible commodities and services will vanish along with enterprises themselves; that 'networkness' or 'networkability' will become a substitute for real production as we currently understand it. The network thus becomes the be-all and end-all of everything, the great solvent or perhaps detergent of history:

For the first time in history, the basic unit of economic organization is not a subject, be it individual... or collective.... the unit is the network, made up of a variety of subjects and organizations, relentlessly modified as networks adapt to supportive environments and market structures. (Castells 1996, p.198)

Having given the network such a momentous role in the history of the future, Castells tries to complete the rather awkward manoeuvre of giving it a real personality or 'culture' of its own. Borrowing from Weber's identification of capitalism as having an 'ethical foundation' and 'spirit', Castells finds himself wondering: 'What is, then, this "ethical foundation of the network enterprise" this "spirit of informationalism"?':

It is a culture, indeed, a patchwork of experiences and interests, rather than a charter of rights and obligations. It is a *multi-faceted, virtual culture*, as in the visual experiences created by computers in cyberspace by rearranging reality.... The network enterprise learns to live within this virtual culture. Any attempt at crystallizing the position in the network as a cultural code in a particular time and space sentences the network to obsolescence, since it becomes too rigid for the variable geometry required by informationalism. (Castells 1996, p.199, original emphasis.)

Whilst this kind of perspective will seem familiar and acceptable to those looking at the future of work through the lens of *cultural* globalization, it is almost impossible to reconcile this highly sytlized and impossibly vague description with any concrete understanding of what the *economic* future of work might be like. Sadly, Castells has conjured up a fantasy image which, as he earlier said of the 'so-called transnationals', belongs 'more to the world of mythical representation... than to the institutionally bounded realities of the world economy'. Are we really to believe that the messy, noisy, painful business of earning a living can be squared with the idea of a 'multi-faceted virtual culture' which only really 'exists' in cyberspace? I think not.

Secondly, and more helpful from the point of view of understanding how internationalization might affect patterns of work in the future, we can abandon the widespread misconception that 'economic globalization' has something to do with integration and convergence towards a single historical and developmental trajectory. Although as Castells says: 'a global economy is something different [from a world economy]: it is an economy with the capacity to work as a unit in real time on a planetary scale' (ibid., p.92), we should remember that the capacity for something to happen in no way guarantees that it will happen. In refining our perception of which processes and which relationships are being subjected to, and are perhaps becoming more intensified by, economic globalization, we have to acknowledge that this is, and is likely to remain, a highly specific and selective process:

> The global economy does not embrace all economic processes in the planet. It does not include all territories, and it does not include all people in its workings, although it does affect directly or indirectly the livelihood of the entire humankind. While its effects reach out to the whole planet, its actual operation and structure concern only segments of economic structures, countries, and regions, in proportions that vary according to the particular position of a country or region in the international division of labour. (Castells 1996, p.102)

7 Work Futures

One of the most striking features of the foregoing discussion is that there are conflicts and challenges *between* the accounts generated by the various perspectives we have been looking at. Challenges and conflicts which give rise to quite different characterizations and emphases in describing what the main features of the future of work will be. Despite our preference for tidy conclusions, these differences make it difficult to produce an entirely satisfactory synthesis of what they have to say on the topic. At one level then, we arrive back where we started and have to conclude that there are many futures of work depending on who one is, where one lives, how much education one has had and so on. Even if some way could be found for accommodating these differences between people living within the same national economic structure, this might tell us very little about the situation of people living in quite different national circumstances.

At another level however, and perhaps more confidently, the preceding discussion does allow us to say some useful things about the advantages and disadvantages of the various approaches and perspectives which are at our disposal, and to reach some reasonably concrete conclusions about the prevailing trends and tendencies out of which the future of work is being forged. It also allows us to look again at the continuing purchase of the narrative accounts of work with which we began our account, and to reflect a little on the themes of continuity and change, and on the relationship between the practical and ideational aspects of work which have been present throughout.

How to Study the Future of Work

A first problem we need to address in deciding what strategy to adopt in studying the future of work is that of understanding the different levels at which conflicts and challenges between the different accounts arise. One issue is that differences are exacerbated by variations in the degree of abstraction which each perspective contains. For example, perspectives which take issues of identity as their central thematic, tend to operate at a much higher level of abstraction than do those centred around workforce segregation. Whilst it is useful and necessary to have both accounts, the kinds of evidence they provide are not actually very compatible since it is difficult to reconcile highly specific empirical material of the kind generated by the SCELI project, with generalized descriptions of selfhood.

Whilst this is partly a consequence of the nature of concepts and ideas involved, it is also a reflection of differences in the preoccupations and interests of those who use them. Whilst this may simply be a matter of personal choice, it is also, in a Weberian sense, a matter of value judgements. People who offer views about the future of work add value or make value judgements about which bits of social practice and social experience are the most important. The concept of globalization for example, is clearly a much broader idea than that of the provision of child care to households.

Determining which is the more *important* concept however, depends on whether one is primarily interested in the abstract dynamics of social development, or on the more immediate and directly practical problems which people are already known to be facing. Whilst feminist contributions to the future of work would acknowledge the impact of global processes on the opportunities and constraints faced by women, they are likely to see these as secondary when compared with the issue of continuing prejudice and marginalization at the day-to-day level. Similarly, the concept of culture is more abstract than the concept of flexible specialization. Although managers always have been concerned about the subjectivities of their employees and more recently have entered the fringes of debates about the 'culture of the enterprise', their concerns about the future of work are prioritized in terms of keeping up with technological change and of developing 'best practice' in their organizations. For cultural theorists, these concerns tend to be framed as being less important than the more intimate questions of the impact of work on people's sense of who they are.

Up to a point, arguments about the extent to which consumption is displacing production as the primary site of people's experience is more a consequence of a general down-grading of academic interest in the latter, rather than a real reflection of any actual decline in its importance. Further still, and in terms of the scope of the account offered in this volume, the perspectives we have been looking at are by no means exhaustive. We could for example, have chosen to include those which are based around issues of social and governmental policy. Here we would find important discussions about the continuing role of the State in providing people with opportunities for work, and whether welfare policies help or hinder social and economic development (e.g. Doyal and Gough 1984, Hutton 1994, Burrows and Loader (eds.) 1994, Joseph Rowntree Foundation 1995, Pierson 1996). We could have included debates around citizenship, communitarianism, and 'the right to work'. This would have allowed us to look more closely at how the individual's position in the division of labour provides access to the public realm with its incumbent rights and responsibilities, and orients them with regard to the institutions of the State (e.g. Van Parijs (ed.) 1992, Glyn and Miliband (eds.)

1994, Jordan 1996). This alerts us to the fact that all accounts of what the future of work will be like are partial and incomplete.

These variations of content and emphasis also have an impact upon the kind of contribution each account can make in describing what the future of work will be like, both in terms of the actual amount of directly relevant commentary, and in terms of the degree to which it challenges the way things are. Theorists of consumption for example, have little to say about the future of work, not because they think it is unimportant but because many of the issues they choose to study lie elsewhere. Conversely, although participants in debates about post-Fordism might have little to say about culture or identity, they are much better placed to comment on the practicalities of work.

If we were conducting a kind of academic audit we might conclude that it would be better to concentrate on one area rather than another so as to achieve the highest yield of what we have selected as the most directly relevant material. In foreclosing our field of enquiry however, we would forfeit important information from other fields. Another of our conclusions then, is that in recent years there has been a forceful attempt to get away from the somewhat narrow approach which characterized the study of work until the late-1970s. The contributions of feminist discourses, and discourses around identity and culture have played an important part in this renewed effort.

Turning to differences in critical purchase, it is also clear that some perspectives are much more critical and proactive in their approach to the future of work then are others. One of the characteristics of feminist accounts for example, is that they have a lot more to say about how the future of work *should be* compared with other accounts. Although those who study the empirical details of gender segregation usefully bring the picture - or at least a fragment of it - into closer focus, they tend to be rather shy when it comes to offering any opinion about what the alternatives might be.

Similarly, and perhaps even more dispassionately, while those who study skill, control and technology at work have opinions about whether this or that type of change will be more beneficial, will provide a better quality of working experience, will contribute to the fuller development of the individual, they tend to adopt a somewhat fatalistic attitude about what is going on. The provision of detailed accounts sometimes seems to act as a substitute for constructive speculation about how improvements might be achieved. Showing even less imagination about what the future of work could be like, and largely preoccupied with meeting the next set of production targets, managers seem to have almost nothing to say on the topic. Of all the accounts we have looked at managerialist accounts sometimes seem to be entirely reactive rather than forward looking. For all the talk about breaking new ground, of taking the lead, of regaining a

239

competitive advantage, we are all too aware that much of this is actually a matter of trying to catch up with producers in the Southeast Asian economies who *did* have new ideas and *did* put them to work.

Whilst there is nothing inherently wrong with being uncritical these preferences for apparent objectivity, detachment and pragmatism do not provide grounds for being prejudicial about those approaches which *do* arise out of a deep sense of wanting to change things. As the empirical evidence we have been looking at shows, there is a clear parallel here between the kind of insecurity and worry that radical suggestions cause within the academy and the kinds of disturbance they cause outside it. As we have seen in our discussion of gender ideologies of work, and of the changing bases of masculine and feminine identities, people feel very uneasy about changing the way things are. For 'tradition' we can read 'paranoia' at the prospect of change. Many people will find it difficult to avoid a deep sense of foreboding at the prospect of abandoning established ideas about work. After all, one of the reasons why these have survived for so long, is precisely because continuity has provided a sense of security.

To challenge people directly about these ideas is tantamount to accusing them of self-delusion, of holding beliefs about work which are deeply flawed. The natural reaction has been to defend the old ideas and, initially at least, to reject the new. A further conclusion then, is that accounts of the future of work which put forward challenging suggestions about what the alternatives might be are bound to be treated with great suspicion and cause considerable unease. Overcoming these genuine feelings of insecurity is one of the most difficult challenges faced by studies of the future of work.

In expressing our preferences about how to study the future of work then, we are arranging the different factors and issues into a kind of analytical and discursive hierarchy. Although at one level we have to regard all accounts as equally valid - they all have something useful to say about the future of work - at a more political level it is difficult not to pin one's colours to a particular mast. Again, although this might seem to be a somewhat esoteric issue only of concern to academics a not dissimilar procedure is also followed by people in general.

Each of the imagined characters we met at the very beginning of our account will have different opinions about what their future of work will be. Some views might seem to be better informed than others, and the number of choices on offer will certainly vary, but it would be quite wrong to dismiss any particular view as being invalid. Pessimistically, the most cogent thing we can say about how to study the future of work is that it is an indeterminate and very messy business which requires us to make difficult choices about which issues are the more important, what kinds of evidence are the most persuasive, and which perspective hits the target most often. Optimistically, we can say that each of these choices

240

generates a number of interesting permutations in describing what the future of work will be like. However fragmentary it might ultimately be, a brief review of the specific conclusions offered within the various analytical perspectives we have been looking at allows us to build up an overall picture of its most likely features.

Describing the Future of Work

If one is approaching the topic from within established sociology of work perspectives, and is primarily interested in issues of skill and control, one would predict that people are likely to get more of the same, but this time with different kinds of skills and different forms of organization of the production process. One would stress that many skills are now hybrid rather than singular, and that at least at the level of conceptual integrity and subjective experience things are getting better rather than worse. One would also describe how these changes are being accompanied by the emergence of integrated control systems based around team- and group-working rather than around hierarchic systems. In both cases however, there are clear and growing divisions between those employed in core jobs and those in peripheral jobs. The relative job security and economic well-being of the former will be heavily contrasted with the largely debilitating and marginalizing experiences of the latter. More and more these differences are structured into the labour market as employers define their need for employees in terms of functional and numerical flexibility. Perceptions of employability now relate more to attributes of future potential and availability than to skills and credentials already held. Investments in training and career development are, and will remain, focused on core employees alone.

Also from within a sociology of work perspective, but this time having a keener interest in technological change, one would focus attention on how the new paradigm of microelectronic technologies now dominates the practicalities of work. Emphasizing the inherent flexibility that this brings to the production process, one would stress that the horizons of possibility regarding ways of working and means of organization are being shifted. One would also describe how although the *content* of these possibilities is different, the *process* of change, characterized by invention, innovation and implementation, is largely a continuation of developments which have been taking place for as long as anyone can remember. Computers are different from steam engines, but the desire to appropriate their use for the purposes of generating profit is largely the same. Confident in the correctness of this thought, one might also stress that as latest developments in artificial intelligence, optical and other kinds of telecommunications, and perhaps genetic engineering reach maturity, they will add further momentum to the on-going process of technical change.

241

Many of the same features would be noted by someone looking at the future of work from a managerial perspective. Taking the priorities of achieving best practice, of reaching 'best in class' status, and of maintaining technological comparability for granted, one would frame one's perception of the future of work in terms of continuing innovation. The problems of anticipating new kinds of consumer demand for goods and services, and of being able to meet these demands in a timely manner, would be uppermost. Together with concerns about relative productivity, much attention would be paid to the global context within which these challenges are being framed. However parochial one's concerns and experiences might seem, reminders of the 'global competitive environment' - real or imagined - will not be very far away. This future of work is thus framed in terms of goals and targets and the strategies to meet them. This is a pragmatic orientation where developments are judged on the grounds of relatively short-term expediency.

In terms of attitudes towards the workforce, latent concerns about work satisfaction and fulfilment are regarded as no less important than in the past, but the degree to which they impinge upon the future organization of work is restricted by relatively unchanging perceptions of costs and benefits. However much one might like the idea of using HRM strategies to the benefit of employees, this will still be regarded as secondary to its role in benefiting the enterprise. In large part changes in organization are driven by the demands of the technology and the skill requirements which this dictates. It might be nice to imagine a situation where all employees feel part of an organization which actually cares about them, is prepared to accommodate their intrinsic concerns, and to offer equal opportunities for training and career advancement, but the reality its that a significant number of tasks actually don't have these capacities.

Whilst a proportion of employees are regarded as important because of their flexibility in offering multiple kinds of core skills, the main attribute of many employees is that other kind of flexibility namely their easy availability and willingness to work variable hours. Only in the core are real people and actual jobs identifiable one with the other. In the periphery, the actual person who does the job is much less important than the fact that the job needs to be done. The chief designer or the head chef have individuality and a true working identity within the enterprise; the person in the packing department or the washer-upper have no such identity since there are any number of other employees who can replace them.

Also centrally concerned with these features but adopting a quite different and much more critical perspective are those who are developing feminist discourses about the future of work. The immediate problem here is of having to make suggestions against a background of established perceptions (both academic and popular) not only of what work is and who should have access to it, but of what constitutes household life. Whilst many of the above contributions have really only had to address the past in a superficial way, and have barely touched upon the role of the household in social reproduction, feminist accounts have had to do a great deal of foundational and reconstructive work even before they can begin looking to the future. From this perspective, the future of work for women is paradoxical. On the one hand it is clear that increasing opportunities for employment may offer greater equality in social and economic status for women. A stronger presence in the workforce, particularly in higher occupations, may help to erode the male prejudices of the past. In their turn these shifts may serve to weaken the grip of gender ideologies as previously dichotomous perceptions of the appropriate roles of men and women are shown to be irrational and divisive.

On the other hand, and as many feminist accounts from within the sociology of work have shown, these shifts in consciousness may not be sufficient to counteract deep-rooted assumptions about the relationship between women and poorly paid, insecure and menial types of work in the periphery. Even though the structured nature of the availability of these kinds of work poses a considerable challenge both to prospective male and female employees, and even though the demands of flexibility might suite the preferences of some women quite well, it remains the case that women will have to work harder, to study longer, and to struggle more if they want to put themselves on a equal footing with men in the future of work.

Feminist perspectives also stress that ultimately, the avoidance of being trapped into meaningless jobs requires the elimination of those kinds of jobs for both women *and* men. From this perspective then, the future of work is seen very much in terms of overcoming immediate practical difficulties and restraints. The shape the future will take will be directly tied to the rate at which equal opportunities are actively driven forward and genuinely implemented. Progress here will in turn depend on introducing practical shifts in the burden and responsibility for social reproduction which currently rests with the household. Without these changes, opportunities in the future of work will remain just as closed and partial as they have been in the past.

Less immediately identifiable as commentators on the future of work are the cultural theorists and the theorists of identity. For someone adopting this perspective, the future of work will be one where work itself has become less important in the balance of people's activities and thus in their sense of who they are. Setting aside concerns for the structural complexities of the labour process, with its aggregations of managers and workers, the skilled and the unskilled, with its topography of core and periphery and its detailed descriptions of new patterns of work, it is the individual who is seen as being the main unit of analysis in the future. All the rest is just the scenery against which the really important business of self-dissection and self-construction takes place. Allowing a certain imprecision and thus working from a somewhat glossed and partial account of practical changes in the labour process, the future of work is one in which people will become increasingly enthusiastic about opportunities for developing new kinds of identity and selfhood.

The demise of the old stereotype of work as a largely rigidifying, limiting and stultifying experience will give way to one in which people develop a new confidence about themselves and their working lives. No longer timid and embarrassed about confronting and transgressing previously accepted dichotomies between maleness and femaleness, between men's work and women's work, or between the realms of work and non-work, we will increasingly identify with ourselves and with the selves of others as consumers rather than as producers. Our sense of who we are in relation to other people will be calibrated less in terms of the jobs we do and more in terms of lifestyle locations. When we ask someone who we are meeting for the first time 'what do you do?', we will no longer be interested mainly in the job they have but in their habits as consumers. Perhaps for the first time then, and having become much more aware of the true extent of our ontologies, we might be able to stop always addressing the self from the point of view of work, and instead to address work from the point of view of the self.

The final discourse we have been looking at, economic globalization, also characterizes the future in terms of continuity and change, order and disorder. Whilst experiences in the modern world are increasingly centred on the intimate realm of the self, they are also, and confusingly, influenced by the distant and the unknown. Whilst we may become more aware of the potential impact of globalization on economic processes and relationships, it remains an open question as to whether this awareness will actually make much of a difference to people's perception of the work that they do. At the level of immediate day-to-day experiences within the workplace, patterns of work and access to employment will continue to be framed largely in terms of local conditions. As far as the larger question of global convergence in economic affairs is concerned, the jury is still out. Some might say that it has not yet been appointed.

Future Narratives?

We began our account by looking at what we labelled the narrative accounts of work put forward by the theorists of industrialism, post-industrialism and post-Fordism. Although the current trend in studying the future of work has been to move away from the story-telling approach and to concentrate instead on particular and more closely prescribed sets of issues and concerns, it has proved almost impossible to repress our tendency to frame the future in terms of the past.

Superficially, this exposes the fact that the distinction between narrative and non-narrative approaches is in any case somewhat bogus since even perspectives such as those around issues of identity which characterize the future in terms of increasing individuality and fragmentation have to locate people in some kind of historical context. As C.Wright Mills observed, for as long as people have biographies - as long as they move chronologically from one year to another - there always will be some kind of history, and thus some kind of narrative which can be told. We may no longer define 'history' in terms of social evolution with its assumptions about the inevitability of progress, but we do still have a sense of ourselves as being participants in a gradual unfolding of time and experience.

Less superficially however, the grip of narrative does tell us some very important things both about what the future of work will be like and how to study it. To begin with, and despite their current neglect, many of the basic themes developed in the classic accounts of economic and social development put forward by Marx, Weber and Durkheim, are just as important at the end of the twentieth century as they were at its beginning. From Marx's account for example, we already know that the positive material and psychological benefits which accrue from working activities are often overshadowed by experiences of inequality and exploitation. Whilst ongoing changes in the way that work is organized have the potential to reduce and perhaps overcome these negative experiences, we have to address the sobering fact that the same kind of optimism has been expressed many times before.

In looking at the future of work we therefore have to be realistic in the expectations we have of it. It would be brave indeed to forecast that the experience of work in the early part of the next century will be characterized by liberation, freedom and fulfilment. Certainly none of the accounts we have been looking at reach this conclusion. What we can say though is that we have a clearer understanding of *why* work is likely to remain an alienating experience for many people. In large part this understanding arises out of a more detailed unpacking of the potential sources of alienation.

In addition to the basic kinds of material compulsion and exploitation analysed by Marx, we can add that the future of work will continue to alienate people if access to, and choice of employment, continue to be restricted by prejudicial expectations and assumptions about who should be doing what kinds of work. Whilst it may be the case that in the future work will be more varied and interesting, more creative and fulfilling, more healthy and rewarding, this will mean nothing at all to the many people who are denied access to these kinds of work. If anything, the excluded, the marginalized and the economically dispossessed will feel the divisions between high and low quality jobs even more acutely than they do already.

245

Even more seriously, and despite the current tendency to assume that access to employment has become unproblematic, the future of work will continue to be characterized by divisions between those with secure employment and those without. This amounts to an extension of the core/periphery model *across* the boundary of employment, between the relatively secure and those on the margins. Although flexibility generates benefits in terms of more varied kinds and patterns of work it also has the effect of institutionalizing the miscellaneous and fragmentary nature of many kinds of work and occupations.

Whilst there are clear indications that so-called non-standard forms of working will become more and more common in the future, it remains to be seen whether other structures such as legal protection for employees, trade union representation, training and career pathways, pensions and other employment-related benefits and so on will develop at the same rate. Whereas for the employer flexibility means 'opportunity', for employees it may mean 'insecurity'. One of the key personal and employment skills of the future will be the ability to cope with job insecurity, uncertainty and change.

This spectre of the divided society reminds us of Durkheim's concerns about the impact of industrialism on the integrity of society. It is undoubtedly more fashionable to characterize these potential divisions in terms of core and periphery, and to explain them as being a necessary and inevitable consequence of industrial development, but the basic point remains that the division of labour is not just a practical thing to do with the specialization of tasks, but is also a social thing which deeply affects the kinds of relationships people form with one another. If it is the case, as the cultural and identity theorists suggest, that the future of work will be characterized by a new and enhanced sense of identity-as-an-individual, then we are bound to ask what impact this will have on the individual as part of society. Perhaps unexpectedly, an increasing sense of wanting to be different from other people will result in a deeper understanding of our dependence on them.

If Durkheim were writing today about the future of work and its role in society, he might suggest that the social tensions caused by the division of labour can never be fully resolved, and that we should look to the realm of consumption as the new site for social solidarity. In the same way that the division of labour in modern society replaced the *conscience collective* of pre-modern society as the main source of social solidarity, perhaps the 'division of consumption' is taking on this role in post-modern society. Instead of continuing to believe that complete social solidarity will emerge from within the realm of work - courtesy of the division of labour, we might suggest that the social solidarity of the future will increasingly depend upon a withering away of this realm altogether; upon its foreshortening and foreclosing in relation and proportion to all the other realms of activity in which we engage. 'True' freedom from work in Marx's sense is not something which is available *within* the realm of work, but must be sought *outside* it.

In reapplying the theoretical and analytical insights developed by Marx and Durkheim we can see that in the future, work will continue to be characterized by an awkward balance between the old and the new, between continuity and change, between new opportunities for some and less promising prospects for others. This tension between what *can* be done and what *should* be done takes us back to Weber's distinction between formal and substantive rationality.

At the practical level, new technologies and means of organizing the labour process are providing powerful new opportunities for expressing formal rationality; if we want to produce such-and-such a commodity, or offer such-and-such a service more efficiently then before, then the practical means of doing so are close at hand. At the level of whether or not such developments are desirable and necessary however, whether it is *substantively* rational to seek out these new opportunities, we have hardly moved forward at all. Weber's pessimism about where the drive for rationality might lead, and Bell, Galbraith's and Beck's concerns about how the economic 'benefits' of acquisitive productivism can be reconciled with the social and environmental 'costs' of acting in this apparently rational way are issues which continue to be studiously ignored. Less pessimistically though, and co-opting this schizophrenic depiction of rationality, we can note that increases in flexibility at the practical level are being accompanied by important new kinds of flexibility at the ideational level.

Ideational flexibility underscores one of the strongest messages to emerge from the foregoing account, which is that by looking at the future of work from a number of different perspectives we can more fully appreciate how perceptions of change are increasingly being expressed and described explicitly in terms of changes in people's expectations, attitudes and beliefs about what work is what role it plays in our lives. Whilst these concerns obviously have practical and pragmatic dimensions since we can not get away from the fact that, for the foreseeable future at least, work will remain our only means of earning a living, they are nonetheless marked by an intellectual desire to explore new possibilities.

Up to a point, we are becoming increasingly disinterested in looking at the 'objective' possibilities of what the future of work might be like in practical terms, and much more interested in developing new ideas about what work *could* be like. For example, from a feminist perspective, the promise of women achieving true equality with men is increasingly being expressed in terms of looking again at the balance between activities inside and outside the household, not only in terms of who is responsible for them, but also in terms of what they *mean*, and in terms of the personal and social value they carry. This desire to put forward imaginative alternatives, and thus to overturn the categorical stereotypes into which various activities are currently classified, is taking place very much at the level of ideas. In demonstrating that gender ideology is socially constructed and thus historically variable, and in showing how material practices of segregation and subordination are linked to these established perceptions, it is plain to see that perceptual and ideational changes are already heavily involved in shaping the future of work for both men and women.

A very similar approach has also emerged from within culturalist and identity perspectives, where again the emphasis is on the framing of expectations and experiences of work specifically in terms of personal meanings and interpretations. Even from within the more traditional sociology of work perspectives, it is clear that in matters of production and work organization, new ideas about how to organize things are tending to prefigure discussions about how to put them into practice. It may well be that the formal techniques of flexible specialization, or of HRM have been explored in more detail than the ideas upon which they are based, but this should not distract us from the fact that someone somewhere developed new ideas and considered it to be substantively rational to put them into practice. It is to be hoped that the much heralded triumph of flexibility in the practical and material sense will be matched by greater flexibility at the level of ideas about what kind of future of work we would like to have.

If, as Marx suggested, humankind only sets itself new tasks when the means of achieving them are available, then perhaps the time has now come for us to discuss again what those tasks should be. Whilst we are still some way short of achieving 'true' liberation from work, the kinds of ideas offered by the various accounts described here might allow us a glimpse of what that sense of liberty entails and so stiffen our resolve to bring it about.

Chapter Notes

Chapter One

1 Kumar is referring here to Charles Darwin's theory of 'natural selection' as presented in his major works *Origin of the Species* (1859) and *The Descent of Man* (1871).

2 The main inventions were Kay's flying shuttle (1733) for weaving, Hargreaves' 'spinning Jenny' (1768), Arkwright's 'water frame' (1769), and Crompton's mule (1779) for spinning yarn, and Cartwright's power-driven loom (1786).

3 For more details see Murphy 1973 Part II. Also useful are Lane 1978, Evans 1983 and Doyle 1992 Part 1.

4 In addition to Ashton, whose book was originally published in 1948, the other 'classic' accounts of are: Arnold Toynbee, *The Industrial Revolution*, published in 1884 and Paul Mantoux, *The Industrial Revolution in the Eighteenth Century*, published in 1906.

5 For more detailed introductions to these debates see: Swingewood 1984; Morrison 1995; Hughes *et al.* 1995; Craib 1997, and McIntosh 1997.

6 There is some dispute on this point, since Marx can be interpreted as suggesting that social or 'class' relations, rather than 'technical relations', are the prime movers in economic and social development. On this understanding, Marx becomes more a theorist of class struggle, than a theorist of the industrial labour process. The capitalist class is able to impose a particular kind of labour process on the rest of society because it has ownership and control over the means of production. Developments within the forces of production - including technological developments - do not therefore have an independent life of their own, but are circumscribed by the class situation in which they occur. For a discussion of this point see: Anderson 1974, Callinicos 1985, and Ransome 1996.

7 It is worth emphasizing again that the vast majority of people *actually do* have these expectations - they are not figments of the sociological imagination. Evidence for this has been very consistent over time. For examples see: Blum 1953, Blauner 1964, Davis and Werling 1964, Goldthorpe *et al.* 1968, Beynon and Blackburn 1972, Mackenzie 1973, Lockwood 1975, Blackburn and Mann 1979, Cullen *et al.* 1980, Fox 1980, and Brown *et al.* 1983. For a fuller discussion see Ransome 1996.

Expectations which are centred around patterns of consumption, lifestyle and identity are discussed in later chapters.

8   In addition to Lowith see Brubaker 1984, Andreski's introduction to Weber 1983, and Andreski 1985.

9   R.H.Tawney makes a similar point: 'The exact analysis of natural conditions, the calculations of forces and strains, the reduction of the complex to the operation of simple, constant, and measurable forces, was the natural bias of an age interested primarily in mathematics and physics' (Tawney 1960, p.249).

10   On this point Marx notes: 'For wages the lowest and the only necessary rate is that required for the subsistence of the worker during work and enough extra to support a family and prevent the race of workers from dying out. According to Smith, the normal wage is the lowest which is compatible with common humanity, i.e. with a bestial existence' (Marx 1975, p.283; Adam Smith, *The Wealth of Nations*, vol.1, p.61).

11   'In fact [the capitalist system] no longer needs the support of any religious forces, and feels the attempts of religion to influence economic life, in so far as they can still be felt at all, to be as much an unjustified interference as its regulation by the state. In such circumstances man's commercial and social interests tend to determine their opinions and attitudes' (Weber 1976, p.72).

12   He defines these terms as follows: 'The totality of beliefs and sentiments common to average citizens of the same society forms a determinate system which has its own life; one may call it the *collective* or *common conscience*... it has specific characteristics which make it a distinct reality'. (Durkheim   1933, pp.79-80) 'What justifies this term [mechanical solidarity] is that... the individual conscience... is a simple dependent upon the collective type and follows all of its movements, as the possessed object follows those of its owner. In societies where this type of solidarity is highly developed, the individual does not appear.... It is quite otherwise with the solidarity which the division of labour produces. Whereas the previous type implies that individuals resemble each other, this type presumes their difference. The first is possible only in so far as the individual personality is absorbed into the collective personality; the second is possible only if each one has a sphere of action which is peculiar to him; that is, a personality. It is necessary, then, that the collective conscience leave open a part of the individual conscience in order that special functions may be established there, functions which it cannot regulate. The more this region is extended, the stronger is the cohesion which results from this solidarity.... And, moreover, the unity of

the organism is as great as the individuation of the parts more marked' (Durkheim 1933, pp.130-1).

13 Durkheim identifies this sense of loss of control and purpose as one of the defining characteristics of 'anomic suicide': 'Egoistic suicide results from man's no longer finding a basis for existence in life; altruistic suicide, because this basis for existence appears to man situated beyond life itself. The third sort of suicide... results from man's activity's lacking regulation and his consequent sufferings. By virtue of its origin we shall assign this last category the name of *anomic suicide*.... In anomic suicide, society's influence is lacking in the basically individual passions, thus leaving them without check-rein [it] has its principal field among... the industrial and commercial world'. (Durkheim 1952, p.258)

Chapter Two

1 For a summary discussion of these terms see: Bell 1974, pp.37-40; Kumar 1978, pp.193-4; and Amin 1994, pp.1-5.

2 Drawing on the work of Browning and Singelmann (1978), Gershuny and Miles also distinguish between 'producer services' which 'span industries providing finance, design, management and legal services, among others, to industries (which may themselves produce goods or services)', 'distributive services', which 'provide transport and communications, as well as storage and sales facilities to other industries', 'social services' which 'provide collectively for some individual needs (health, education, etc.), and for some aspects of social order (the police and related functions)', and finally 'personal services', constituting a mixture of 'declining, individually-organised activities like domestic services, together with capital-intensive and often monopolistic activities like some entertainments and hotels' (Gershuny and Miles 1983, pp.13-14).

3 Kumar suggests that it would be useful to distinguish not only *between* the primary (extractive industries), secondary (industrial) and tertiary (service) sectors, but *within* the latter between a tertiary sector composed of well-established and unremarkable services in finance, commerce and administration, and a *quaternary* sector composed of the more recent so-called 'semi-professions' in education, social work and health services, and providers of leisure, entertainment and recreation services. He agrees with Bell that it is within the latter that we find the 'professional, technical and scientific groups' whose emergence constitutes 'the

essential underlying movement to post-industrialism' (Kumar 1978, p.212).

4   There are of course exceptions to this general rule as is demonstrated by the growing support, initially by a minority and later more generally, for anti-nuclear, environmental and other social movement organizations. The Campaign for Nuclear Disarmament was formally constituted in London in 1958, and Greenpeace was founded in Vancouver in 1969. For more details see: Minion and Bolsover (eds.) 1983, Marx and McAdam 1994.

5   Although we are following Gilbert *et al.*'s analysis here, other authors have attached slightly different labels to the perspectives which have contributed to the Fordism/post-Fordism debate. In his introduction to these debates for example, Amin (1994), divides his analysis between the regulationists, the neo-Schumpterians, and the flexible specialization approach. Elam (1994) prefers the labels neo-Marxist (referring to the regulationists), neo-Schumpterian, and neo-Smithian (referring to Piore and Sabel's work on the emergence of flexible specialization). In the conclusion to this chapter, it will be argued that although each approach differs in its emphasis and in its analysis of causality, there is a high degree of correspondence between these perspectives regarding the *key factors* involved. The alternative points of departure tend to lead towards very parallel conclusions.

6   In his analysis of the political consequences of 'privatism and autonomy', Lodziak draws attention to the double-sided nature of this phenomenon: 'It is clear that the experienced lack of autonomy steers people towards the private sphere, and can result in apolitical self-absorption. But there is also a sense in which privatism can be seen to reflect an attempt to exercise autonomy.... opportunities are opening up for the development of this capacity in the private sphere' (Lodziak 1995, p.91).

7   This is of course a direct repetition of the trends identified by Marx in the transition towards 'Modern Industry' during the mid-eighteenth century: 'Manufacture produced the machines, by means of which Modern Industry abolished the handicraft and manufacturing systems in those spheres of production that it first seized upon'. (Marx 1954 *Capital I*, p.361) See also Braverman 1974.

8   For an illustrative example of the adoption of the just-in-time system in the UK, see Turnbull 1988. For a discussion of the impact of these developments on working relationships, see Hyman and Streek 1988, Rubery and Wilkinson (eds.) 1994, Grint and Woolgar 1997. For an

analysis of the impact of these developments at the level of the international economy see Dicken 1992.

9   This analysis draws heavily on concepts developed by Antonio Gramsci. For a full account of these see Ransome 1992.

Chapter Three

1   For further discussion of how 'skill' can be defined see Gallie 1991 and Vallas 1990. In more recent research reported by Gallie (1996), 'skill' is assessed or measured in terms of 'multiple indicators' including formal qualifications, training and experience.

2   Braverman's book *Labor and Monopoly Capital* (1974) instigated a new phase of empirical and analytical studies into the nature and organization of work in industrial capitalist societies which lasted well into the 1980s. The issues of 'skill' and 'control' - which we will be looking at shortly - were central to these debates. The best summaries are still those provided in Wood, (ed.) 1982, and Thompson, 1983). The impact of technological change on the labour process had featured in an earlier wave of research known as the 'technological implications approach' during the 1950s and 1960s. Main contributions were provided by: W.F.Whyte 1949 and 1951; Rice 1958; Trist *et al.* 1963; Walker and Guest 1952; Turner 1956; Blauner 1964; Woodward 1958 and 1965; Mallet 1963; Naville 1963 and Gallie 1978.

3   This list is taken from Christie *et al.* who report that the employers they surveyed, were having 'severe problems in recruiting experienced staff and new graduates or trainee technicians in these areas' (Christie *et al.* 1990, p.90). They continue that: 'Much of the most common difficulty, experienced by nearly half the users in all four of the surveys, has been lack of people with specialist microelectronics expertise. The kind of expertise most crucially lacking is microelectronics engineers'. (Christie *et al.* 1990, p.11)

4   It is interesting to note that these authors make a direct connection between changes in the skills mix, and the type of knowledge required: 'With a greater skills mix in the workplace, more workers are able to cope with a greater variety of tasks both in operations and in maintenance.... Multiple skills are increasingly in demand; for example, technicians often work in common design and development groups, and have to co-operate across occupational boundaries, with theoretical knowledge in a range of fields matched by practical and diagnostic

skills'. (Campbell and Warner 1992, p.17) This reiterates the earlier point that the current technological paradigm is heavily based on theoretical knowledge.

5   Comparing data collected in three surveys carried out during the 1980s and 1990s, Gallie is able to show not only that levels of skills have increased, but that rate of increase in these levels has become progressively more marked during this period. For full details of the research see Gallie 1996.

6   Looking at the situation in the UK for example, Campbell and Marsden conclude: 'It is argued that training policies and practices have suffered through insufficient attention being paid to the links between these three problem areas. The 'fragmented' approach to training that has resulted has meant even less emphasis than before on intermediate craft and technical skills based on certified vocational training. Rather than seeing the problems at each end of the skills market as symptomatic of too weak an intermediate skill base, decision-makers have tended to conclude the opposite. They do not perceive the problem to be in the intermediate area at all, but that the focus of training strategy should be on the one hand the relieving of graduate skill shortages, and on the other the achievement of minimum standards of employability from what in Britain may now be termed the "skills underclass"' (Campbell and Warner 1992, pp.199-200).

7   For a useful summary of the definitions of control see Francis 1986, pp.106-17. Drawing on organization theory, Francis suggests a four-fold definition of control: 'The first control issue... is that of co-ordinating different elements of a complex task performed by various individuals within some form of a division of labour when the individuals are indifferent between the range of alternative actions they might be instructed to engage in. 'Control 2'... is about coping with the free-rider problem.... Our last two control types are each concerned with control over the effort-reward bargain' (Francis 1986, pp.108-9).

8   Braverman comments for example, that: 'The division of labour in capitalist industry is not at all identical with the phenomenon of the distribution of tasks, crafts, or specialities of production throughout society, for while all known societies divided their work into productive specialities, no society before capitalism systematically subdivided the work of each productive speciality into limited operations. This form of the division of labour becomes generalised only within capitalism' (Braverman 1974, p.70).

9   The essence of scientific management is summarized by Taylor in his description of 'the task idea': 'The work of every workman is fully planned out by the management at least one day in advance, and each man receives in most cases complete written instructions, describing in detail the task which he is to accomplish, as well as the means to be used in doing the work.... This task specifies not only what is to be done, but how it is to be done and the exact time allowed for doing it.... Scientific management consists very largely in preparing for and carrying out these tasks' (Taylor *Principles of Scientific Management*, 1967, pp.39/63; quoted in Braverman 1974, p.118). For a discussion see Edwards 1979. For a more theoretical treatment see Silverman 1970.

10 Galbraith describes the components of the motivating system as follows: 'The name for [this type of motivation] must be coined and I propose to call it *adaptation*. Adaptation, it will be evident, has much to do with the urge for power in a world of oganization. Compulsion, pecuniary compensation, identification and adaptation can motivate an individual either separately or in combination. Their collective influence I shall refer to as the motivating system. The strength of any given motivation or of the motivating system will be measured by the effectiveness with which it aligns the individual with the goals of the organization' (Galbraith 1972, p.132).

11 For a detailed discussion of the implications of networking see: *Scientific American*, 'Communications, Computers and Networks', vol.265 no.3 (Special Issue, September 1991), and 'Business Computing - A Special Report', *The Independent*, 15 September 1992.

12 For a detailed discussion of BPR see *New Technology, Work and Employment*, 'Business Process Re-Engineering', Special issue, vol.10, no.2, 1995.

13 In the UK for example, union membership declined from 13.3 million in 1979 to 9.1 million in 1992, while the number of unions fell from 453 to 268. Between 1979 and 1989. Union density (the actual number of union members as a proportion of the active workforce) fell from 56.9 to 44.2 per cent ('Trade union membership and density 1992-93', *Employment Gazette* vol.102, no.6, June 1994, table 1; and Kessler and Bayliss 1992, p.138). Amongst the most important factors affecting union membership are: (i) men are more likely to be union members than are women (at 38 per cent compared to 31 per cent in 1993). The *rate of decline* in membership was also higher for men falling from 44 per cent in 1989 to 38 per cent in 1993 compared with a fall amongst women from 33.0 per cent to 31.0 per cent; (ii) full-time workers are almost twice as likely to

be union members than are part-time workers (43 per cent compared with 22 per cent in 1989); (iii) manual workers are more likely to be union members than are non-manual workers (43 per cent compared with 35 per cent in 1989). Manual-worker union membership fell sharply from 43 per cent in 1989 to 36 per cent in 1993) while membership amongst non-manual workers remained constant at around 35 per cent, and (iv) union membership is much higher amongst public sector workers than it is amongst private sector workers ('Trade union membership and density 1992-93', *Employment Gazette* vol.102, no.6, June 1994, table 6). These factors clearly suggest that a general shift away from full-time, male-dominated employment in manufacturing towards part-time female-dominated employment in services is bound to result in continuing volatility in bargaining strength of unions and their members.

14   Storey and Sisson note for example, that: 'There is evidence... that where team briefings and [quality controls] and the like have been introduced, they face indifference or even hostility from middle line managers; suggestions are all too often not followed up and meetings are not held or are perfunctory affairs' (Storey and Sisson 1991, p.171).

Chapter Four

1   For representative discussions of the detailed material see: Beechey 1987; Beechey and Perkins 1987; Crompton and Jones 1984; Dex 1985 and 1987; Gilbert and Arber (eds.) 1992; Hamilton and Barrett (eds.) 1987; Martin and Roberts 1984; Penn *et al.* (eds.) 1994; Rees 1992; and Tilly and Scott 1987.

2   Some authors go so far as to suggest that since many of these activities are, or could just as easily be performed as waged work in the formal economy, the distinction between 'production' and 'reproduction' is rather misleading. Walby decides for example, 'to define the area usually described as "reproduction" as production, since it is work' (Walby 1990, p.62).

3   For further discussion, and in addition to Charles 1993 and Walby 1990, see: Secombe 1974, 1975, Barker and Allen (eds.) 1976, Wilson 1977, Humphries 1977a, 1977b and 1981, and Brenner and Ramas 1984.

4   Many of the research findings referred to below derive from the various studies which made up the Social Change and Economic Life Initiative (SCELI) which was carried out in six British travel-to-work-areas between 1985 and 1990. The overall survey included around 6000

respondents, while the various follow-up surveys included somewhat smaller numbers of respondents. For an explanation of the surveys and the methods used see Duncan Gallies's 'Forword' and 'Methodological Appendix' which appears for example in Scott (ed.) 1994.

5   We should note here that Hakim (1993) has argued that some claims about the timing of recent rises in economic activity amongst women may be inaccurate to the extent that they confuse increases in the *number* of jobs with the proportion of *total work time* accounted for by women: 'The much trumpeted rise in women's employment in Britain consisted entirely of the *substitution of part-time for full-time jobs* from 1951 to the later 1980s.... The overall picture is thus one of stability in women's economic activity rates from 1851, and possibly before that, until 1971, certainly well after the Second World War' (Hakim 1993, pp.101/102, original emphasis).

6   A similar conclusion emerges from recent survey data. Amongst those questioned: 'The proportion of women working full time was at a similar level in 1973 and 1993 (34 per cent and 35 per cent respectively) but there has been a rise in the proportions working part time. In 1973, 23 per cent of all women aged 16-59 were doing part-time work compared with 30 per cent in 1993' (*General Household Survey* 1993, p.54).

7   Compared to the UK rate of part-time employment as a percentage of total employment of 24 per cent in 1993, higher rates were to be found in the Netherlands (33 per cent); Switzerland (28 per cent); Norway (27 per cent), and Sweden (25 per cent). Lower rates were to be found in Denmark (22 per cent); Japan (21 per cent); the US and Canada (17 per cent); Germany and France (12 per cent), and Spain and Italy (6 per cent). Data taken from 'The OECD Jobs Study', 1995, chart E.

8   For representative discussions see: Hakim 1979; Cockburn 1983; Dex 1985, pp.130-41; Beechey and Perkins 1987, pp.137-42; Milkman 1987; and Burchell and Rubery 1989.

Chapter Five

1   This survey is carried out by Social and Community Planning Research (SCPR). The 1984, 1985, and 1986 surveys were based on the opinions of 1800 respondents, selected at random 'to yield a representative sample of people living in Britain aged 18 and over at the time of the survey'. Since 1987 the sample has been increased to 3100 respondents. For more

details about the sampling procedure and data see: Jowell *et al.* (eds.) 1984-1990.

2   A powerful account of this sense of despair and desperation comes from an unemployed ex-army officer during the 1930s: '"I used to sit down and think, think, think, of everything under the sun, trying to find the reason for my misery, the state of the world, the futility of existence, and what was going to be the end of it all. Like many people when they reach the depths of despair, I thought about suicide; but something told me that it would not be the end of my troubles, but only the beginning, and I shuddered to think of a worse state of man than utter hopelessness, helplessness and dejection"' (Beales and Lambert (eds.) 1973, p.132).

3   Referring back to our earlier discussion of Weber for example, we can note that one of the reasons why these working communities are so solidaristic is precisely because the work-based and non-work-based sources of identity of the people who lived there were very closely matched. These linkages are much less common in places where the type of employment is mixed and the workforce is mobile.

4   Picking up on a number of themes expressed by 'consciousness-raising groups' within the emerging 'men's movement' of the 1970s and 1980s, this author suggests that men have a mission, if not a duty, to release themselves from the psychological grip of an increasingly devalued masculinity: 'In exploring the cultural roots of our masculinity, we are not simply meeting the challenge of feminism, but we are learning to define what we need and want for ourselves, individually and collectively, in a world in which we dare to value and appreciate, without the fear of being punished. This means learning how we have become the men that we are. In our time this personal exploration of masculinity, however painful and embarrassing, has become a crucial task' (Seidler 1989, p.21).

5   On the issue of technology as a means of control both inside and outside the household see also Cockburn 1985, Wajcman 1991, Gray 1992, and Silverstone and Hirsch (eds.) 1992.

6   There is now a massive literature which examines the emergence and nature of consumption. Useful points of departure include: Gardner and Sheppard 1989, Miller 1987, Miller (ed.) (1995), Keat *et al.* (1994), Keat and Abercrombie (eds.) (1991), Cross 1993, Fine and Leopold 1993, Heelas and Morris (eds.) 1993, Featherstone 1991, Rojek and Turner (eds.) (1993), Rojek 1995, McCracken 1990, Gabriel and Lang (1995). Specifically on consumption and identity see Du Gay 1996, Mort 1996, Lunt and Livingstone 1992, Friedman (ed.) 1994.

7   These ideas have of course given rise to a wave of counter-critique both within and outside cultural studies. See for example: Gane 1991a and 1991b, Kellner 1989, Robert Hughes 1990, Callinicos 1989. Specifically on the issue of class analysis, see the debates between Saunders and Warde, and other papers in Burrows and Marsh (eds.) 1992, and Hamnett *et al.* (eds.) 1989, Lee and Turner 1996.

8   This effort went hand in hand with what has been called 'the crisis of masculinity'. For a way into these discussions see: Brod (ed.) 1987, Mangan and Walvin (eds.) 1987, Kimmel 1987, Chapman and Rutherford (eds.) 1988, Morgan 1990, Seidler (ed.) 1991, Hall 1992, and Roper and Tosh (eds.) 1992.

Chapter Six

1   In technical terms, this process follows Marx's general formula of capital, MCM1, where M stands for Money capital and liquid financial assets, C stands for Commodity capital, meaning capital that is tied-up in various 'concrete' forms such as factories and capital goods in the labour process, and where M1 stands for expanded money capital. For a full discussion see Arrighi 1994, pp.5-10. Marx's 'General Formula for Capital' is set out in *Capital I*, 1954, pp.145-63.

2   It should also be noted that the systemic cycles of specifically *capital accumulation* identified by Arrighi produce a slightly different historical periodization than those of recent long-wave theories which generally trace the first wave only as far back as the late-eighteenth century. For Arrighi: 'Four systemic cycles of accumulation will be identified, each characterized by a fundamental unity of the primary agency and structure of the world-scale process of capital accumulation: a Genoese cycle, from the fifteenth to the early seventeenth centuries; a Dutch cycle, from the late sixteenth century through most of the eighteenth century; a British cycle, from the latter half of the eighteenth century through the early twentieth century; and a US cycle, which began in the late nineteenth century and has continued into the current phase of financial expansion' (Arrighi 1994, p.6).

3   Francks points out that the term *zaibatsu* 'is written with Chinese characters meaning 'financial clique/faction'.... The four great pre-war Japanese zaibatsu, known after their founder's company [were] Mitsubishi, Sumitomo and Yasuda....' (Francks 1992, p.227) She also notes that a similar term '*chaebol*' is used in South Korea, for example,

the conglomerates Hyundai and Daiwoo, and *caifa* in Taiwan, for example Tatung (ibid., p.266 n.10). For a useful description of these types of organization see Francks 1992, pp.227-39, Castells 1996, Dicken 1992.

4   As Hirst and Thomspon point out, there is a tendency not to distinguish very precisely between multi- and trans-national companies. For example, Arrighi distinguishes between the *teritorially*-oriented joint-stock chartered companies of the late-nineteenth century, and the *functionally*-oriented corporations of the twentieth century (Arrighi 1994, pp.73-4), while Waters identifies TNCs in terms of various kinds of 'alliance arrangements between firms' such as 'equity swaps, technology transfers, production licensing, the division of component manufacture and assembly, market sharing, or 're-badging' (Waters 1995, p.79). For further discussion of these criteria see Dicken 1992, pp.48ff. In the following account I am following the strict definition given by Hirst and Thompson.

Bibliography

Abbott, P. and Wallace, C., (1992), *The Family and the New Right*, London: Pluto.

Ackers, P., Smith, C. and Smith, P., (eds.), (1996), *The New Workplace and Trade Unionism*, London: Routledge.

Aglietta, M., (1979), *A Theory of Capitalist Regulation*, London: New Left Books.

Ainley, P. and Corney, M., (1990), *Training for the Future: The rise and fall of the Manpower Services Commission*, London: Cassell.

Amin, A., (ed.), (1994), *Post-Fordism: A Reader*, Oxford: Blackwell.

Amin, A., (1994), 'Post-Fordism: Models, Fantasies and Phantoms of Transition', in Amin (ed.), (1994), pp.1-39.

Amin, A. and Thrift, N., (eds.), (1994), *Globalization, Institutions, and Regional Development in Europe*, Oxford: Oxford University Press.

Amin, A. and Thrift, N., (1994), 'Living in the Global', in Amin and Thrift (eds.), (1994), pp.1-22.

Amin, S., (1980), *Class and Nation*, New York: Monthly Review Press.

Anderson, M., (1971), *Family Structure in Nineteenth Century Lancashire*, Cambridge: Cambridge University Press.

Anderson, M., Bechhofer, F. and Gershuny, J., (eds.), (1994), *The Social and Political Economy of the Household*, Oxford: Oxford University Press.

Anderson, P., (1974), *Passages from Antiquity to Feudalism*, London: New Left Books.

Anderson, R.J., Hughes, J.A. and Sharrock, W.W., (1987), *Classic Disputes in Sociology*, London: Hyman.

Andreski, S., (1985), *Max Weber's Insights and Errors* (International Library of Sociology), London: Routledge, Chapman and Hall.

Annual Abstract of Statistics, Central Statistical Office: no. 117 (1981); no.127 (1991); no.131 (1996), London: HMSO.

Appelbaum, E. and Albin, P., (1989), 'Computer rationalization and the transfromation of work: lessons from the insurance industry', in Wood, S. (ed.), (1989), pp.247-265.

Arrighi, G., (1994), *The Long Twentieth Century: Money, Power, and the Origins of Our Times*, London: Verso.

Atkinson, J. and Meager, N., (1986), *Changing Working Patterns: How companies achieve flexibility to meet new needs,* London:National Economic Development Office (NEDO).

Bahro, R., (1984), *Red and Green,* London: Verso.

Bahro, R., (1985), *The Alternative in Eastern Europe,* London: Pan Books.

Baran, P. and Sweezy, P., (1968), *Monopoly Capital,* Harmondsworth: Penguin Books.

Barker, D.L. and Allen, S., (eds.), (1976*), Dependence and Exploitation in Work and Marriage,* London: Longman.

Barrett, M., (1980), *Women's Oppression Today: Problems in Marxist Feminist Analysis,* London: Verso.

Barron, M. and Norris, G.M., (1976), 'Sexual divisions and the dual labour market', in Barker and Allen (eds.), 1976.

Baudrillard, J., (1983), *Simulations,* New York: Semiotext.

Baudrillard, J., (1986), *Forget Foucault,* New York: Semiotext.

Bauman, Z., (1992), *Intimations of Postmodernity,* London: Routledge.

Beales, H.L. and Lambert, R.S., (eds.), (1973), *Memoirs of the Unemployed,* Wakefield: EP Publishing Limited. Originally published 1934 by Victor Gollancz.

Beaumont, B.P., (1993), *Human Resource Management: Key concepts and skills,* London: Sage.

Beauvoir, Simone de ., (1972), *The Second Sex,* Harmondsworth: Penguin Books.

Beck, U., (1992), *The Risk Society: Towards a New Modernity,* London: Sage, (originally published 1986).

Beechey, V., (1979), 'On Patriarchy', *Feminist Review,* no. 3, pp.66-82.

Beechey, V., (1987), *Unequal Work,* London: Verso.

Beechey, V. (1982), 'The sexual division of labour and the labour process: A critical assessment of Braverman', In Wood, S. (ed.), 1982, pp.54-73.

Beechey, V. and Perkins, T., (1987), *A Matter of Hours: Women, part-time work and the labour market,* Cambridge: Polity Press.

Bell, D., (1974), *The Coming of Post-Industrial Society: A venture in social forecasting,* London: Heinemann Educational.

Bell, D., (1976), *The Cultural Contradictions of Capitalism,* London: Basic Books.

Bell, R.M.B., (1972), *Changing Technology and Manpower Requirements in the Engineering Industry,* Research Report no.3. EITB and Sussex University Press.

Berman, M., (1982), *All that is Solid Melts into Air,* London: Verso.

Bessant, J.R., Bowen, J.A.E., Dickson, K.E. and Marsh, J., (1981), *The Impact of Microelectronics: A Review of the Literature,* Technology Policy Unit, University of Aston, Birmingham; London: Frances Pinter.

Beynon, H. and Blackburn R.M., (1972), *Perceptions of Work: Variations Within a Factory*, London: Cambridge University Press.

Blackburn, R.M. and Mann, M., (1979), *The Working Class in the Labour Market*, London: Macmillan.

Blauner, R., (1964), *Alienation and Freedom: The Factory Worker and his Industry*. Chicago: University of Chicago Press.

Blum, F. (1953), *Towards a Democratic Work Process*, New York: Harper and Bros.

Bly, J., (1992), *Iron John: A book about men*, New York: Addison-Wesley.

Bosanquet, N., (1983), *After the New Right*, London: Heinemann.

Bourdieu, P., (1984), *Distinction*, London: Routledge and Kegan Paul.

Bowring, F., (1996), 'Misreading Gorz', *New Left Review*, vol.217 (May/June 1996).

Boyer, R. and Mistral, J., (1983), *Accumulation, Inflation, Crises*, Paris: PUF

Braun, E. and MacDonald, S., (1982), *Revolution in Miniature: The History and Impact of Semiconductor Electronics*, (2nd Edition), Cambridge: Cambridge University Press.

Braverman, H., (1974), *Labor and Monopoly Capital: The Degredation of Work in the Twentieth Century*, New York: Monthly Review Press.

Brenner, J. and Ramas, M., (1984), 'Rethinking women's oppression', *New Left Review*, no.144, pp.33-71.

Brighton Labour Process Group, (1977), 'The Capitalist Labour Process', *Capital and Class*, no.1.

Brod, H., (ed.), (1987*), The Making of Masculinites: The New Men's Studies*, London: Allen and Unwin.

Brown, R.K., Curran, M. and Cousins, J. (1983), *Changing Attitudes to Employment?*, (research paper no.40), Department of Employment: HMSO.

Browning, H.C. and Singelmann, J., (1978), 'The transformation of the US labour force: The interaction of industry and occupation', *Politics and Society*, 8 (7-4), pp. 481-509.

Brubaker, R., (1984), *The Limits of Rationality*, London: Allen and Unwin.

Bulmer, M., (ed.), (1975), *Working-Class Images of Society*, London: Routledge and Kegan Paul.

Burawoy, M., (1979), *Manufacturing Consent: Changes in the Labour Process under Monopoly Capitalism*, Chicago: University of Chicago Press.

Burchell, B. and Rubery, J., (1989), 'Segmented jobs and segmented workers: an empirical investigation', *SCELI Working Papers*, no.13, Nuffield College, Oxford.

Burchell, B. and Rubery, J., (1994), 'Divided Women: Labour market segmentation and gender segregation', in Scott (ed.), (1994), pp.80-120.

Burns, T. and Stalker, G.M., (1961), *The Management of Inovation*, London: Tavistock.

Burrows, R. and Loader, B., (eds.), (1994), *Towards a Post-Fordist Welfare State?*, London: Routledge.

Burrows, R. and Marsh, C., (eds.), (1992), *Consumption and Class; Divisions and Change*, London: Macmillan.

Butler, J., (1990), *Gender Trouble: Feminism and the Subversion of Identity*, London: Routledge.

Callinicos, A., (1985), *Marxism and Philosophy*, Oxford: Oxford University Press.

Callinicos. A., (1989), *Against Postmodernism: A Marxist Critique*, Cambridge: Polity Press.

Campbell, A. and Warner, M., (1992), *New Technology, skills and management: Human resources in the market economy*, London: Routledge.

Campbell, C., (1987), *The Romantic Ethic and the Spirit of Modern Consumerism*, Oxford: Blackwell.

Carrigan, T., Connell, R.W. and Lee, J., (1985), 'Toward a New Sociology of Masculinity', *Theory and Society*, vol.14, no.5, pp.551-604.

Castells, (1996), *The Rise of the Network Society*, Oxford: Blackwell.

Castles, S. and Miller, M.J., (1993), *The Age of Mass Migration*, Basingstoke: Macmillan.

Census of Employment 1981, 1984, 1987, 1989. Final results published in *Employment Gazette*: December 1983; September 1987; October 1989, and April 1991.

Chapman, R. and Rutherford, J., (eds.), (1988), *Male Order: Unwrapping Masculinity*, London: Lawrence and Wishart.

Charles, N., (1993), *Gender Divisions and Social Change*, Hemel Hempstead: Harvester Wheatsheaf.

Christie, I., Northcott, J. and Walling, A., (1990), *Employment Effects of New Technology in Manufacturing*, London: Policy Studies Institute.

Cockburn, C., (1983), *Brothers: Male Dominance and Technological Change*, London: Pluto Press.

Cockburn, C., (1985), *Machinery of Dominance*, London: Pluto Press.

Cohen, P.S., (1968), *Modern Social Theory*, London: Heinemann.

Coleman, J.C. and Warren-Adamson, C., (eds.), (1992), *Youth Policy in the 1990s: The way forward*, London: Routledge.

Connell, R.W., (1983), *Which Way is Up?*, Sydney: George Allen and Unwin.

Connell, R.W., (1987), *Gender and Power: Society, the person and sexual politics*, Oxford: Polity Press.

Connell, R.W., (1995), *Masculinites*, Oxford: Polity Press.

Coombs, R.W., (1984), 'Long-Term Trends in Automation', in Marstrand, P. (ed.), (1984), pp.146-162.

Cooper, C.M. and Clark, J.A., (1982), *Employment, Economics and Technology: The Impact of Technological Change on the Labour Market*, Brighton: Wheatsheaf.

Corti, L. and Dex, S., (1995), 'Highly Qualified Women', in *Employment Gazette*, vol.103, no.3, pp.115-121.

Craib, I., (1997), *Classical Social Theory: An Introduction to the Thought of Marx, Weber, Durkheim and Simmel*, Oxford: Oxford University Press.

Crompton, R. and Jones, G., (1984*), White Collar Proletariat: Deskilling and Gender in Clerical Work*, London: Macmillan.

Crompton, R. and Reid, S., (1982), 'The Deskilling of clerical work', in Wood, S., (ed.), (1982), pp.163-178.

Crompton, R. and Sanderson, K., (1990), *Gendered Jobs and Social Change*, London: Unwin Hyman.

Crompton, R., Gallie, D. and Purcell, K., (eds.), (1996), *Changing Forms of Employment: Organisations, skills and gender*, London: Routledge.

Cross, G., (1993), *Time and Money: The Making of Consumer Culture*, London: Routledge.

Cullen, I., Hammond, S. and Haimes, E., (1980), *Employment and Mobility in Inner Urban Areas*, Principal Report to the SSRC of Project HR 5884, London: Bartlett School of Architecture and Planning.

Daniel, W.W., (1974), *A National Survey of the Unemployed*, PEP Broadsheet vol.40, no.546.

Daniel, W.W., (1987), *Workplace Industrial Relations and Technological Change*, London: Frances Pinter.

David, D.S. and Brannon, R., (1976), *The Forty-Nine Percent Majority: The Male Sex Role*, Reading, MA: Addington-Wesley.

Davis, L.E. and Werling, R., (1960), 'Job design factors', *Occupational Psychology*, vol. XXXIV, no.2, pp.109-132.

Day, R.B., (1976), 'The theory of the Long Cycle: Kondratiev, Trotsky, Mandel', *New Left Review*, no.99 (Sep-Oct 1976), pp.67-82.

De La Monthe, J.R., (1986), 'Financial Services', in Smith A.D. (ed.), (1986), pp 55-118.

Delphy, C., (1984), *Close to Home*, London: Hutchinson.

Dennehy, C. and Sullivan, J., (1977), 'Poverty and Unemployment in Liverpool', in Field (ed.), (1977), pp.56-77.

Dertonzos, M.L., Lester, R.K. and Solon, R.M., (1989), *Made in America: Regaining the Productive Edge*, Cambridge: Mass.: MIT Press.

Devor, H., (1989), *Gender Bending: Confronting the Limits of Duality*, Bloomington: Indiana University Press.

Dex, S., (1985), *The Sexual Division of Work: Conceptual revolutions in the Social Sciences*, Brighton: Harvester Books.

Dex, S., (1987), *Women's Occupational Mobility: A Lifetime Perspective*, London: Macmillan.

Dicken, P., (1992), *Global Shift: The Internationalization of Economic Activity*, London: Paul Chapman Publishing (second editon).

Dickens, P., Forsgren, M. and Malmberg, A., (1994), 'The Local Embeddedness of Transnational Corporations', in Amin and Thrift (eds.), (1994), pp.23-45.

Dixon, C., (1991), *South East Asia in the World-Economy*, Cambridge: Cambridge University Press.

Donaldson, L., (1985), *In Defence of Organisation Theory*, Cambridge; Cambridge University Press.

Donaldson, N., (1991), *Time of our Lives: Labour and Love in the Working Class*, Sydney: Allen and Unwin.

Dosi, G., Freeman, C., Nelson, R., Silverberg, G. and Soete, L., (eds.), (1988), *Technical Change and Economic Theory*, London: Frances Pinter.

Doyal, L. and Gough, I., (1984), 'A Theory of Human Needs', *Critical Social Policy*, no.10, pp.6-38).

Doyal, L. and Gough, I., (1991), *A Theory of Human Need*, London: Macmillan.

Doyle, W., (1992), *The Old European Order 1660-1800*, Oxford: Oxford University Press (second edition; first edition published 1978).

Du Gay, P., (1996), *Consumption and Identity at Work*, London: Sage.

Ducatel, K., (1995), 'The future of low-skilled jobs', in Metcalf, H., (ed.), (1995), pp.56-84.

Duffy, A. and Pupo, N., (1992), *Part-Time Paradox: Connecting Gender, Work and Family*, Toronto: McClelland and Stewart.

Dunford, M., (1989), 'Technopoles, Politics and Markets: The development of electronics in Grenoble and Silicon Glen', in Sharp and Holmes (eds.), (1989), pp.80-118.

Dunne, G., (1997), *Lesbian Lifestyles: Women's work and the politics of sexuality*, Basingstoke: Macmillan.

Dunning, J., (1981), *International Production and the Multinational Enterprise*, London: Allen and Unwin.

Dunning, J., (1993), *Multinational Enterprises in a Global Economy*, Wokingham: Addison-Wesley.

Durkheim, E., (1933), *The Division of Labour in Society*, trans., G. Simpson, New York: Free Press. This second edition first published in 1902, Paris: Alcan. First edition published in 1893.

Durkheim, E., (1952), *Suicide: A Study in Sociology*, trans., J.A.Spaulding and G.Simpson, edited and introduced by G.Simpson, London: Routledge and Kegan Paul, (second edition). First edition published in 1897.

Durkheim, E., (1964), *The Rules of Sociological Method*, trans., S. Solovay and J.H. Mueller, edited by G.E.G. Catlin, London: Glencoe Free Press. This edition first published 1938. First edition published in 1895.

Eco, U., (1986), *Faith and Fakes*, London: Secker and Warberg.

Edwards, R., (1979), *Contested Terrain: The Transformation of the Workplace in the Twentieth Century*, London: Heineman.

Eisenberg, P. and Lazarsfield, P.F., (1938), 'The psychological effects of unemployment', *Psychological Bulletin*, 1938.

Eisenstein, Z., (ed.), (1979), *Capitalist Patriarchy and the Case for Socialist Feminism*, London: Monthly Review Press.

Elam, M., (1994), 'Puzzling out the Post-Fordist debate: Technology, markets and insitutions', in Amin (ed.), (1994), pp.43-70. Originally published in *Economic and Industrial Democracy*, (1990), vol.11 no.1, pp.9-37.

Elger, T. and Fairbrother, P., (1992), 'Inflexible flexibility: A case study of modularisation', in Gilbert *et al.*, (eds.), (1992), pp.89-106.

Emmott, B., (1993), 'Everybody's Favourite Monsters', *The Economist* 27/3 (supplement).

Employment Gazette, 'Labour disputes in 1993', Department of Employment, vol. 102, no.6, June 1994, London: HMSO.

Employment Gazette, 'Trade union membership and density 1992-93', Department of Employment: June 1994, London: HMSO.

Ernste, H. and Meier, V., (eds.), (1992), *Regional Development and Contemporary Industrial Response: Extending Flexible Flexible Specialisation*, London: Belhaven.

Esser, J. and Hirsch, J., (1994), 'Post-Fordist regional and urban structure', in Amin, A. (ed.), (1994), pp.71-97. Originally published in *International Journal of Urban and Regional Research*, 1989, vol.13, no.3, pp.417-436.

Eurostat, *Annual Review 1970-1979, 1976-1985*, EC Brussels: 1986.

Eurostat, *Basic Statistics of the Community*, EC Brussels: 1988, 1989 and 1991.

Evans, E.J., (1983), *The Forging of the Modern State: Early Industrial Britain 1783-1870*, London: Longman.

Evetts, J., (ed.), (1994), *Women and Career: Themes and Issues in Advanced Industrial Societies*, London: Longman.

Featherstone, M., (1991), *Consumer Culture and Postmodernism*, London: Sage.

Featherstone, M., (ed.), (1992), *Cultural Theory and Cultural Change*, London: Sage.

Featherstone, M., Lash, S. and Robertson, R., (eds.), (1995), *Global Modernities*, London: Sage.

Ferman, L. and Gordus, J.P, (eds.), (1979), *Mental Health and the Economy*, Kalamazoo, Mich.: Upjohn Institute.

Field, F., (ed.), (1977), *The Conscript Army: A Study of Britain's Unemployed*, London: Routledge and Kegan Paul.

Fine, B., (1992), *Women's Employment and the Capitalist Family*, London: Routledge.

Fine, B. and Leopold, E., (1993), *The World of Consumption*, London: Routledge.

Fineman, S., (1983), *Whte Collar Unemployment: Impact and Stress*, Chichester: John Wiley and Sons.

Fineman, S.. (ed.), (1987), *Unemployment: Personal and Social Consequences*, London: Tavistock Publications.

Forester, T., (ed.), (1980), *The Microelectronics Revolution: The Complete guide to the New Technology and its Impact on Society*, Oxford: Basil Blackwell.

Forester, T., (ed), (1985), *The Information Technology Revolution*, Oxford: Basil Blackwell.

Fox, A., (1980), 'The meaning of work', in Salaman and Esland (eds.), 1980, pp.139-191.

Francis, A., (1986), *New Technology at Work*, Oxford: Clarendon.

Francis, D., (1987), 'The Great Transition', in Anderson *et al.*, (1987), pp.1-35.

Francks, P., (1992), *Japanese Economic Practice: Theory and Practice*, London; Routledge.

Frank, A.G., (1971), *Capitalism and Underdevelopment in Latin America*, (revised edition), Harmondsworth: Penguin Books. Originally published 1967, New York: Monthly Review Press.

Frankel, B., (1987), *The Post Industrial Utopians*, Cambridge: Polity Press.

Freeman, C., (1984), 'Keynes or Kondratiev?', in Marstrand P., (ed.), (1984), pp.103-23.

Freeman, C., (ed.), (1985), *Technological Trends in Employment: vol.4 Engineering and Vehicles*, (SPRU) Aldershot: Gower.

Freeman, C. and Perez, C., (1988), 'Structural crisis of adjustment, business cycles and investment behaviour', in Dosi *et al.*, (eds.), 1988.

Freeman, C., Clark, J.A. and Soete, L., (1982), *Unemployment and Technical Innovation: A Study of Long Waves and Economic Development*, London: Frances Pinter.

Friedman, A.L., (1977), *Industry and Labour: Class Struggle at Work and Monopoly Capital*, London:Macmillan.

Friedman, J., (ed.), (1994), *Consumption and Identity*, Chur, Switzerland: Harwood Academic.

Fromm, E., (1955), 'The Human Implications of Instinctivistic Radicalism', *Dissent* vol.2, no.4, pp.342-349.

Gabriel, Y. and Lang, G., (1995), *The Unmanageable Consumer: Contemporay Consumption and its Fragmentation*, London: Sage.

Galbraith, J.K., (1969), *The Affluent Society* London: Hamish Hamilton, (second revised edition). First published in 1958.

Galbraith, J.K., (1972), *The New Industrial State*, London: Andre Deursch. First published in 1967.

Galbraith, J.K., (1994), *The World Economy since the Wars: A Personal View*, London: Sinclaire-Stevenson.

Gallie, D., (1978), *In Search of the New Working Class: Automation and Social Integration within the Captalist Enterprise*. London: Cambridge University Press.

Gallie, D., (1991), 'Patterns of skill change: Upskilling, deskilling or the polarization of skills?', *Work, Employment and Society*, vol.6, no.3, pp.319-351.

Gallie, D., (1996), 'Skill, gender and the quality of employment', in Crompton *et al.*, (eds.), (1996), pp.133-159.

Gallie, D. and Vogler, C., (1993), 'Labour Market Deprivation, Welfare, and Collectivism', in Gallie *et al.*, (eds.), (1993), pp.299-336.

Gallie, D., Marsh, C. and Vogler, C., (eds.), (1993), *Social Change and the Experience of Unemployment*, Oxford: Oxford University Press.

Gallie, D., Penn, R. and Rose, M., (eds.), (1996), *Trade Unionism in Recession*, Oxford: Oxford University Press.

Gane, M., (1991a), *Baudrillard: Critical and Fatal Theory*, London: Routledge.

Gane, M., (1991b), *Baudrillard's Bestiary*, London: Routledge.

Garber, M., (1992), *Vested Interests: Cross-Dressing and Cultural Anxiety*, London: Routledge.

Gardner, C. and Sheppard, J., (1989), *Consuming Passion - The Rise and Fall of Retail Culture*, London: Unwin Hyman.

Garner, R., (1996), *Contemporary Movements and Ideologies*, New York: McGraw Hill.

General Household Survey, (1993), Office of Population, Censuses and Surveys (OPCS), London: HMSO.

George, M., (1973), 'From 'Goodwife' to 'Mistress': The transformation of the female in bourgeois culture', *Science and Society*, vol.37, no.2, pp.152-177.

Gershuny, J.I., (1979), 'The informal economy: Its role in industrial society', *Futures*, Febuary, pp.3-15.

Gershuny, J.I., (1993), 'The Psychological Consequences of Unemployment: An Assessment of the Johoda Thesis', in Gallie *et al.*, (eds.), (1993), pp.213-230.

Gershuny, J.I. and Miles, I.D., (1983), *The New Service Economy: The Transformation of Employment in Industrial Societies*, London, Frances Pinter.

Gershuny, J.I. and Pahl, R.E., (1979), 'Work outside employment: Some preliminary speculations', *New Universities Quarterly*, vol.34, no.1, pp.120-135.

Gershuny, J.I, Godwin, M. and Jones, S., (1994), 'The Domestic Labour Revolution: A process of lagged adaptation?', in Anderson *et al.* (eds.), (1994), pp.151-197.

Giddens, A., (1972), *Politics and Sociology in the Thought of Max Weber*, London: Hutchinson.

Giddens, A., (1990), *The Consequences of Modernity*, Cambridge: Polity Press.

Giddens, A., (1991), *Modernity and Self-Identity: Self and Society in the Late Modern Period*, Cambridge: Polity Press.

Giddens, A., (1992), *The Transformation of Intimacy: Sexuality, Love and Eroticism in Modern Societies*, Cambridge: Polity Press.

270

Giddens, A. and Held, D., (eds.), (1982), *Classes, Power and Conflict: Classical and Contemporary Debates*, London: Macmillan.

Giddens, A. and Mackenzie, G., (1982), *Social Class and the Division of Labour*, Cambridge: Cambridge University Press.

Gilbert, N. and Arber, S., (eds.), (1992), *Women and Working Lives: Divisions and Change*, London: Macmillan.

Gilbert, N., Burrows, R. and Pollert, A., (eds.), (1992), *Fordism and Flexibility: Divisions and Change*, Basingstoke: Macmillan.

Gilpin, R., (1987), *The Political Economy of International Relations*, Princetown: Princetown University Press.

Gittins, D., (1985), *The Family in Question*, Basingstoke: Macmillan.

Glendenning, C. and Millar, J., (eds.), (1987), *Women and Poverty in Britain*, Hemel Hempstead: Harvester Wheatsheaf.

Glucksmann, M., (1986), 'In a classs of their own?: Women workers in the new industries in inter-war Britain', *Feminist Review*, no.24, pp.7-39.

Glyn, A. and Miliband, D., (eds.), (1994), *Paying for Inequality: The Economic Cost of Social Injustice*, London: Rivers Oram Press.

Godelier, M., (1980), 'Language and History; Work and its Representations: A research proposal', *History Workshop Journal*, issue 10 (Autumn 1980), pp.164-174.

Goldthorpe, J.H., (1979), 'Herbert Spencer', in Raison, T., (ed.), (1979), *The Founding Fathers of Social Science*, London: Scholar Press. (Revised edition, originally published by Penguin, 1969).

Goldthorpe, J.H., Lockwood, D., Bechhofer, E. and Platt, J., (1968), *The Affluent Worker: Industrial Attitudes and Behaviour*, Cambridge: Cambridge University Press.

Gorz, A., (ed.), (1976), *The Division of Labour: The Labour Process and Class-structure in Modern Capitlaism*, Brighton: Harvester Press.

Gorz, A., (1982), *Farewell To The Working Class: An Essay on Post-Industrial Socialism*, trans., M. Sonenscher, London: Pluto Press. Originally Published 1980, as *Adieux au Proletariat*. Paris, Editions Galilee.

Gorz, A., (1985), *Paths to Paradise: On the Liberation from Work*, trans., by M.Imre, London: Pluto Press.

Gorz, A., (1989), *Critique of Economic Reason*, trans., G. Handyside and C. Turner, London: Verso. Originally published as: *Metamorphoses du Travail*: Quete du sens, Galilee, 1988.

Gough, J. (1992), 'Where's the value in "post-Fordism"?', in Gilbert *et al.*, (eds.), (1992), pp.31-45.

Gray, A., (1992), *Video Playtime: The Gendering of a Leisure Technology*, London: Routledge.

Grint, K., (1991), *The Sociology of Work: An introduction*, Cambridge: Polity Press.

Grint, K. and Woolgar, S., (1997), *The Machine at Work, Technology, Work and Organization*, Cambridge: Polity Press.

Guest, D.E., (1991), 'Human resource management: its implications for industrial relations and trade unions', in Storey (ed.), 1991, pp.41-55.

Habermas, J., (1976), *Legitimation Crisis*, London: Heineman.

Hakim, C., (1979), 'Occupational Segregation: A Comparative Study of the Degree and Pattern of the Differentiation Between Man's and Women's Work in Britain, the United States and Other Countries', *Research Paper* no.9, Department of Employment.

Hakim, C., (1993), 'The Myth of Rising Female Employment', *Work, Employment and Society*, vol. 7, no.1, pp.97-120.

Hall, C., (1992), *White, Male and Middle Class*, Cambridge: Cambridge University Press.

Hall, S. and Jacques, M., (eds.), (1989), *New Times: The Changing Face of Politics in the 1990's*, London: Lawrence and Wishart.

Hall, S., (1987), *Invisible Frontiers: The Race to Synthesize a Human Gene*, New York: Atlantic Monthly Press.

Hamilton R. and Barrett M., (eds.), (1987), *The Politics of Diversity: Feminism, Marxism and Nationalism*, London: Verso.

Hamnett, C., McDowell, L. and Saarre, P., (eds.), (1989), *The Changing Social Structure*, London: Sage.

Hampson, N., (1990), *The Enlightenment*, Harmondsworth, Penguin Books.

Handy, C., (1976), *Understanding Organizations*, Harmondsworth: Penguin Books.

Handy, C., (1989), *The Age of Unreason*, London: Business Books.

Harris, O. and Young, K., (1981), 'Engendered Structures: Some problems in the analysis of reproduction', in Kahn and Llobera (eds.), (1981), pp.109-147.

Hartmann, H., (1979), 'Capitalism, patriarchy, and job segregation by sex', in Eisenstein (ed.), 1979.

Hartmann, H., (1981), 'The unhappy marriage of Marxism and Feminism: towards a more progressive union', in Sargent, L. (ed.), 1981. Originally published in *Capital and Class*, 1979, no.8, pp.1-33.

Harvey, D., (1989), *The Condition of Postmodernity*, Oxford: Oxford University Press.

Hayes, J. and Nutman, P., (1981), *Understanding the Unemployed: The Psychological Effects of Unemployment*, London: Tavistock Publications.

Heelas, P. and Morris, P., (eds.), (1992), *The Values of Enterprise Culture*; The Moral Debate, London: Routledge.

Henley Centre for Forecasting, (1986) *Planning for Social Change*, vol.1: London.

Herzberg, F., (1968), *Work and the Nature of Man*, New York: Staples Press.

Hill, J., (1978), 'The psychlogical impact of unemployment', *New Society*, 19 Jan. 1978, pp.118-120.

Hirst, P. and Thompson, G., (1996), *Globalization in Question: The International Economy and the Possibilities of Governance*, Cambridge: Polity Press.

Holmes, B., 'Literacy and Numeracy: What cause for concern?', *Employment Gazette*, March 1989, pp.133-139.

Horkheimer, M. and Adorno, T., (1972), *Dialectic of Enlightenment*, New York: Herder and Herder.

Hughes, J.A., Martin, P.J. and Sharrock, W.W., (1995), *Understanding Classical Sociology: Marx, Weber, Durkheim*, London: Sage.

Hughes, R., (1990), *Nothing if not Critical*, London: Harper Collins.

Humphries, J., (1977a), 'The working class family, women's liberation and class struggle: the case of nineteenth-century British history', *The Review of Radical Political Economics*, vol.9 no.3.

Humphries, J., (1977b), 'Class struggle and the persistence of the working-class family', *Cambridge Journal of Economics*, vol.1, pp.241-258.

Humphries, J., (1981), 'Protective legislation, the capitalist state, and working-class men: the case of the 1842 Mines Regulations Act', *Feminist Review*, no.7, pp.1-34.

Hutton, W., (1994), *The State We're In*, London: Jonathan Cape.

Hyman, R. and Streek, W., (eds.), (1988), *New Technology and Industrial Relations*, Oxford: Basil Blackwell.

Illich, I., (1971), *De-Schooling Society*, London: Calder and Boyers.

Illich, I., (1973), *Tools for Conviviality*, London: Calder and Boyers.

Illich, I., (1975), *Medical Nemesis: The Expropriation of Health*, London: Calder and Boyers.

Irwin, S., (1995), *Gender and Household Resourcing: Changing relations to work and family*, Leeds, School of Sociology and Social Policy Gender Analysis and Policy Unit Working Paper no.12.

273

Jahoda, M., (1982), *Employment and Unemployment: A Social-Psychological Analysis*, Cambridge: Cambridge University Press.

Jahoda, M., Lazarsfeld P.H. and Zeisel, H., (1971), *Marienthal: The Sociography of an Unemployed Community*, Aldine Atherton Inc. Originally published 1933 as *Die Arbeitsolosen von Marienthal*.

Jameson, F., (1991*)*, *Postmodernism, or The Cultural Logic of Late Capitalism*, London: Verso.

Jenson, J., (1989), 'Paradigms and Political Discourse: Protective Legislation in the USA and France before 1914', *Canadian Journal of Political Science*, 22, pp.235-258.

Jessop, B., (1992a), 'Post-Fordism and Flexible Specialization: incommensurable, contradictory, complementary, or just plain different perspectives?', in Ernste and Meier (eds.), (1992), pp.25-44.

Jessop, B., (1992b), 'Fordism and post-Fordism: critique and reformulation', in Storper and Scott (eds.), (1992), pp.43-65.

Jessop, B., (1994), 'Post-Fordism and the State', in Amin, A. (ed.), (1994), pp.251-279.

Jones, D., 'Vehicles', in Freeman (ed.), (1985), pp.128-87.

Jordan, B., (1996), *A Theory of Poverty and Social Exclusion*, Cambridge: Polity Press.

Joseph Rowntree Foundation, (1995), *Inquiry into Income and Wealth*, York: Joseph Rowntree Foundation.

Jowell, R., Witherspoon, S. and Brook, L., (eds.), (1989), *British Social Attitudes Annual Reports*: 1984, 1985, 1986, 1987, 1988/89 and 1990, Social and Community Planning Research (SCPR), Aldershot: Gower.

Kahn, J.S. and Llobera, J.R., (eds.), (1981), *The Anthropology of Pre-capitalist Societies*, London: Macmillan.

Kalvin, P. and Jarrett, J. E., (1985), *Unemployment: Its Social Psychological Effects*, Cambridge: Cambridge University Press.

Kasl, K.V. and Cobb, S., (1979), 'Some mental health consequences of plant closing and job loss', in Ferman and Gordus, (eds.), 1979, pp.139-192.

Keat, R. and Abercrombie, N., (eds.), (1991), *Enterprise Culture*, London: Routledge.

Keat, R., Whitely, N. and Abercrombie, N., (eds.), (1994), *The Authority of the Consumer*, London: Routledge.

Keefe, T., (1984), 'The stress of unemployment', *Social Work*, May-June 1984, vol.29, no.3, pp.264-268.

Keep, E., (1991), 'Corporate training strategies: the vital component?, in Storey (ed.), 1991, pp.109-125.

Keep, E. and Mayhew, K., (1995), 'Training ploicy for competitiveness: time for a new perspective?', in Metcalf, H., (ed.), (1995), pp.110-114.

Kellner, D., (1989), *Jean Baudrillard: From Marxism to post-Modernism and Beyond*, Cambridge: Polity Press.

Kelly, K., (1995), *Out of Control: The Rise of Neo-biological Civilization*, Menlo Park, C.A.: Addison-Wesley.

Kenwood, A.G. and Lougheed, A.L., (1992), *The Growth of the International Economy 1820-1990: An introductory text*, London: Routledge (third edition).

Kerr, C., Dunlop, J., Harbison, F. and Myers, C., (1973), *Industrialism and Industrial Man*, Harmondsworth: Penguin Books.

Kessler, S. and Bayliss, F., (1992), *Contemporary British Industrial Relations*, London: Macmillan.

Kimmel, M., (1987), *Changing Men*, London: Sage.

Klein, V., (1965), *Britain's Married Women Workers*, London: Routledge and Kegan Paul.

Kondratiev, N., (1935), 'The Long Waves in economic life', *Review of Economic Statistics*, 17, pp.105-115.

Kumar, K., (1978), *Prophecy and Progress: The Sociology of Industrial and Post-Industrial Society*, Harmondsworth: Penguin Books.

Kumar, K., (1983), *Prophecy and Progress: The Sociology of Industrial and Post-Industrial Society*, Harmondsworth: Penguin Books (originally published 1978).

Kumar, K., (1995), *From Post-Industrial to Post-Modern Society: New Theories of the Contemporary World*, Oxford: Blackwell.

Lampard, R., (1993), 'An Examination of the Relationship between Marital Dissolution and Unemployment', in Gallie *et al.*, (eds.), (1993), pp. 264-298.

Lane, P., (1978), *The Industrial Revolution: The Birth of the Modern Age*, London: Weidenfeld and Nicholson.

Lash, S. and Urry, J., (1987), *The End of Organized Capitalism*, Cambridge, Polity Press.

Lash, S. and Urry, J., (1994), *Economies of Signs and Space*, London: Sage.

Laslett. P., (1977), *Family Life and Illicit Love in Earlier Generations: essays in historical sociology*, Cambridge: Cambridge University Press.

Lee, D. and Newby, H., (1983), *The Problem of Sociology*, London: Hutchinson.

Lee, D.V. and Turner, B.S., (1996), *Conflicts About Class: Debating inequality in late industrialism*, London: Longman.

Legge, K., (1991), 'Human resource management: a critical analysis', in Storey (ed.), 1991, pp.19-40.

Leman, S., (1992), 'Gender, technology and flexibility in the UK mail order industry', in Gilbert *et al.*, (eds.), (1992), pp.118-133.

Lenin, V.I., (1970), *Imperialism, The Highest Stage of Capitalism*, Peking: Foreign Language Press. Originally published 1916.

Levy, M., (1966), *Modernization and the Structure of Societies*, Princeton: Princeton University Press.

Lewis, J., (1984), *Women in England 1870-1950*, Hemel Hempstead: Harvester Wheatsheaf.

Lewis, J., (1992), *Women in Britain since 1945: Women, Family, Work and the State in the Post-War Years*, Oxford: Blackwell.

Lipietz, A., (1985), *The Enchanted World: Inflation credit and the world crisis*, London: Verso.

Lipietz, A., (1987), *Mirages and Miracles: the crisis of global Fordism*, London: Verso.

Lipietz, A., (1994), 'Post-Fordism and Democracy', in Amin, A. (ed.), (1994), pp.338-357.

Littler, C., (1982), 'Deskilling and changing structures of control', in Wood, S. (ed.), (1982), pp.122-145.

Livi-Bacci, M., (1993), *The Changing Course of Migration*, Paris: OECD.

Lockwood, D., (1975), 'Sources of variation in working-class images of society', in Bulmer, M. (1975), pp.16-31. Originally published 1966, *Sociological Review*, vol.14 no.3, pp.249-267.

Lodziak, C., (1995), *Manipulating Needs, Capitalism and Culture*, London: Pluto Press.

Lodziak, C. and Tatman, J., (1997), *Andre Gorz: A critical introduction*, London: Pluto Press.

Lovering, J., (1994), 'Employers, the Sex-Typing of Jobs, and Economic Restructuring', in Scott (ed.), (1994), pp.327-355.

Lowith, K., (1982), *Max. Weber and Karl Marx*, edited and introduced by T. Bottomore and W. Outhwaite, trans., H. Fantel, London: George Allen and Unwin. German original published 1932.

Lunt, P.K. and Livingstone, S.M., (1992), *Mass Consumption and Personal Identity*, Buckingham: Open University Press.

MacCannell, D. and MacCannell, J.F., (1993), 'Social Class in postmodernity: simulacrum or return of the real?', in Rojek and Turner (eds.), (1993), pp.124-145.

Mackenzie, G. (1973), *The Aristocracy of Labour: The position of skilled craftsmen in the American class structure*, Cambridge: Cambridge University Press.

Macpherson, C.B., (1962), *The Political Theory of Possessive Individualism*, Oxford: Oxford University Press.

Mager, N.N., (1987), *The Kondratieff Waves*, New York: Praeger.

Main, B., (1994), 'The Labour Market: Friend or Foe?', in Anderson *et al.* (eds.), (1994), pp.133-148.

Mallet, S., (1963), *La Nouvelle Classe Ouvriere*, Paris: Editions du Seuil.

Mallet, S., (1975), *The New Working Class*, trans., A. and B. Shepherd, London: Spokesman Books. French original published 1963.

Mandel, E., (1975), *Late Capitalism*, trans., Joris De Bres, London: New Left Books.

Mangan, J.A. and Walvin, J., (eds.), (1987), *Manliness and Morality*, Manchester: Manchester University Press.

Mann, M, (1986), 'Work and the work ethic', in Jowell *et al.* (eds.), (1986), pp.17-29.

Marcuse, H., (1964), *One Dimensional Man*, London: Abacus.

Marginson, P., (1991), 'Change and continuity in the employment structure of large companies', in Pollert (ed.), (1991), pp.32-45.

Marglin, S. (1976), 'What do bosses do? The origins and functions of hierarchy in capitalist production', in Gorz, A., (ed.), (1976).

Marglin, S. (1982), 'What do bosses do? The origins and functions of hierarchy in capitalist production', (abridged) in Giddens and Held 1982, pp.285-298. Full version originally published 1974, *Review of Radical Political Economics* 6(2), pp. 60-92.

Marsden, D., (1982), *Workless: An Exploration of the Social Contract Between Society and the Worker*, London: Croom Helm.

Marsden, D. and Ryan, P., (1989), 'Initial Training, Labour Market Structure and Public Policy in Britain and the FRG', Paper presented at Training Agency Conference on International Comparisons of Vocational Education and Training for Intermediate Skills, Manchester, September.

Marstrand P., (ed.), (1984), *New Technology and the Future of Work and Skills,* Proceedings of a Symposium organised by Section X at the Annual Meeting of the British Association for the Advancement of Science, August 1983, London: Frances Pinter.

Martin, R. and Roberts, C., (1984*)*, *The Women and Employment Survey: A Lifetime Perspective*, London: HMSO.

Martin, R. and Wallace, J., (1984), *Working Women in Recession: Employment Redundancy and Unemployment*, Oxford: Oxford University Press.

Marx, G., and McAdam, D., (1994), *Collective Behaviour and Social Movements*, Englewood Cliffs, N.J.:Prentice Hall.

Marx, J, L., (ed.), (1989), *A Revolution in Biotechnology*, Cambridge: Cambridge University Press.

Marx, K., (1954), *Capital I*, London: Lawrence and Wishart.

Marx, K., (1959) *Capital III*, London: Lawrence and Wishart.

Marx, K., (1963), *Early Writings*, trans., T.B. Bottomore, London: C.A. Watts and Co.

Marx, K. (1975), *Early Writings*, introduction by L.Colletti, trans., R. Livingstone and G. Benton, Harmondsworth: Penguin.

Marx, K. and Engels, F., (1952), *Manifesto of the Communist Party*, Moscow: Progress Publishers.

Marx, K. and Engels, F., (1970), *The German Ideology, Part One* (with selections from Parts Two and Three, together with Marx's 'Introduction to a Critique of Political Economy'), ed., C.J. Arthur, London: Lawrence and Wishart.

Maslow, A.H., (1970), 'A theory of human motivation', in Vroom, V.H. and Deci, E.L. (eds.), (1970), originally published 1943, in *Psychological Review*, vol.50, pp.370-396.

McCracken, G., (1990), *Culture and Consumption: New Approaches to the Symbolic Character of Consumer Goods and Activities*, Bloomington: Indiana University Press.

McHugh, P., Merli, G. and Wheeler, W.A., (1995), *Beyond Business Process Reengineering: Towards the Holonic Enterprise*, Chichester: John Wiley and Sons.

McIntosh, I., (1997), *Classical Sociological Theory: A Reader*, Edinburgh, Edinburgh University Press.

McLellan, D., (ed.), (1977), *Karl Marx Selected Writings*, Oxford: Oxford University Press.

Meager, N. and Williams, M., (1994), *The Case for National Equality in Employment Targets*, Brighton: Institute for Manpower Studies.

Meek, R., (1973), *Studies in the Labour Theory of Value*, London: Lawrence and Whishart.

Metcalf, H., (ed.), (1995), *Future Skill Demand and Supply*, London:Policy Studies Institute.

Milkman, R., (1987), *Gender at Work: The Dynamics of Job Segregation by Sex during World War Two*, Illinois: University of Illinois Press.

Miller, D., (1987), *Material Culture and Mass Consumption*, Oxford: Basil Blackwell.

Miller, D., (ed.), (1995), *Acknowledging Consumption*, London: Routledge.

Millward, N., (1994), *The New Industrial Relatinos?* London: Policy Studies Institute.

Mingione, E., (1991), *Fragmented Societies*, Oxford: Basil Blackwell.

Minion, J. and Bolsover, P., (1983), *The CND Story*, Campaign for Nuclear Disarmament, London: Alison and Busby.

Morgan, D., (1990), *Unmasking Masculinity: A critical Autobiography*, London: Unwin Hyman.

Morris, L., (1990), *The Workings of the Household*, Cambridge: Polity Press.

Morrison, K., (1995), *Marx, Durkheim, Weber: Formations of Modern Social Thought*, London: Sage.

Mort, F., (1996), *Cultures of Consumption: Masculinities and social space in late Twentieth-Century Britain*, London: Routledge.

Murphy, B., (1973), *A History of the British Economy 1086-1970*, London: Longman.

Murray, R., (1989a), 'Fordism and Post-Fordism' in Hall,S. and Jacques, M., (eds.), (1989), pp.38-53. Originally published in *Marxism Today*, October 1988.

Murray, R., (1989b), 'Benetton Britain: The New Economic Order, in Hall, S. and Jacques, M., (eds.), (1989), pp.54-64. Originally published in *Marxism Today*, November 1985.

Myrdal, A and Klein, M., (1956), *Women's Two Roles*, London: Routledge and Kegan Paul.

Naville, P., (1963), *Vers L'automatisme social?*, Paris: Editions du Seuil.

New Technology, Work and Employment, 'Business Process Re-Engineering', Special issue, vol.10, no.2, 1995.

Nicholas, K., (1986), *The Social Effects of Unemployment in Teesside*, Manchester: Manchester University Press.

Oakley, A., (1974), *The Sociology of Housework*, London: Martin Robinson.

OECD (Organization for Economic Co-operation and Development), (1994), *The OECD Jobs Study: Implementing the Strategy*, OECD.

OECD (Organization for Economic Co-operation and Development), (1995), *Economic Outlook*, no.58, OECD.

Offe, C., (1985), *Disorganized Capitalism: Contemporary Transformations of Work and Politics*, Cambridge: Cambridge University Press.

Ohmae, K., (1985), *Triad Power: The Coming Shape of Global Competition*, New York: Free Press.

Pahl, J., (1985), *Private Violence and Public Policy: The needs of battered women and the response of the public services*, London: Routledge and Kegan Paul.

Pahl, J., (1989), *Money and Marriage*, Basingstoke: Macmillan.

Pahl, R.E., (1984), *Divisions of Labour*, Oxford: Basil Blackwell.

Pahl, R.E., (ed.), (1988), *On Work: Historical, comparative and theoretical perspectives*, Oxford: Basil Blackwell.

Pahl, R.E. and Wallace, C.D., (1984), 'Household work strategies in economic recession', in Redclift and Mingione (1984), pp.189-227.

Penn, R., (1992), 'Flexibility in Britain during the 1980s: Recent empirical evidence', in Gilbert *et al.*, (eds.), (1992), pp.66-80.

Penn, R., Rose, M. and Rubery, J., (eds.), (1994), *Skill and Occupational Change*: Oxford: Oxford University Press.

Perez, C., (1983), 'Structural changes and the assimilation of new technologies in the economic and social systems: A contribution to the current debate on Kondratiev Cycles', *Futures*, October 1983. See also *Futures*, vol.13, no.4 (August 1981) Special Issue.

Perez, C., (1985), 'Micro-electronics, Long-waves and World Structural Systems: New perspectives for developing countries', *World Development,* vol.13, no.3.

Petchesky, R.P., (1986), *Abortion and Women's Choice*, London: Verso.

Pfeil, F., (1995), *White Guys: Studies in Postmodern Domination and Difference*, London: Verso.

Pierson, C., (1996), *Beyond the Welfare State? The New Political Economy of Welfare*, Cambridge: Polity Press.

Piore, M.J. and Sabel, C.F., (1984), *The Second Industrial Divide*: Possibilities for Prosperity, New York: Basic Books.

Plant, L. Lesser, M. and Taylor-Gooby, P., (1980), *Political Philosophy and Social Welfare: Essays on the Normative Basis of Welfare Provision*, London: Routledge and Kegan Paul.

Plummer, K., (ed.), (1981), *The Making of the Modern Homosexual*, London: Hutchinson.

Pollert, A., (1981), *Girls, Wives, Factory Lives*, Basingstoke: Macmillan.

Pollert, A., (1991), 'The Orthodoxy of Flexibility', in Pollert (ed.), (1991).

Pollert A., (ed.), (1991), *Farewell to Flexibility?*, Oxford: Blackwell.

Pollert, A., (1996), 'Gender and Class Revisited; Or, the poverty of 'Patriarchy'', *Sociology*, Vol.30, No.4. pp.639-659.

Portwood, D., (1985), 'Careers and Redundancy', *The Sociological Review*, Aug 1985, vol.33, no.3, pp.449-468.

Rainnie, A. and Kraitham, D., (1992), 'Labour market change and the organisation of work', in Gilbert *et al.*, (eds.), (1992), pp.49-65.

Ransome, P., (1992), *Antonio Gramsci: A New Introduction*, Hemel Hempstead: Harvester Whearsheaf.

Ransome, P., (1995), *Job Security and Social Stability: The impact of mass unemployment on expectations of work*, Aldershot: Avebury.

Ransome, P., (1996*)*, *The Work Paradigm: A theoretical investigaion of concepts of work*, Aldershot: Avebury.

Rees, T., (1992), *Women and the Labour Market*, London: Routledge.

Reich, R., (1991), *The Work of Nations*, New York: Random House.

Rice A.K., (1958), *Productivity and Social Organisation*, London: Tavistock.

Robertson, R., (1992), *Globalization, Social Theory and Global Culture*, London: Sage.

Rojek, C., (1995), *Decentring Leisure: Rethinking Leisure Theory*, London: Sage.

Rojek, C. and Turner, B.S., (eds.), (1993), *Forget Baudrillard?*, London: Routledge.

Roper, M. and Tosh, J., (eds.), (1992), *Manful Assertions: Masculinities in Britain since 1800*, London: Routledge.

Rose, M., (1975), *Industrial Behaviour: Theoretical development since Taylor*, London: Allen Lane.

Rosenau, J., (1980), *The Study of Global Interdependence*, New York: Nichols.

Rubery, J. and Wilkinson, F., (1994), *Employer Strategy and the Labour Market*, Oxford: Oxford University Press.

Rubery, J., Horrell, S, and Burchell, B., (1994), 'Part-time Work and Gender Inequality in the labour Market', in Scott (ed.), (1994), pp.205-234.

Rustin, M., (1989), 'The politics of Post-Fordism: Or, the trouble with 'New Times', *New Left Review* no.175, (May/June 1989), pp.54-77. A shortened version was subsequently published as 'The trouble with New Times' in Hall and Jacques (eds.), 1989, pp.303-320.

Sabel, C.F., (1984), *Work and Politics: The division of labour in industry*, Cambridge: Cambridge University Press. (First published 1982).

Salaman, G., (1981), *Class and Corporation*, London: Fontana.

Salaman, G. and Esland, G., (eds.), *The Politics of Work and Occupations*, Milton Keynes: Open University Press.

Sargent, L., (ed.), (1981), *Women and Revolution*, London: Pluto Press.

Sayers, S., (1987), 'The need to work', *Radical Philosophy*, no.46, (Summer 1987), pp,17-26, reprinted in Pahl (ed) (1988), pp.722-741.

Schuller, T., (1991), 'Financial participation', in Storey (ed.), 1991, pp.126-136.

Schumacher, E.F., (1974), *Small is Beautiful: A Study of Economics as if People Mattered*, London: Abacus.

Schumpeter, J.A., (1989), *Essays on Entrepreneurs, Innovations, Business Cycles, and the Evolution of Capitalism*, edited by R.V. Clemence, Oxford: Transaction Publishers.

Schwartz Cowan, R., (1989), *More Work for Mother: The Ironies of Household Technology from the Open Hearth to the Microwave*, London: Free Association Books.

Scientific American, vol.265, no.3, (September 1991), Special Issue: 'Communications, Computers and Networks'.

Scott, A.J. and Storper, M., (eds.), (1992), *Pathways to Industrialization and Regional Development*, London: Routledge.

Scott, A.M., (1994a), 'Gender Segregation and the SCELI Research', in Scott (ed.), (1994), pp.1-38.

Scott, A.M., (ed.), (1994), *Gender Segregation and Social Change: Men and Women in Changing Labour Markets*, Oxford: Oxford University Press.

Scott, J., (1988), *Gender and the Politics of History*, New York: Columbia University Press.

Secombe, W., (1974), 'The housewife and her labour under capitalism', *New Left Review*, no.83.

Secombe, W., (1975), 'Domestic labour: Reply to critics', *New Left Review*, no.94.

Seidler, V, J., (1989), *Rediscovering Masculinity: Reason, Language and Sexuality*, London: Routledge.

Seidler, V.J., (ed.), (1991), *The Achilles Heel Reader: Men, Sexual Politics and Socialism*, London: Routledge.

Sève, L., (1978), *Man in Marxist Theory and the Psychology of Personality*, trans., J.McGreal, Hassocks: Harvester Press. Originally published 1974.

Sharp, M., (1989), 'Biotechnology in Britain and France: The evolution of policy', in Sharp and Holmes (eds.), (1989), pp.119-159.

Sharpe, M., and Holmes, P. (eds.), (1989), *Strategies for New Technology: Case studies from Britain and France*, London: Philip Allan.

Silverman, D., (1970), *The Theory of Organisations: A Sociological Framework*, London: Heineman.

Silverstone, R. and Hirsch, E., (eds.), (1992), *Consuming Technologies: Media and Information in Domestic Spaces*, London: Routledge.

Simmel, G., (1978), *The Philosophy of Money*, London: Routledge and Kegan Paul.

Sklair, L., (1991), *Sociology of the Global System*, London: Harvester Wheatsheaf.

Smith, Adam, (1863), *The Wealth of Nations: An inquiry into the nature and causes of the wealth of Nations*, Edinburgh: Adam and Charles Black.

Smith, A.D., (ed.), (1986), *Technological Trends and Employment: vol.5 Commercial Service Industries*, (SPRU) Aldershot: Gower.

Smith, C., (1991), 'From 1960s automation to flexible specialisation: a *deja vu* of technological panaceas', in Pollert, A., (ed.), (1991), pp. 138-157.

Smith, R. (1987), *Unemployment and Health: A Disaster and a Challenge*, Oxford: Oxford University Press.

Social Trends, no.18 (1988); no.19 (1989); no.21 (1991); no.25 (1995), London: HMSO.

Soete, L., (ed.), (1985), *Technological Trends and Employment: vol.3 Electronics and Communications*, (SPRU), Aldershot: Gower.

Soper, K., (1981), *On Human Needs: Open and Closed Debates in a Marxist Perspective*, Brighton: Harvester Press.

Spencer, H., in Thompson, K. and Tunstall, J., (eds.), (1971), *Sociological Perspectives: Selected Readings*, Harmondsworth: Penguin.

Spybey, T., (1996), *Globalization and World Society*, Cambridge: Polity Press.

Stallings, B., (1993), 'The New International Context of Development', Madison, WIS: University of Wisconsin, *Working Paper Series on the New International Context of Development*, no.1.

Stamp, P. and Robarts, S., (1986), *Positive Action: Changing the workplace for women'*, London: National Council for Civil Liberties.

Stevenson, N., (1995), *Understanding Media Cultures*, London: Sage.

Stewart, F., (1992), 'The adolescent consumer', in Coleman and Warren-Anderson (eds.), 1992, pp.203-226.

Storey, J., (ed.), (1991), *New Perspectives on Human Resource Management*, London: Routledge.

Storey, J., (ed.), (1994), *New Wave Manufacturing Strategies: Organizational and Human Resource Management Dimensions*, London: Paul Chapman Publishing.

Storey, J. and Sisson, K. (1991), 'Looking to the future', in Storey (ed.), 1991, pp.167-183.

Storper, M. and Scott, A.J., (eds.), (1992), *Pathways to Industrialisation and Regional Development*, London: Routledge.

Swingewood, A., (1984), *A Short History of Sociological Thought*, London: Macmillan.

Tawney R.H., (1982), *The Acquisitive Society*, Brighton: Wheatsheaf (originally published 1921 by G.Bell and Sons).

Tawney, R.H., (1960), *Religion and the Rise of Capitalism: An Historical Study*, (Holland Memorial Lectures, 1922). London: John Murray. Originally published 1926.

Taylor, F.W., (1967), *Principles of Scientific Management*, New York. First published 1911.

Taylor, R., (1994), *The Future of the Trade Unions*, London: Andre Deutsch.

Thompson, E.P., (1963), *The Making of the English Working Class*, London: Victor Gollancz.

Thompson, E.P., (1967), 'Time, work discipline and industrial capitalism', *Past and Present*, no.38, pp.56-97.

Thompson, P., (1983), *The Nature of Work: An Introduction to debates on the Labour Process*, London: Macmillan.

Thompson, P. and McHugh, D., (1990), *Work Organisations: A Critical Introduction*, London: Macmillan.

Tilly, L. and Scott, J., (1987), *Women, Work and Family*, London: Methuen.

Toffler, A., (1970), *Future Shock*, New York: Random House.

Toffler, A., (1980), *The Third Wave*, New York: William Morrow.

Touraine, A., (1974), *The Post Industrial Society*, London: Random House. First published 1969 as *La Societe post-industrielle*, by Les Editions Denoel S.A.R.L, Paris.

Trist, E.L., *et al.*, (1963), *Organisational Choice*, London: Tavistock Institute of Human Relations.

Turnbull, P.J., (1988), 'The Limits to "Japanisation" - Just-in-Time, Labour relations and the UK Automobile Industry', *New Technology, Work and Employment*, vol3. no.1, pp.7-20.

Turner, A.R., (1956), *The Foreman on the Assembly Line*, Cambridge, Mass.: Harvard University Press.

Turner, B.S., (1984), *The Body and Society*, Oxford: Blackwell.

Turner, B.S., (1992), *Regulating Bodies*, London: Routledge.

Turner, B.S., 'Baudrillard for Sociologists', in Rojek and Turner (eds.), (1993), pp.70-87.

United Nations Industrial Development Organisation (UNIDO), *Industry and Development Global Report*: 1988/1989 (Vienna 1988), 1989/1990, (Vienna 1989).

United Nations *World Investment Report 1993*, 'Transnational Corporations and Intgrated International Production', (1993), New York: United Nations.

United Nations, (1995a), *The World's Women in 1995: Trends and Statistics*, New York: United Nations.

United Nations, (1995b), *World Economic and Social Survey*, New York: United Nations.

United Nations, *Economic Survey of Europe in 1994-1995*, New York: United Nations.

Vallas, S.P., (1990), 'The concept of skill', *Work and Occupations*, vol.17, no.4, pp.379-398.

Van Parijs, P., (ed.), (1992), *Arguing for Basic Income: The Ethical Foundations for a Radical Reform*, London, Verso.

Veblen, T., (1925), *The Theory of the Leisure Class*, London: Allen and Unwin.

Vogler, C., (1994), 'Segregation, Sexism, and Labour Supply', in Scott (ed.), (1994), pp.39-79.

Vroom, V.H., (1964), *Work and Motivation*, New York: John Wiley and Sons.

Wajcman, J., (1991), *Feminism Confronts Technology*, Cambridge: Polity Press.

Wajcman, J., (1996), 'Women and Men Managers', in Crompton *et al.*, (eds.), 1996, pp.259-277.

Walby, S., (1986), *Patriarchy at Work: Patriarchal and Capitalist Relation in Employment*, London: Pluto Press.

Walby, S., (ed.), (1988), *Gender Segregation at Work*, Milton Keynes: Open University Press.

Walby, S., (1990), *Theorising Patriarchy*, Oxford: Blackwell.

Walby, S., (1997), *Gender Transformations*, London: Routledge.

Walker, R., (1989), 'Machinery, labour and location', in Wood. S., (ed), (1989), pp.59-90.

Walker R. and Guest R., (1952), *Man On the Assembly line*, Cambridge, Mass.: Harvard University Press.

Wallerstein, I., (1974), *The Modern World-System I: Capitalist Agriculture and the Origins of the European World-Economy in the Sixteenth Century*, New York: Academic Press.

Wallerstein, I., (1979), *The Capitalist World-Economy*, Cambridge: Cambridge University Press.

Wallerstein, I., (1980), *The Modern World System II: Mercantilism and the Consolidation of the European World-Economy, 1600-1750*, New York: Academic Press.

Walsh, T., (1991), '"Flexible" employment in the retail and hotel trades', in Pollert (ed.), 1991, pp.104-115.

Waters, M., (1995), *Globalization*, London: Routledge.

Weber, M., *On the Methodology of the Social Sciences* (1949 edition edited by Shils, E.A. and Finch, Glencoe, Ill.).

Weber, M., *Economy and Society*, (1956 German Edition) quoted in Mommsen 1974.

Weber, M., (1968), *Gesammelte Politische Schriften*, Tubingen: Johannes Winckelmann.

Weber, M. (1976), *The Protestant Ethic and the Spirit of Capitalism*, trans., Talcott Parsons, London: Allen and Unwin. This translation originally published in 1930.

Weber, M., *Economy and Society*, (1978 edition edited by Roth, G. and Wittich, C., Berkeley: University of California Press).

Weber, M., (1983): *Max Weber on Capitalism, Bureaucracy and Religion: A Selection of Texts*, edited and in part newly translated by Stanislav Andreski, London: Allen and Unwin.

Weber, M., (1992), *The Protestant Ethic and the Spirit of Capitalism*, trans., Talcott Parsons (1930), introduction by Anthony Giddens, London: Routledge.

Wells H.G., (1905), *A Modern Utopia*, London: The Literary Press.

Westergaard, J., Noble, I. and Walker, A., (1989), *After Redundancy: The Experience of Economic Insecurity*, Cambridge: Polity Press.

Whittington, R., (1991), 'The fragmentation of industrial R & D', in Pollert (ed.), (1991), pp.84-103.

Whyte, F.W., (1949), 'The social structure of the restaurant', *American Journal of Sociology*, 54, pp.302-310.

Whyte, F.W., (1951), 'Small groups and large organisations', in Rohrer J.H. and Sherif, M. (1951) *Social Psychology at the Crossroads*, New York: Harper and Row.

Wilson, E., (1977), *Women and the Welfare State*, London: Tavistock.

Winter, M.F. and Robert, E.R., (1980), 'Male dominance, late capitalism, and the growth of instrumental reason', *Berkeley Journal of Sociology*, pp.249-80.

Witz, A., (1988), 'Patriarchal relations and patterns of sex segregation in the medical division of labour', in Walby (ed.), (1988).

Wolff, C., (1979), *Bisexuality*, London: Quartet.

Wood, S., (ed.), (1982), *The Degradation of Work? Skill, Deskilling and the Labour Process*, London: Hutchinson.

Wood, S., (ed.), (1989), *The Transformation of Work?*, London: Routledge.

Woodward, J., (1958), *Management and Technology*, London: HMSO.

Woodward, J., (1965), *Industrial Organisations: Theory and Practice*, London: Oxford University Press.

Zimbalist, A., (ed.), (1979), *Case Studies on the Labor Process*, London: Monthly Review Press.